Metaphor of Emotions in English

Hituzi Linguistics in English

No. 1 *Lexical Borrowing and its Impact on English*   Makimi Kimura-Kano
No. 2 *From a Subordinate Clause to an Independent Clause*   Yuko Higashiizumi
No. 3 *ModalP and Subjunctive Present*   Tadao Nomura
No. 4 *A Historical Study of Referent Honorifics in Japanese*   Takashi Nagata
No. 5 *Communicating Skills of Intention*   Tsutomu Sakamoto
No. 6 *A Pragmatic Approach to the Generation and Gender Gap in Japanese Politeness Strategies*   Toshihiko Suzuki
No. 7 *Japanese Women's Listening Behavior in Face-to-face Conversation*   Sachie Miyazaki
No. 8 *An Enterprise in the Cognitive Science of Language*   Tetsuya Sano et al.
No. 9 *Syntactic Structure and Silence*   Hisao Tokizaki
No. 10 *The Development of the Nominal Plural Forms in Early Middle English*   Ryuichi Hotta
No. 11 *Chunking and Instruction*   Takayuki Nakamori
No. 12 *Detecting and Sharing Perspectives Using Causals in Japanese*   Ryoko Uno
No. 13 *Discourse Representation of Temporal Relations in the So-Called Head-Internal Relatives*   Kuniyoshi Ishikawa
No. 14 *Features and Roles of Filled Pauses in Speech Communication*   Michiko Watanabe
No. 15 *Japanese Loanword Phonology*   Masahiko Mutsukawa
No. 16 *Derivational Linearization at the Syntax-Prosody Interface*   Kayono Shiobara
No. 17 *Polysemy and Compositionality*   Tatsuya Isono
No. 18 *fMRI Study of Japanese Phrasal Segmentation*   Hideki Oshima
No. 19 *Typological Studies on Languages in Thailand and Japan*   Tadao Miyamoto et al.
No. 20 *Repetition, Regularity, Redundancy*   Yasuyo Moriya
No. 21 *A Cognitive Pragmatic Analysis of Nominal Tautologies*   Naoko Yamamoto
No. 22 *A Contrastive Study of Responsibility for Understanding Utterances between Japanese and Korean*   Sumi Yoon
No. 23 *On Peripheries*   Anna Cardinaletti et al.

Hituzi Linguistics in English

24

Ayako Omori

—

Metaphor of Emotions in English

—

With Special Reference to the Natural World and the Animal Kingdom as Their Source Domains

HITUZI
SYOBO

Copyright © Ayako Omori 2015
First published 2015

Author: AYAKO OMORI

All rights reserved. Except for the quotation of short passages for the purposes of criticism and review, no part of this publication may be reproduced, stored in a retrieval system, or transmitted in any form or by any means, electronic, mechanical, photocopying, recording or otherwise, without the written prior permission of the publisher.

In case of photocopying and electronic copying and retrieval from network personally, permission will be given on receipts of payment and making inquiries. For details please contact us through e-mail. Our e-mail address is given below.

Hituzi Syobo Publishing

Yamato bldg. 2f, 2-1-2 Sengoku
　Bunkyo-ku Tokyo, Japan 112-0011
Telephone: +81-3-5319-4916
Facsimile: +81-3-5319-4917
e-mail: toiawase@hituzi.co.jp
http://www.hituzi.co.jp/
postal transfer: 00120-8-142852

ISBN978-4-89476-740-9
Printed in Japan

To Hiroko, Yasunobu, Michiko and Taishun

Acknowledgements

This doctoral thesis owes a great deal to a large number of people, to whom I could never fully express my gratitude.

First of all, I am heartily grateful to my supervisors during my undergraduate and graduate school days, Seisaku Kawakami and Yoshimitsu Narita. Seisaku Kawakami enlightened the inexperienced young student on the cognitive mechanism of language use. Yoshimitsu Narita led me to develop many ideas and have my own thinking sharpened. I will never forget their invaluable guidance and warm encouragement I have received over the years.

I would also like to sincerely thank the examiners of my thesis. Yukio Oba, the chief examiner, was exceedingly generous with his time, effort and suggestions. Sadayuki Okada, the co-examiner, and Seisaku Kawakami, the external examiner, supplied thoughtful and detailed comments.

I have been blessed with excellent colleagues at Osaka University, where I have been privileged to work for the past twenty-five years. The academic community has provided a supportive and energetic atmosphere, one of the most fruitful places to study and research. I owe a profound debt of gratitude to Hideki Watanabe, a leading member of a study group on rhetoric I organized thirteen years ago, who gave me extensive comments and kindly criticism on various drafts of the manuscript as a whole. Without his insight and generosity, this would have been rather myopic and less historically grounded research. Chapters IV and V of this book are a product of joint researches on animal metaphors with him. I am also grateful to Trane DeVore, Gerry Yokota, and Andrew Murakami-Smith for their important comments on large portions of the manuscript. Their attentions have enabled me to make far fewer errors than I would have made on my own. Shin-ichiro Watanabe, who coedited with Risto Hiltunen at the University of Turku *Approaches to Style and Discourse in English* published by Osaka University Press, gave me an opportunity to contribute to the anthology. A revised version of the contribution forms Chapter I of this book. Ichiro Koguchi, a member of our joint research projects, significantly influenced my observation about Miltonic similes, which resulted in Chapter VI. Tomoji Tabata kindly helped me access the British National Corpus and instructed me on the use of the corpus software program. Tomoko Okita and Yoko Yumoto have unfailingly been generous and warm-hearted, and were delighted with my obtainment of a doctoral degree as if it were their own.

The rest of the book, Chapters II and III, owes much to Raymond W. Gibbs Jr., Professor at the University of California, Santa Cruz, and Paul Wilson, Visiting Professor in the Department of English Language and Applied Linguistics at the University of Łódź. Ray Gibbs, Editor of *Metaphor and Symbol*, supplied invaluable and illuminating comments on an early draft of my article appearing in Volume 23 of the journal, the original of Chapter II. Paul Wilson, Editor of *Dynamicity of Emotion Concepts* published by Peter Lang, invited me to contribute to the collection of papers written by specialists from linguistics, psychology and philosophy, and provided helpful comments on an early draft of my paper, which led to a study reported in Chapter III of this book.

I have been fortunate in studying English language and literature under several professors emeriti at Osaka University. Their stimulating lectures and personal communications with them have been a constant source of energy and inspiration: many thanks and acknowledgement to Toshio Saito, Mitsunori Imai, Minoru Fujita, Akira Tamai, and Hisashi Ishida. I am also thankful to the late Haruhiko Fujii with fond memories of his impressive lectures on *Beowulf*, Milton and Shakespeare, and humorous and intellectual conversations I enjoyed with him.

I am deeply indebted to my seniors in the academic world: Yoshihiko Ikegami, Masaaki Yamanashi, Minoru Nakau, Yukio Hirose, Ken-ichi Seto, and Toshio Ohori, for their special insights, sound advice, and strong encouragement. Sincere thanks are also due to my friends: Makimi Kano and Yoshitaka Kozuka. Discussions with them have consistently been inspiring and valuable.

This research was partially supported by the Grants-in-Aid for Scientific Research of Japan Society for the Promotion of Science (JSPS). Grant numbers: 12610491 (2000–2003), 19520422 (2007–2010), and 23520582 (2011–). The publication of this book is supported by Grant-in-Aid for Publication of Scientific Research Results of JSPS. Grant number: 265068 (2014).

Ayako Omori
September 2013

Contents

Acknowledgements   VII

Introduction: Looking into the Human Mind

0.1	Development of metaphor studies	1
0.2	Cognitive metaphor theory and natural language data	2
0.3	The aim and the framework of the present study	7

CHAPTER I
Water Metaphors in English Poetry

1.1	Introduction	11
1.2	The driving force for poetic metaphor	11
1.3	Similarity revisited: a brief overview of traditional theories on metaphor	14
1.4	The flow of thoughts: a conceptual metaphor for understanding mental activities	17
1.4.1	SLUGGISHNESS OF MIND IS STAGNANT WATER	19
1.4.2	ACTIVE THOUGHT IS RUNNING WATER	20
1.4.3	PASSIONATE THOUGHT IS SURGING WAVES	22
1.4.4	LINGERING THOUGHT IS EBB AND FLOW OF THE TIDE	23
1.4.5	INTROVERTED PASSION IS A WHIRL	24
1.4.6	ABUNDANT MANIFESTATION OF THOUGHT IS OVERFLOWING WATER	26
1.5	Conclusion	28

CHAPTER II
Emotion and Four Elements

2.1	Introduction	31

2.2	Kövecses' (1990, 2000) view of prevalent metaphors of emotion and the emotion prototype	31
2.3	A corpus study of emotion concepts	33
2.3.1	Queries to the FLUID IN A CONTAINER metaphor and the emotion prototype	33
2.3.2	Intuition vs. corpus data	34
2.3.3	Metaphorical expressions for the uncontrollability of emotion	35
2.3.4	A cognitive model and its theoretical implications	38
2.3.5	"Temperature" of emotion	40
2.4	Attributes of emotion prototype and prototypical emotions	43
2.5	Conclusion	46
Appendix		48

CHAPTER III

Conventional Metaphors for Antonymous
Emotion Concepts

3.1	Introduction	55
3.2	Retrieving metaphors for emotions from the corpus	56
3.3	Pleasure and sadness	56
3.3.1	The antonymous relationships between PLEASURE and SADNESS	56
3.3.2	The search results	57
3.3.3	Commonalities and disparities between PLEASURE and SADNESS	59
3.4	Hope, fear, and despair	63
3.4.1	The HOPE-FEAR relationships and HOPE-DESPAIR relationships	63
3.4.2	The search results	65
3.4.3	Commonalities and disparities among HOPE, FEAR and DESPAIR	66
3.4.4	The distinctive traits of HOPE, FEAR and DESPAIR	66
3.4.5	Synonymous relationships between FEAR and DESPAIR	70
3.5	Conclusion	73
Appendix		75

CHAPTER IV
Emotions and Animal Metaphors

4.1	Introduction	99
4.2	Animal idioms for emotions	99
4.2.1	Meaning of idioms and conceptual metaphors	99
4.2.2	Idioms including animal terms for emotions	101
4.3	Animal metaphors in poetry	105
4.3.1	Sommer and Weiss (1996)	105
4.3.2	FEAR and HOPE in the *OED*	109
4.3.3	Traditional metaphors of FEAR in the *OED*	111
4.3.4	Metaphoric coherence in texts	114
4.4	Conclusion	117

CHAPTER V
Bestiality and Humanity through Animal Metaphors

5.1	Introduction	121
5.2	Generic terms for the animal and their metaphoric meanings	121
5.3	Specific terms for animals and their metaphoric meanings	125
5.4	Metaphors evoking animal behaviors	130
5.5	Conclusion	136
Appendix		139

CHAPTER VI
Case Study: Lucifer's Metamorphosis in Milton's *Paradise Lost*

6.1	Introduction	161
6.2	The change of Satan's figure and his acts	162
6.3	Conceptual metaphors related to the changes of Satan's figure	163
6.3.1	Phase 1: Satan's rebellion against God	163
6.3.2	Phase 2: Satan's agony in Hell and plot to revenge on God	164
6.3.3	Phase 3: Satan's escape from Hell and flight to the new world	167
6.3.4	Phase 4: Satan's arrival on the earth	168

6.3.5	Phase 5: Satan's invasion upon Paradise and unsuccessful approach to Eve	170
6.3.6	Phase 6: Satan's temptation accomplished	174
6.3.7	Phase 7: Satan's return to Hell and divine punishment inflicted upon him	176
6.4	Metaphor and Satan's emotion	178
6.4.1	Satan's awareness of falling down and his anguish (1)	179
6.4.2	Satan's awareness of falling down and his anguish (2)	180
6.4.3	Satan wandering between good and evil	181
6.5	The power of Milton's rhetoric	184

Conclusion:
Entering in at the Strait Gate

Bibliography	193
Index	201

Introduction:
Looking into the Human Mind

0.1 Development of metaphor studies

Metaphor studies trace back to Greek and Roman antiquity. Throughout the history of Western Rhetoric, metaphor has been regarded as "a sort of happy extra trick with words," and "a grace or ornament or added power of language, not its constitutive form" (cf. Richards 1936: 90). After the passage of centuries, via Richards' (1936) and Black's (1962) insightful descriptions of metaphor as intercourse of thoughts, George Lakoff and his collaborators focused attention on metaphor from a cognitive linguistic point of view in the later 20th century. Since then, interdisciplinary approaches to rhetoric have been emphasized, as clearly shown by the three anthologies of metaphor studies published by Cambridge University Press: the first and second editions of *Metaphor and Thought* in 1979 and 1993 (hereafter *MT1* and *MT2*), and *The Cambridge Handbook of Metaphor and Thought* in 2008 (hereafter *CHMT*).

The range of researchers has been considerably extended in these three decades. Twenty-two scholars joined the project of *MT1*, while thirty-four researchers contributed to *CHMT*. No contributor of *MT1* participated in the publication of *CHMT*, and only four authors of *MT2* are also in *CHMT*: Raymond W. Gibbs, Jr., Dedre Gentner, Sam Glucksberg, and George Lakoff. The number of essays is twenty-one in *MT1*, while twenty-eight in *CHMT*. And the universities where the contributors of *MT1* are affiliated are in the USA, England, Canada, and Italy, whereas those of *CHMT* belong to universities in as many as nine countries: Holland, Israel, France, Germany and Hungary along with the aforementioned four.

Research methodology has also developed in these thirty years. Published a year earlier than Lakoff and Johnson's *Metaphors We Live by* (1980), *MT1* had already directed its attention to the relationship of metaphor and thought, as indicated in the title of the book. This attention was an anticipation of Lakoff and Johnson's view that "[M]etaphor is pervasive in everyday life, not just in language but in thought and action" (*Metaphors We Live By*, p.3). In fact, most of the contributors of *MT1*, leading philosophers, psychologists, linguists, and educators, had attended a multidisciplinary conference on metaphor and thought held at the University of Illinois at Urbana-Champaign in 1977, and their contributions to *MT1* were substantially revised versions of papers presented at the conference. The diversity of their research domains shows that metaphor is a phenomenon that cuts across a wide range of human activity. However, the scholars at that time regarded metaphor as a tool for communication and thought (cf. "Educational Uses of Metaphor" by Thomas G. Sticht, *MT1* 474–485), and they conducted speculative researches treating a small number of single sentences like "Encyclopedias are gold mines" ("The Role of Similarity in Similes and Metaphors" by Andrew Ortony, the editor, *MT1* 186–201), "Marriage is a zero-sum game" ("More about Metaphor" by Max Black, *MT1* 19–43), "Richard is a gorilla" ("Metaphor" by John R. Searle, *MT1* 92–123), etc.

The researches appearing in *CHMT*, on the other hand, do not treat metaphor as a mere tool. According to them, metaphor is rather a contributor toward human cognition, communication and culture. Metaphor is regarded as primarily "conceptual" in nature, an underlying system of communicative practice. The emergence of the concept of *conceptual metaphor* is a great product of the literature on metaphor in the last three decades. Conceptual metaphors generally consist of a series of conventional mappings which relate aspects of two distinct conceptual domains: a source domain and a target domain. This concept makes a contrast with a *linguistic metaphor*, or a metaphorical expression. Linguistic metaphors are natural outcome of the metaphorical patterns of thinking of human beings. This viewpoint has developed metaphor study from a *multi*-disciplinary to an *inter*-disciplinary approach. Many metaphor researchers address origins of metaphor, that is, the brain, the body, and the culture of the human being. Their interest are in the interaction of metaphor, thought and culture: how metaphorical expressions — both linguistic and non-linguistic — are influenced, supported, or constrained by mechanisms of thought, individual experiences, and the underlying culture of human societies. This approach is called "cognitive metaphor theory."

0.2 Cognitive metaphor theory and natural language data

Cognitive metaphor theory has traditionally presented speculative accounts of the relationship between metaphor and thoughts. Most of the linguistic data that Lakoff and Johnson and their followers use have been either constructed by the researchers' intuition, or elicited from informants. The latest trend of corpus linguistics, however, has warned about the dangers of those introspective examples, emphasizing the importance of naturally-occurring data. Deignan, in her highly suggestive work titled *Metaphor and Corpus Linguistics* (2005), states that "more specific, illuminating and possibly more accurate findings are to be made when we forget what people *can* say, and instead study in detail what they *do* say" (p. 224), and points out three advantages of corpus observation of language in use over intuitive language analysis (pp. 85–87). Firstly, unlike human memory that is limited in ability, a computer is "far better equipped to both store and search large amounts of text, performing endlessly repetitive tasks swiftly and accurately." Secondly, machine-readable corpora allow us to access a stock of typical word meanings, collocations and grammatical patterns, while human beings themselves are, strangely enough, "not good at describing their own language production," as demonstrated in corpus researchers' and lexicographers' report that they regularly find uses of words that they would not have predicted. Thirdly, whereas no one knows all the words of their language or their meanings in use, corpus data help us to "provide a less subjective analysis of language than unsupported intuition." Deignan has shown that some of the linguistic metaphors cited by cognitive scholars as realizations of conceptual metaphors they postulate are, in fact, rare or non-existent in authentic language data in large corpora, and that metaphor types frequently seen in corpora are overlooked or neglected by cognitive linguists. She has also indicated that cognitive studies on metaphor have disregarded the fact that some important grammatical aspects in the source and the target domains are different from each other (See also Lindquist 2009, Ch. 6; and Semino 2008, Ch. 6).

Are natural language data in corpora, then, to be characterized as of a different nature from introspective data produced by researchers or informants? To this question Turner (1991) answers by emphasizing a powerful and pervasive conceptual connection between the concept of MIND and that of WRITING:

> Records are understood as a sort of external memory, and memory as internal records. Writing is understood as thinking on paper, and thought as writing in the mind. By means of this conceptual connection, the written work is taken as a substitute for or even as a distillation of the author: the author's mind is an endless paper on which he writes, making mind internal writing; and the book he writes is external mind, the external form of that writing. The writing is therefore conceived of as having a voice, one that speaks to us, and to which we respond.... This makes the everyday metonymic reference to writing by its author's name — as in "Plato is on the top shelf" — seem so natural.
>
> (Turner 1991: 246)

His argument suggests that human introspection and linguistic expressions are two sides of the same coin: natural language data are closely connected to invented or elicited data by researchers' or informants' intuition. It should be noted, however, that a corpus is a large *collection* of linguistic expressions. That is, a rich accumulation of expressed introspection of people constitutes the entire body of a large corpus. A frequently-used pattern of language retrieved from a corpus is, as it were, "a greatest common divisor" of introspections of people whose expressions are gathered into that corpus.

Then, what significance does that "greatest common divisor" have for cognitive studies on metaphor? Briefly speaking, cognitive linguistics attempts to investigate cognitive mechanisms of human beings through access to linguistic data. Evans and Green (2006) aptly describe the research stance that cognitive linguists take:

> Cognitive linguists, like other linguists, study language for its own sake; they attempt to describe and account for its systematicity, its structure, the functions it serves and how these functions are realized by the language system. However, an important reason behind why cognitive linguists study language stems from the assumption that language reflects patterns of thought. Therefore, to study language from this perspective is to study patterns of conceptualisation. Language offers a window into cognitive function, providing insights into the nature, structure and organisation of thoughts and ideas. The most important way in which cognitive linguistics differs from other approaches to the study of language, then, is that language is assumed to reflect certain fundamental properties and design features of the human mind.
>
> (Evans and Green 2006: 5)

If language is a reflection of the human mind and offers a window into cognitive function, then cognitive linguists, even if their aim is to clarify patterns of human conceptualization, should never forget to study language "for its own sake," nor underestimate the importance of natural language data in use. Cognitive metaphor theory, as Lakoff and Turner (1989) put it, regards metaphor as "conventional," "accessible to everyone," and "an integral part of our ordinary everyday thought and language" (p. xi). Putting the basic assumption of cognitive linguistics and its view of metaphor together, we can conclude that it is ordinary and conventional examples of metaphor that provide a trustworthy and convincing evidence for a cognitive metaphor theory.

Then, what is a "conventional" example of metaphor? For a linguistic pattern is to be regarded as conventional, it should pass through a filter of the society. In other words, it should be recognized as a conceivable usage by members of that society. Many orientational metaphors, such as "my spirits *rose*," "I *fell* into a depression," "She is an *upstanding* citizen," and "That was a *low* trick" (Lakoff and Johnson 1980: 15–16), are good examples of conventional usage, for they are based on bodily experiences and human culture, and are therefore widely accepted.

Expressions which have passed through a filter of time are also regarded as conventional. Great works of literature are accepted for a long time, and felicitous phrases in those works remain alive in people's memory. Take a famous quotation from Shakespeare, "All the world's a stage, / and all the men and women merely players" (*As You Like It* 2.7), for example. This passage is well-known precisely because one of our remarkably basic ways of understanding human life is the LIFE-AS-A-PLAY metaphor (cf. Lakoff and Turner 1989: 20–22), and according to this conceptual metaphor we regard the passage as convincing. Biblical phrases, proverbs and idioms have also passed through a filter of time. When we read the famous words of Jesus, "Enter ye in at the strait gate: for wide is the gate, and broad is the way, that leadeth to destruction, and many there be which go in thereat: Because strait is the gate, and narrow is the way, which leadeth unto life, and few there be that find it" (Matthew 7: 13–14), we understand it through the LIFE-AS-A-JOURNEY metaphor: this passage refers to "alternative paths through life which lead to different destinations in the hereafter" (Lakoff and Turner 1989: 9).

On the other hand, a metaphorical expression that is introspectively produced cannot always pass through a filter of the society or time. McGlone (1996) conducted experiments in which he produced metaphorical statements and asked his participants to generate paraphrases of those statements. One of his inventions is "Dr. Moreland's lecture was a 3-course meal for the mind," which is intended to be a realization of the conceptual metaphor IDEAS ARE FOOD. Elicited paraphrases by his participants include "Dr. Moreland's lecture was a full tank of gas for the mind" and "The lecture was an intellectual rose garden." Those sentences by McGlone and his participants are all highly novel and innovative, far from conventional or ordinary. Some researchers may justify the novel and innovative metaphors like these as evidence of cognitive metaphor theories. McGlone's and his participants' sentences above undoubtedly reflect conceptual mappings from the concept of FOOD, FUEL, or A FLOWER to KNOWLEDGE or INFORMATION provided by a lecture. However, an invented example, based on introspection of an individual and thus regarded novel and innovative, only offers a window into the mind of *that person alone*. Conventional expressions, on the other hand, offer windows into the minds of *people in general*. And it must be stressed that the cognitive linguistic view of metaphor originally puts a high value on those conventional expressions. As Deignan (2005) argues, innovative examples "can perhaps be justified on the grounds that the conventionality or otherwise of the metaphors is immaterial — both demonstrate mental links, and the researchers' aims are to gather information about thought, rather than about language. However, much literature in the conceptual metaphor tradition places emphasis on the ubiquity of metaphor in everyday, conventional language" (p. 111).

Therefore, the more conventional, and the less innovative, linguistic data are, the more suitable it is for cognitive metaphor studies, as the figure below shows:

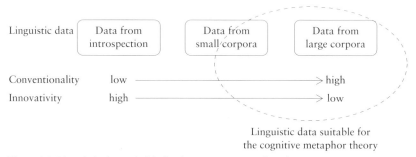

Figure 0.1: Linguistic data suitable for the cognitive metaphor theory

Here, linguistic data are divided into three types: data from introspection, from small corpora, and from large corpora.[1] An invented example derived from introspection of an individual is low in conventionality and high in innovativity. A linguistic pattern frequently used in a large corpus, on the other hand, is highly conventional and non-innovative, and thus more suitable for a cognitive study on metaphor.[2] Data from small corpora, placed in the middle, are relatively small accumulations of texts, both in machine-readable and printed forms, such as a work (or works) written by a specific writer, collected speeches of a specific statesman, and so on.[3] This figure indicates that some of the data from small corpora are adequate for cognitive metaphor studies, while others are not. Not all the data retrieved from a small corpus can synchronically or diachronically infiltrate into people's minds. If a linguistic metaphor passes through the synchronic and/or diachronic filter and remains in people's memory, then it proves to be an accurate realization of their metaphoric thought pattern, revealing itself to be suitable for a cognitive metaphor study.

Deignan's (2005) suggestions are exceedingly meaningful in that they shed light on the importance of large corpora as reliable data for confirmation of the cognitive metaphor theory. Her criticism is not directed at the theoretical framework itself but at the data which the cognitive literature has traditionally used. Her argument implies that a linguistic theory should not isolate itself from the reality of language use.

0.3 The aim and the framework of the present study

The present study is an investigation of the structure of conceptual metaphors for the emotions. The research was conducted using British National Corpus (BNC), a one-hundred-million word corpus of present-day British English, and smaller corpora such as literary works like English poetry and dictionaries. Focusing on both ordinary and literary language data, I attempt to take account of the systematic nature of metaphor in language and thought.

Thought process can be divided into two types: active and passive. The former, including understanding, judging and problem-solving, is a mental process which a human advances and handles volitionally. Jäkel (1995) persuasively argues on those active thought processes by postulating a conceptual metaphor "MENTAL ACTIVITY IS MANIPULATION" as a complex cognitive model in which several sub-metaphors form a coherent system. Emotion, on the other hand, is to be characterized by "passivity" in that it is an autonomous mental process, which we are almost powerless to resist. The passivity is exemplified by corpus citations like "the tide of emotion was *irresistible, surging through her* like great waves" and "he ran a hand through his hair, *unable to deal with the sudden wave* of emotion the conversation had brought with it," which describe the uncontrollability of emotion (see Section 2.3.3). The present study concentrates on the passive mental process of emotion, trying to present metaphor models for understanding them.

There are various source domains for understanding emotion. Zoltán Kövecses, who has published influential works on metaphors for emotion for the last two decades, enumerates source domains used for conceptualization of emotion: CONTAINER, NATURAL FORCE AND PHYSICAL FORCE, SOCIAL SUPERIOR, OPPONENT, CAPTIVE ANIMAL, INSANITY, DIVIDED SELF, BURDEN, ILLNESS, and so on (1990, 2000, etc.). Among them, he regards the domain of CONTAINER as "the major metaphorical source domain" (2000: 37). A research of mine (2008), however, examines a substantial number of corpus examples in the form of "[source-domain nominal] + *of* + [target-domain nominal]," [4] and reveals that the source domain most frequently mapped onto the target domain of EMOTION is NATURAL PHENOMENA, and that the major source sub-domain is A HUGE MASS OF MOVING WATER IN THE NATURAL WORLD like SEA and RIVER.

The first half of the present study, therefore, concentrates on the conceptual domain of NATURAL PHENOMENA. Chapter I is a study on WATER metaphors describing the mental activity of emotion in English poetry. Detailed analyses of works written by renowned poets, like Wordsworth, Blake, Tennyson, Poe, and others, show that they instantiate conceptual metaphors in which several aspects of water in the natural world are coherently mapped onto aspects of emotions. Chapter II reports the corpus study on conventional metaphors of the type "[source-domain nominal] + *of* + [target-domain nominal]" stated above. Through observation of a number of citations retrieved from BNC, I propose an alternative to the long-accepted idea on the prototype of emotion formed by the introspective method adopted in traditional cognitive linguistic studies. Chapter III concentrates on specific emotions like PLEASURE, SADNESS, HOPE, FEAR, and DESPAIR. I adopt the same corpus methodology as the preceding chapter for retrieval and analysis of conventional metaphors used to talk about those emotions, and indicate that semantic relationships between antonymous pairs of emotion concepts can be characterized in terms of whether or not a particular aspect of a source domain, or the domain itself, is used in metaphorical mappings.

The second half of the present study focuses on the conceptual domain of ANIMAL as a source used to describe emotion. Animal metaphor is ubiquitous: animals are fairly familiar to us human beings, and we have wide, accumulated knowledge of this domain. The study shows how various qualities of various animals are linked to aspects of human emotions in metaphorical mappings. In Chapter IV I observe animal metaphors in English idioms and poetic texts retrieved by dictionaries, and consider a systematic nature of correspondences between source and target domains. Chapter V is a study on quadruped metaphors, with special reference to the Great Chain of Being, a widespread cultural model providing a background to European literature and the history of ideas, which Lakoff and Turner (1989) mentioned in their investigation into the cultural understanding of the relationship between the animal and the human. Chapter VI is a case study on *Paradise Lost*. I construct a highly schematic reading of a number of epic similes in the Miltonic work. Vehicles used in those similes refer to a wide range of things in the natural world, from celestial entities to base animals, which vividly describe how Satan attempts to take revenge on God and gradually changes his own figure and emotion as he gets closer to his goal. I postulate conceptual metaphors indicating a Christian view of the world, and investigate a relationship between those conceptual metaphors and the descriptions of Satan's change.

Notes

1 Similarly, Deignan (1997: 22) divides evidence for the conceptual metaphor theory into three types, stating that "first, in the field of cognitive science, researchers test speakers' understanding and responses to metaphors in texts, often comparing this to literal language (see, for example, Gibbs and O'Brien 1990; Gibbs 1993). The second type of evidence is typified by much of the work done by Lakoff and his co-researchers, which is based on introspective studies of linguistic expressions. Third, other studies of linguistic expressions are based on

corpora of various kinds (see, for example, van Teeffelen 1994; Rohrer 1995; Patthey-Chavez et al. 1996)."
2 See, for example, Stefanowitsch and Gries eds. (2006), an anthology of corpus-based studies on the linguistic and cognitive nature of metaphoric mappings.
3 Among the studies using data from small corpora is Charteris-Black (2004), who manually analyzed the metaphorical expressions in a corpus of fifty-one inaugural speeches by US presidents from George Washington to Bill Clinton, categorizing them according to their source domains.
4 Bednarek (2008) also pays attention to conventional expressions of the type "[nominal] + *of* + [nominal]", stating that "Considering left-hand collocation with *affection*, *of* and *with affection* are very common patterns. With *of affection*, a frequent pattern is N *of affection*, most nouns belonging to a number of distinct semantic subsets," and lists several semantic subsets like "showing" (ex. *display of affection*, etc.), "quantity" (ex. *his lack of affection*, etc.), "warmth" (ex. *the fire of affection*, etc.), "force" (ex. *surge of affection*, etc.), and "expressor" (ex. *gesture of affection*, etc.) (pp. 122–123).

CHAPTER 1
Water Metaphors in English Poetry

1.1 Introduction

Lakoff and Johnson's (1980) influential study of metaphor started a new current in cognitive linguistics. This powerful current has produced interesting studies directed toward an investigation of the functions and structure of metaphor as an integral part of our everyday thought and language. Lakoff and Turner (1989) analyse poetic metaphor from the standpoint that metaphor is a primary tool for shaping our everyday understanding of everyday events, and that poetic language illuminates the processes that guide our comprehension and imagination. This chapter, taking its position in this current of cognitive linguistic research on metaphor, constitutes a further exploration into an important factor in the formation of metaphor in our cognitive processes through focusing on a particular style of expressing various conditions of the human mind.

1.2 The driving force for poetic metaphor

Lakoff and Turner (1989) refute traditional views that metaphor is something that belongs to poetry and that poetry is alienated from everyday language, and argue that poetic metaphor deals with central and indispensable aspects of human conceptual systems (p. 215). Their work takes its title, *More than Cool Reason*, from a line in Shakespeare's *Midsummer Night's Dream*:

(1) Hippolyta: 'Tis strange, my Theseus, that these lovers speak of.
    Theseus: More strange than true; I never believe
    These antique fables, nor these fairy toys.
    Lovers and madmen have such seething brains,
    Such shaping fantasies, that apprehend

More than cool reason ever comprehends.
(*Midsummer Night's Dream* V. i. 1–6. Italics mine.)

Here Theseus characterizes the brains of lovers and madmen. He goes on to say that poets, just like lunatics and lovers, are "of imagination all compact" (ibid. 8), conveying his idea of the work of poets as follows:

(2) The poet's eye, in a fine frenzy rolling,
Doth glance from heaven to earth, from earth to heaven;
And as imagination bodies forth
The forms of things unknown, the poet's pen
Turns them to shapes and gives to airy nothing
A local habitation and a name.
(Ibid. 12–17.)

Lakoff and Turner contrast Theseus's discussion of poetry and Hippolyta's words "But all the story of the night told over, / And all their minds transfigur'd so together, / More witnesseth than fancy's images, / And grows to something of great constancy" (ibid. 23–26), and evaluate her opinion highly: "Hippolyta correctly sees that Theseus's dichotomy is mistaken: poets see more than 'fancy's images,' something that 'grows to great constancy'" (Lakoff and Turner 1989: 215–216). By "Theseus's dichotomy," they seem to mean the division between truth and fantasy, or reason and imagination. The king of Athens regards the poets' way of thinking as involved with the latter of these binary pairs. He assumes that poets form unsubstantial fantasy by using imagination at their command, and express the phantom, "airy nothing," in poetic words. In his opinion, the process of poetic composition has nothing to do with truth or reason; on the contrary, he identifies poets' imagination with "frenzy," i.e. with a disorder of the mind.[1]

To this traditional view of poets one of *the poets* expresses a strong objection:

(3) This was a Poet — It is That
Distills amazing sense
From ordinary Meanings —
And Attar so immense

From the familiar species
That perished by the Door —
We wonder it was not Ourselves
Arrested it — before —
(Emily Dickinson, "This was a Poet – It is That.")

In this short piece, we can note two points which are in stark contrast to Theseus's view: that expressions in poetry are composed of ordinary everyday language, and that the ability to distil an amazing sense from their ordinary meanings is not particular to poets. Poetic expressions are in fact "familiar" flowers which blossomed and "perished by the Door." The "amazing sense" that the poet intends by the use of the ordinary words is not a provisional one, set up only for the nonce, but is *inherent* in the "ordinary Meanings" of the words and can be "distilled" from them like fragrant "Attar" from familiar flowers. The ability to distil it is common to us all, as is shown by Dickinson's remark: "We *wonder* it was not Ourselves / Arrested it — before —."

These points made by Dickinson are in complete agreement with the views of cognitive linguists on poetic metaphor. Poetic language is never beyond ordinary language. To put it another way: rhetorical expressions in poetry are not products of the workings of the mind deviating from ordinary reason. Poetic works, to be sure, are products of artistic talent. But this does not mean that we ordinary people differ from poets in composing thought. Great poets, as Lakoff and Turner (1989: Preface) put it, "use basically the same tools we use," i.e. an imaginative way of thinking common to all human beings.

The word "cool" modifying "reason" in (1) briefly expresses Theseus' view on the ordinary reason: it is used there in the sense "not heated by passion or emotion." [2] From a cognitive linguistic point of view, however, *passion* and *emotion* are not alien to the workings of the minds of ordinary people. The emotional aspect of the mind plays an important role in human cognitive processes, whose workings provide a driving power for bringing our imagination into full play. With regard to the sense of the word "imagination" in Example (2), the *Oxford English Dictionary* gives an insightful definition as follows: [3]

(4) imagination
    4. The power which the mind has of forming concepts beyond those derived from external objects (the 'productive imagination').
    b. The creative faculty of the mind in its highest aspect; the power of framing new and striking intellectual conceptions; poetic genius.

As is suggested by this definition, the power of imagination which produces concepts for unsubstantial things should be characterized as a high intellectual ability, not as the working of "frenzy" incompatible with normal reason. Thus poets' emotional experiences, which generate imagination, the creative faculty, and lead to poetic metaphors, are to be regarded as an important factor in *intellectual* conceptualization. In the following sections, the working of metaphor for creative conceptualization will be investigated through a brief survey of various studies of metaphor and through examples of poetic works.

1.3 Similarity revisited: a brief overview of traditional theories on metaphor

Many writers on the rhetorical use of language, from the Greek philosophers to contemporary linguists, have argued over metaphor from various points of view; nevertheless agreement has not been reached even over basic issues concerning the definition of metaphor. One such issue is the question whether metaphor is based on similarity.

The idea that metaphor arises from the cognition of similarity has been advocated by many scholars, from Aristotle on down: "the ability to forge a good metaphor shows that the poet has an intuitive perception of the similarity in dissimilars" (*Poetics*, pp. 40–41). Jakobson (1956) classifies various cases of aphasia into two basic groups, *similarity disorder* and *contiguity disorder*, and characterizes two different forms that normal discourse can take as *metaphoric* and *metonymic*, thus associating metaphor with similarity. Leech (1969) places special emphasis upon the likeness perceived between the tenor — what is actually under discussion — and the vehicle — the image or analogue in terms of which the tenor is represented — as the *only* contributing factor in metaphoric transference. Ricoeur (1977) takes a similar view: metaphor reveals the logical structure of *the similar* because, in the metaphorical statement, *the similar* is perceived despite difference, in spite of contradiction. Comparison Theory also presupposes resemblances as the grounds for metaphor, and relates metaphors to similes, i.e. comparison statements in which these resemblances are formulated (Miller (1979)).

There are some theories, on the other hand, which utterly deny that metaphor is based on similarity. Richards (1936), whose view is called Interaction Theory by Black (1962, 1979), cites Denham's [4] lines on the Thames, in which the flow of the poet's thoughts is compared to the river: "O could I flow like thee, and make thy stream / My great exemplar as it is my theme! / Though deep, yet clear; though gentle, yet not dull; / Strong without rage, without o'erflowing, full." Richards' observation on the senses and implications of *deep*, *clear*, *gentle*, *strong* and *full*, as they apply to a stream and to a mind, did not reveal any resemblance between vehicle and tenor counting. He takes the vehicle as "an excuse for saying about the mind something which could not be said about the river" (p. 122). Black (1962, 1979) modifies and develops Richard's view that the peculiar modification of the tenor which the vehicle brings about is even more the work of their unlikenesses than of their likenesses. He also finds difficulty in turning up any literal resemblance between tenor and vehicle, and regards it as a main function of metaphor to create the similarity rather than to formulate some similarity antecedently existing.

This extreme disagreement stems from the casual and facile use by these writers of the terms *similarity* and *resemblance*. What Interaction Theorists mean by these terms has to do with the physically measurable attributes of the external objects, such as the depth of the river (i.e. measurement from the surface to the bottom) as seen in Richards' analysis. What is necessary here is a shift in focus. Although the depth of a river and that of a human mind are physically dissimilar to each other, the poet must have felt *something* in common. Otherwise, he would not have been able to associate the two. To clarify the nature of similarity in metaphor, we have to consider other aspects of meaning besides the physical senses that cause the semantic anomaly.

Cognitive linguistic theories focus on how meanings reflect human experiences, i.e. our cognition of entities in the external world.[5] Our experiences of the world are inevitably influenced by our own sensations and sensibilities, which form a basis for thinking and for using language. With regard to similarity in metaphor, Lakoff and Turner express their view as follows: "Metaphor always results in a similarity of image-schema structure between the source and target domain. This is by no means the traditional Similarity Position. But it is a theory in which similarity of a limited special kind does play a role" (1989: 123). On the basis of their argument, I would like further to consider the relationship between our emotional experience and concepts formed in our minds. As I have argued elsewhere (Omori 1996), a concept formed through our experience of an external entity has three aspects: *encyclopaedic knowledge*, a mental system constituted by intellectual judgements on the entity; *perceptual information*, gained through sensory experiences of the entity; and *emotional reaction*, a feeling we hold in our mind when we experience the entity.

These three aspects are closely interrelated and influence each other. Encyclopaedic knowledge depends on perceptual information, in that it consists of the accumulation of this information organized intellectually into a system. Emotional reaction also depends on perceptual information in that the reaction derives from the information. And there may be cases where folk beliefs or superstitions about an entity transmitted in a particular culture are accumulated in one's encyclopaedic knowledge, and this knowledge influences one's emotional reaction to the entity. This close and apparently intricate relationship among the three aspects of a concept, however, does not mean that it is hard to draw a line of demarcation between them. On the contrary, we can sharply distinguish the natures of those aspects by their definitions shown above. It should be noted that when a concept is realized as a word, all of the three aspects do not necessarily function as the meaning of the expressed word. Consider for example the meaning of the word "amethyst" in the following poem:

(5) I held a jewel in my fingers
    And went to sleep.
    The day was warm, and winds were prosy;
    I said: "'T will keep."
    I woke and chid my honest fingers, —
    The gem was gone;
    And now an *amethyst* remembrance
    Is all I own.

(Emily Dickinson, "The Lost Jewel." Italics mine.)

The girl is convinced in her dream vision that the jewel is in her fingers. She wakes up to find it was an illusion, but the phantom still remains with purple brilliancy in her remembrance. What does the poet intend to imply by the word "amethyst" in line seven? Her chief purpose is certainly not to specify the object referred to by the two generic terms, "jewel" (line one) and "gem" (line six). Our encyclopaedic knowledge of the gemstone contributing toward the referential function of the word *amethyst* is not directly involved in the meaning of the expression in (5). "An amethyst remembrance" rather seems to mean the vivid remembrance of the beauty of transparent purple colour shining in her hand, and of her tranquil pleasure in cherishing it as a treasure. The word *amethyst* is a loan from the Greek $\dot{\alpha}\mu\acute{\epsilon}\theta\upsilon\sigma\tau\sigma\varsigma$ meaning *not drunken*, a notion that the stone was a preventive of intoxication.[6] The amethyst is also assumed to symbolize sincerity, and is also associated with a number of superstitions; it is also regarded as a love charm, as a potent influence in improving sleep, and so on.[7] Such symbolic and cultural significance, which may be due to the impression one gains from the soft and calm brilliance of the jewel, perhaps functions as an element of the meaning of "amethyst" in (5). In any case, the meaning of the word reflects the poet's emotional reaction to the amethyst as well as her perceptual information about it. Both are integral parts of the concept of the gemstone formed in her mind.

This is also the case with words used metaphorically, with no direct referential function.[8] Let us return to the meaning of the expressions "deep," "clear," and others in Denham's lines cited by Richards for the purpose of supporting his view that metaphor is not based on similarity. We should reconsider each of them in terms of the aspects of the concepts of *stream* and *mind* formed through our sensory and emotional experiences. Through those experiences, we learn to metaphorically see, for example, the depth of the human mind as we physically see that dimensional quality of the river. We will be able to confirm the existence of similarity in Denham's metaphor when we compare our aesthetic and emotional reactions to the river and to the mind. The similarity here resides not in physically measurable attributes of the external objects but in the concepts formed in our mind.

1.4 The flow of thoughts: a conceptual metaphor for understanding mental activities

In the previous section, I proposed a new way of characterizing similarity as the basis of metaphor. There is a possible argument against my view: that the aesthetic and emotional reactions to the depth and clarity of the Thames are but temporary, subjective responses at the moment of seeing the stream, and thus cannot be regarded as factors contributing to metaphorical conceptualization. To answer such an attempt to refute my view, I would like to present several pieces of evidence that there is a predominant and ubiquitous mode of expression whereby the human mind is in every way compared to stream:

(6) a. the *stream* of consciousness
 b. *fluency* of thought
 c. *tidal waves* of passion
 d. a sudden *flood* of joy
 e. Words *rolled* from his lips like a *cataract*.
 f. I sat near the grave, full to *overflowing* with grief.
 g. He felt a *surge* of sympathy for her.
 h. *Still waters run deep.* (A proverbial saying, meaning that people who are shy or do not say much often have very strong feelings or interesting ideas.) [9]

Taken out of context, the italicized words describe various modes of water flow, but in these phrases or sentences they all express mental activities. The sentence in (6e) tells about "words" uttered from someone's lips, but words rolling like a cataract reflect an active movement of thought, for an utterance is caused by concepts that come to mind. The expressions in (6) explicitly show that we understand some modes of our mental activities coherently in terms of modes of flow. There are many words for modes of flowing water whose definitions in dictionaries in general contain descriptions of thoughts or feelings, or which make up phrases collocating with words for mental activities (ex. *flow of spirits*, *stream of thought*). Typical examples are as follows:

>(noun/verb) flood, flow, foam, overflow, roll, stream, surge, tide, wave, whirl
>(adjective) fluent, stagnant, tidal

I therefore suggest that there is a conceptual metaphor that governs and structures a way to understand mental activities:

(I)   A MENTAL ACTIVITY IS A FLOW OF WATER.

Conceptual metaphor is a notion proposed by George Lakoff and his research partners, Mark Johnson and Mark Turner. It is characterized as a major factor in the formation of a conceptual system. Lakoff et al. claim that how we think, what we experience and what we do in our daily lives is governed by metaphor; they list a number of conceptual metaphors, including TIME IS MONEY as a basis of our understanding of time and LIFE IS A JOURNEY for understanding our life.

In the preceding section I argued that the meaning of a word used metaphorically reflects aspects of the corresponding concept formed through sensory and emotional experience of the entity in question. Here I would like to posit that our sensory and emotional experiences are also influential in the formation of conceptual metaphors that govern our thought and action. Consider for example the formation of TIME IS MONEY and LIFE IS A JOURNEY in our mind. In everyday life we accumulate feelings that money is precious, too good to be wasted. Our cognition that these feelings are accordant with the feelings we have toward time contributes to the mapping of the concept of MONEY onto TIME. LIFE IS A JOURNEY is also formed through our feeling of hope at the beginning of the journey, the feelings of joy, pain, and anxiety along the way, and a sense of fulfilment we experience when we arrive at the destination. When we experience the same kinds of feelings on each occasion in our life, the concepts of JOURNEY and LIFE are linked together in our mind. These emotional reactions play an important role in the meanings of expressions based on the conceptual metaphors, such as "Thank you for your time," "I lost a lot of time when I got sick," "We're at a crossroads," and "It's been a long, bumpy road."

The same is true of A MENTAL ACTIVITY IS A FLOW OF WATER, advanced above. I now discuss in detail certain quotations from British and American poets, which will hopefully demonstrate that these expressions are all based on this conceptual metaphor, and consider the emotional aspects concerned in its formation, by proposing a set of subordinate metaphors which are comprised within that basic conceptual metaphor:

(I-i)   SLUGGISHNESS OF MIND IS STAGNANT WATER.
(I-ii)   ACTIVE THOUGHT IS RUNNING WATER.
(I-iii) PASSIONATE THOUGHT IS SURGING WAVES.
(I-iv)   LINGERING THOUGHT IS EBB AND FLOW OF THE TIDE.
(I-v)   INTROVERTED PASSION IS A WHIRL.

(I-vi) ABUNDANT MANIFESTATION OF THOUGHT IS OVERFLOWING WATER.

1.4.1 SLUGGISHNESS OF MIND IS STAGNANT WATER

I first discuss the following lines, metaphorically expressing sluggishness of mind:

(7)   I dwelt alone
    In a world of moan,
    And *my soul was a stagnant tide*,
    Till the fair and gentle Eulalie became my blushing bride —
    Till the yellow-haired young Eulalie became my smiling bride.
              (Edgar Allan Poe, "Eulalie," ll. 1–5. Italics mine.)

(8)   Milton! thou should'st be living at this hour:
    England hath need of thee: *she is a fen*
    Of stagnant waters: altar, sword, and pen,
    Fireside, the heroic wealth of hall and bower,
    Have forfeited their ancient English dower
    Of inward happiness. We are selfish men;
    Oh! raise us up, return to us again;
    And give us manners, virtue, freedom, power.
              (William Wordsworth, "London, 1802," ll. 1–8. Italics mine.)

The man in Example (7) lived in miserable solitude until a fair and gentle woman named Eulalie became his bride. The English people described in Example (8), both officially and privately, and in both civil and military affairs, have lost their inward happiness and are lacking in manners, virtue, freedom and power, being swayed by selfishness. In describing such depression or discouragement, the two poets — one American and one British — coincidentally or rather inevitably imagine stagnant water.

    What similarity is to be recognized between a depressive state of mind and the stagnancy of water? Wordsworth in (8) equates England with a fen. Fens, as backwaters or other forms of stagnant waters, are strongly associated with filthy colour, stinking smell, as a medium of bog moss or annoying mosquitoes. Comparing the mental state of people in England to a fen, the poet sees the inertia-ridden England, where egotism or sluggishness was prevailing, through those unpleasant images of a fen. Unpleasantness like this is generally felt in reaction to apathy, dilatoriness, lethargy or inertness of mind. This is illustrated by the adjective *muddy* which can be used to express those mental states, as in "Day after day my lessons fade, / My intellect gets *muddy*" (Thomas Hood,

"Lament of Toby," ll. 37–38, italics mine) and in the last speech given by Katherina: "A woman moved is like a fountain troubled, / *Muddy*, ill-seeming, thick, bereft of beauty" (William Shakespeare, *The Taming of the Shrew*, V. ii. 141–142, italics mine).

Furthermore, it should be noted that the expressions in (7) and (8) seem to be concerned with the discomfort we usually experience when we see that the water has *no power of action*. Consider another example:

(9) She fears him, and will always ask
What fated her to choose him;
She meets in his engaging mask
All reasons to refuse him;
But what she meets and what she fears
Are less than are *the downward years,*
Drawn slowly to the foamless weirs
Of age, were she to lose him.
(Edwin Arlington Robinson, "Eros Turannos," ll. 1–8. Italics mine.)

The woman described in Example (9) exceedingly fears the cheerless days in the future that would certainly come if she were to lose the man. The expression "the downward years, / Drawn slowly to the foamless weirs / Of age" refers to the dismal days in old age, when nothing would move her heart. As human beings are by nature social animals, a life in utter solitude without any human interaction is hard to endure; it is regarded as a spiritual death. With actual death in sight, fear of the apathetic condition caused by solitude is still stronger for the aged. Robinson here identifies this negative feeling of people faced with solitude and death, spiritual or actual, with the inexplicable horror at the water, pulled by gravity, going downward slowly and unstoppably towards a weir, dammed up and stopping without foam as if it were dead.

The images of stagnant water employed by these eminent poets well testify to our general emotional reactions: the discomfort and fear we experience in seeing filthy and/or motionless water, and our equation of these negative feelings towards this state of water with feelings towards an inert state of mind. It is this cognitive process that enables a mapping of STAGNANT WATER onto SLUGGISHNESS OF MIND.

1.4.2 ACTIVE THOUGHT IS RUNNING WATER

In the next lines the poet compares himself to a sea, and his love named Juliet to a river:

(10) Give me thy soul, Juliet, give me thy soul!
   I am a bitter sea, which drinketh in
   The sweetness of all waters, and so thine.
   Thou, like a river, pure and swift and full
   And freighted with the wealth of many lands,
   With hopes, and fears, and death and life, *dost roll*
   Against *the troubled ocean* of my sin.

   (Wilfred Scawen Blunt,
   "Asking for Her Heart — The Same Continued," ll. 1–7. Italics mine.)

This metaphorical expression consisting of the contrast between the sea and the river is based on the different aesthetic and emotional reactions towards the two. Here the man's own soul is identified with the sea, bitter and troubled. The sea is the last stop of all waters, and consumes everything; thus it cannot be thought of as clear. His awareness that his own soul is debased by sin inevitably reminds him of the troubled sea, for his soul and the sea seem to him equally dirty. The river, on the other hand, is regarded as pure, even though it is full and "freighted with the wealth of many lands, / With hopes, and fears, and death and life;" probably because the water runs swiftly in a given direction, washing everything without stagnating. The comparison of Juliet's soul to a rolling river is based on the aesthetic judgement of the swift water, the feeling of yearning toward its purity, and the cognition that his emotional reaction to the woman's pure active thought is consistent with his reaction to the running water.

The following verse cited from Blake describes how the poet unifies himself with the surrounding nature:

(11) When the green woods laugh, with the voice of joy
   And *the dimpling stream runs laughing by*,
   When the air does laugh with our merry wit,
   And the green hill laughs with the noise of it.
   ...
   Come live & be merry and join with me,
   To sing the sweet chorus of Ha, Ha, He.

   (William Blake, "Laughing Song." Italics mine.)

When the visionary poet sees the beautiful natural scenery with delight, his mind's ear definitely hears the laughing voices of the green woods, the stream, the air, and the hill. In his subjective perception here, his mind and the scenery seem to be interacting: his happiness makes the river, the woods, and everything around him raise the voice of joy, and their laughing voices move him to sing the sweet chorus of "Ha, Ha, He." Focusing our attention on his perception of the river, we observe that he feels extremely comfortable with the way the stream runs dimpling, and equates the water flow with his own thoughts running lightly and cheerfully. We can see in this poem a bi-directional mapping of ACTIVE THOUGHT and RUNNING WATER, a mapping based on the joyful feeling commonly experienced toward active thought and toward running water.

1.4.3 Passionate thought is surging waves

The movement of waters in a furious sea is a menace to human beings. This implication of the overwhelming power of the raging waves is obvious in the following piece of Tennyson:

(12) Break, break, break,
    On thy cold gray stones, O Sea!
    And I would that my tongue could utter
    The thoughts that arise in me.
    ...
    Break, break, break
    At the foot of thy crags, O Sea!
    But the tender grace of a day that is dead
    Will never come back to me.
                        (Alfred Tennyson, "Break, break, break.")

Here the poet is mourning the death of his friend. The repetition of the imperative "Break" toward the sea, alluding to his *broken-hearted* state, shows that he earnestly seeks a sense of unity with the rough sea. He looks back over "the tender grace of a day" he spent with the friend, painfully aware that the precious time will never come back. Tossed about by the uncontrollable grief of losing the dearest friend, he identifies his passion with the surging waves.

The next lines contain a more explicit metaphor:

(13) ... and we
    Who lived, and moved, and sinned in thee
    Stand on the crumbling shores of life,
    Where *waves of sorrow, guilt, and strife*
    Come rolling, surging, foaming on —
        (Janet Hamilton, "Midnight Thoughts at the Close of 1864," ll. 29–33. Italics mine.)

On the last night of the year 1864, the sixty-nine year old Scottish poet is giving herself up to deep emotion toward the closing year. Speaking to the year itself, addressing it as "thee," the old woman looks back the days she lived. Then the negative aspects of the human mind, such as sorrow, guilt and strife, enter her consciousness in overwhelming volume and strength. With the sense of being oppressed by them, she imagines the intensity of waves rolling, surging, and forming on. The metaphorical mapping of SURGING WAVES onto PASSIONATE THOUGHT is based on our emotional reaction to them: the furiousness and uncontrollability we feel equally toward the intensity of the surge and that of the passion.[10]

1.4.4 LINGERING THOUGHT IS EBB AND FLOW OF THE TIDE

One of the characteristic movements of seawater is reiteration: the repeated washing of the waves upon the shore and the tide's ebb and flow. Perception of the reiteration of water can also result in the metaphorical comprehension of a mental activity:

(14) For, alas! alas! with me
 The light of Life is o'er!
 No more — no more — no more —
 (*Such language holds the solemn sea*
 To the sands upon the shore)
 Shall bloom the thunder-blasted tree,
 Or the stricken eagle soar!
  (Edgar Allan Poe, "To One in Paradise," ll. 14–20. Italics mine.)

The man has lost his love, to whom he devoted his utmost affection, as is shown by the lines "Thou wast all that to me, love,/ For which my soul did pine" (ll. 1–2). Comparing himself to "the thunder-blasted tree" and "the stricken eagle," the bereaved man is now suffering profound grief for the death of his "light of Life." The echoing voice "No more — no more — no more —" symbolically expresses the recurring mental pain due to the strong consciousness that the happy days will not come back any more. The poet, provoked by the voice of his own mind, imagines waves of the solemn sea that repeatedly wash up against the shore. The solemnity is due to the immensity of the natural force dominating the movement of the seawater. The italicized lines show that his experience of the sense of loss coming to him again and again is equal in his mind to the experience of seeing the irresistible power of nature to move the huge amount of water back and forth.

(15) Listen! you hear the grating roar

>   Of pebbles which the waves draw back, and fling,
>   At their return, up the high strand,
>   Begin, and cease, and then again begin,
>   With tremulous cadence slow, and bring
>   The eternal note of sadness in.
>   Sophocles long ago
>   Heard it on the Ægæan, and it brought
>   Into his mind *the turbid ebb and flow*
>   *Of human misery*; we
>   Find also in the sound a thought,
>   Hearing it by this distant northern sea.
>   (Matthew Arnold, "Dover Beach," ll. 9–20. Italics mine.)

Here the poet describes the tranquil sea washing against Dover Beach. Struck with admiration at the scenery, as shown in "The sea is calm to-night./ The tide is full, the moon lies fair/ Upon the straits" (ll. 1–3), he listens to the restless waves. Then his sensitive ear detects "the eternal note of sadness" in the grating roar of pebbles which the waves draw back and fling up the high strand. The mournful sound reminds him of Sophocles, who also heard the waves of the Aegean and associated the roar with lingering human misery.

These examples show that we regard our experience of a lingering thought seizing us repeatedly as something equal to the restless movement of waves or the ebb and flow dominated by the gravity and changes in weather condition. This cognitive process is influenced by our feeling that we are unable to resist the solemn power of nature that brings the eternal reiteration. We feel the same kind of resistless force in the reiteration of the waves and that of a thought. That is clearly shown by the fact that the metaphorical expressions based on LINGERING THOUGHT IS EBB AND FLOW OF THE TIDE can collocate with the word *resistless*, as in "the strong ebb and flow / Of the resistless tides of joy and woe" (Julia Caroline Ripley Dorr, "Supplication," ll. 38–39).

1.4.5 INTROVERTED PASSION IS A WHIRL

Among various modes of water flow, a whirl has a tremendous power against which we would never be able to struggle and would be swallowed up if caught in it. We sometimes experience a mental activity triggered off by the same kind of power.

> (16) Ruth does not speak, — she does not stir;
>   But she gazes down on the murderer,
>   Whose broken and dreamful slumbers tell

Too much for her ear of that deed of hell.
She sees the knife, with its slaughter red,
And the dark fingers clenching the bearskin bed!
What thoughts of horror and madness whirl
Through the burning brain of that fallen girl!
(John Greenleaf Whittier, "Mogg Megone," ll. 420–427. Italics mine.)

The girl named Ruth stares silently at the murderer in his drunken sleep. His dark fingers and the bloodstained knife he is grasping bring horror and madness to the girl's mind. In contrast to her stiffened body, her thoughts circulate with rapidity and force. The italicized line reflects the feeling that the introverted movement is overpowering and completely out of her control.

The next excerpt is from a poem which describes two friends, a man and a woman, who say good-by after enjoying a cheerful fireside conversation on a winter night. When she lays her hand in his with frank farewell, eyes meet eyes, and suddenly the two realize that they have been blind in not seeing how their souls have grown dear each to each:

(17) Only a moment of supreme surprise,
Delirious joy crushed down by heaviest pain,
And then each conscious soul, too sadly wise,
Took up the burden of its bonds again.
How could he hope to hide his new-born woe
Where *pleasures whirl* and mad ambitions press?
Or in the petty cares which women know,
How could she look for peace or happiness?
Driven as by a flaming sword, he turned,
And in the instant, as he left the place,
Into his wildered brain her image burned,
And all the wordless anguish of her face.
(Elizabeth Akers Allen, "A Winter Night," ll. 21–32. Italics mine.)

A moment after this intense experience of supreme surprise, and the pain as well as the bliss of love, the two, too sadly wise, take up the burden of their respective bonds again, and part from each other with their feelings repressed. Focusing on what has occurred in the mind of the man, we can note that his sudden delirious pleasure of love, repressed by the force of wisdom or prudence which is conscious of the burden of their bonds, finds nowhere to go, turns inward and moves furiously in a circle like a whirl.

This furious movement of thought reminds us of a conceptual metaphor advanced by Lakoff (1987: 383):

(II) THE BODY IS A CONTAINER FOR THE EMOTIONS.[11]

In this conceptual metaphor we hear a distant echo of the biblical idea of a person as a receptacle of God's mercy and wrath.[12] In dignified or archaic style according to biblical use, the noun *vessel* is employed to denote a person or the body, as in *the weaker vessel*.[13] Here I would like to claim that (II) is a combination of the following two metaphors:

(III) A BODY IS A CONTAINER FOR THE MIND.
(IV) A MIND IS A CONTAINER FOR THE THOUGHTS AND EMOTIONS.

We can characterize (III) as the basis for instance of "A sound mind *in* a sound body," and (IV) as the basis for such expressions as "*Open* your mind to some new thoughts," "Do you have anything *in* mind for the next term's class?" and "Out of sight, *out of* mind."[14] The formation of the metaphorical expressions in Examples (16) and (17) can be clearly understood in terms of the conceptual metaphor A MENTAL ACTIVITY IS A FLOW OF WATER combined with (IV). In the case of (17), where "pleasures whirl," it is his prudence that functions as a lid for the container MIND. His thought with energy of motion is confined in the container completely sealed up, and thus cannot help whirling in the mind with centripetal force. In (16), where "thoughts of horror and madness whirl," it is probably her anxiety that the murderer might wake up that functions as a lid for her mind. Thus she cannot vent her horror or madness freely, and her passionate thoughts cannot but move within the container rapidly in a circle. The irresistible force we feel in introverted passion results from such external pressure, like some external force which generates the staggering power of whirl.

1.4.6 ABUNDANT MANIFESTATION OF THOUGHT IS OVERFLOWING WATER

We have seen above that the generation of INTROVERTED PASSION IS A WHIRL, subordinate to A MENTAL ACTIVITY IS A FLOW OF WATER, is related to A MIND IS A CONTAINER FOR THE THOUGHTS. The same holds true of another subordinate metaphor, i.e. ABUNDANT MANIFESTATION OF THOUGHT IS OVERFLOWING WATER.

(18) God's splendor round his head did glow,
　　Because *his heart did overflow*
　　With pity for another's woe —
　　Such goodness God alone could know.
　　　　　(Thomas Holley Chivers, "The Fallen Temple," ll. 17–20. Italics mine.)

The lines above are quoted from a poem which pays tribute to the memory of the dead man. The poet praises him, saying "Beside God's throne he takes his seat" (l. 16), because during his lifetime he always developed and displayed tender feeling of pity for another's woe. His abundant manifestation of pity is grasped here by the image of water overflowing the vessel of his mind.

The next lines describe a man in rapture over winning the heart of his beloved:

(19) Unenvied celibacy quiet feigns,
   And vaunts the unshared banquet of the soul,
   But *all his joy spring from the brimming bowl.*
   ...
   When soul expansive grasps the blissful boon,
   Dear woman's heart — and love by rolling years
   Is nurtured — and smiles the hymeneal moon
   In ceaseless glow, like stars along the spheres
   Cinctured by the flushing radiance of June;
   Primeval hope her Eden vestures wears,
   Exuberant pleasure cheers the heart of feeling,
   And silver streams o'er laughing lawns are stealing.
           (Summer Lincoln Fairfield, "Inosculation," ll. 22–40. Italics mine.)

The supposed sexual connotations put aside, this example also shows clearly that the poet's understanding of mind is based on the conceptual metaphors A MENTAL ACTIVITY IS A FLOW OF WATER and A MIND IS A CONTAINER FOR THE THOUGHTS. The pleasure of the man described here exceeds the capacity of the vessel of his mind and springs out of "the brimming bowl." The word "exuberant" modifying "pleasure" in line 39 has meanings associated with water flow, as defined in *the OED*:

(20) exuberant, *a.*
   3. Of a fountain, stream, etc.: Overflowing.
   4. *fig.* a. Of affections, joyous emotions, beneficence, vitality, health, or their manifestations: Overflowing, abounding.

This definition suggests that the word is used to describe the state of happiness in general besides the movement of overflowing water. From this an inference is drawn that the feeling of satisfaction with affections, joyous emotions, beneficence etc. is equated in the cognitive process with the satisfaction we feel on seeing the water springing up and overflowing, and that this process enables the understanding ABUNDANT MANIFESTATION OF THOUGHT in terms of OVER-

FLOWING WATER.

It is perhaps illustrative to give a cursory comparison here between the concepts of OVERFLOWING WATER and WHIRL. They are similar in that they are both used to conceptualize strong feelings. With various examples, however, a striking difference emerges between them which we did not expect. The concept of OVERFLOWING WATER is chiefly used for expressing positive attitudes of the mind, as shown in *the OED* definition of the word *exuberant* in (20), and in such expressions as "To make the coming hour o'erflow with joy / And pleasure drown the brim" (William Shakespeare, *All's Well That Ends Well*, II. v. 46–47) and "And now was my heart full of joy, mine eyes full of tears, and mine affections running over with love to the Name, People, and Ways of Jesus Christ" (John Bunyan, *The Pilgrim's Progress*, Section IX). The concept of WHIRL, on the other hand, is used for understanding mental attitudes both positive and negative — thoughts of horror, of madness, of the delirious pleasure of love etc. — as shown in the examples above. This difference comes from the nature of our emotional reactions to overflowing water and to whirl. We gain positive impressions from overflowing water, whereas our impression of whirl is neutral, without leaning toward positive or negative feelings. Probably it is because water can overflow only if there is no obstacle to the motion, such as a lid of a container which would seal it up completely. A vision of water enabled to move and overflow freely reminds us of our comfort in being allowed to manifest our feelings freely and finding them accepted by those whom we are involved with. These emotional aspects influence our understanding of positive attitudes of mind in terms of overflowing water.

1.5 Conclusion

Metaphorical expressions in poetry give us insight into the cognitive process of metaphorical conceptualization. Through observing poetic metaphors, this chapter has investigated the cognitive process behind the particular style of expression of mental activities using words for water flow. The analysis has revealed that there is a mode of thought in which various mental activities are coherently understood in terms of a conceptual metaphor, A MENTAL ACTIVITY IS A FLOW OF WATER, and that this metaphor is organized via our emotional reactions to varied states of water. I have proposed six subordinate metaphors which specify our way of understanding mental activities by comparing them to (i) stagnant water, (ii) running water, (iii) surging waves, (iv) ebb and flow of the tide, (v) a whirl, and (vi) overflowing water. The organization of these conceptual metaphors correlates with the emotional aspects of our concept of WATER FLOW: (i) stagnant water is uncomfortable and fearful; (ii) running water is comfortable, evoking yearning; (iii) surging waves are furious and uncontrollable and thus we feel tossed about by them; (iv) ebb and flow of the tide are reminiscent of human incompetence through their eternality; (v) a whirl, accumulating energy inwardly with its spiral movement, is irresistible; and (vi) overflowing water is rich and satisfying. They are based on our aesthetic and emotional experiences on the conditions of water. We recognize that we show the same sort of reactions when we experience mental activities such as (i) sluggishness of mind, (ii) active thought, (iii) passionate thought, (iv) lingering thought, (v) introverted passion, and (vi) abundant manifestation of thought. This recognition enables mapping of A FLOW OF WATER onto A MENTAL ACTIVITY.[15]

Our sensory and emotional experiences of the environment contribute crucially toward the organization of conceptual metaphors and the linguistic expressions based on them. Many of the most significant poets understand this and express their poetic feelings fluently, using ordinary words and activating ordinary conceptual metaphors. I would like to conclude this chapter by quoting from the Poet Laureate whom I mentioned earlier: "All good poetry is the spontaneous overflow of powerful feelings" (William Wordsworth, "Preface" to *Lyrical Ballads*).[16]

Notes

1 The *Oxford English Dictionary* defines the sense of "frenzy" 2 as follows, citing the line in question as one example: "Agitation or disorder of the mind likened to madness; a state of delirious fury, rage, enthusiasm, or the like; also, wild folly, distraction, craziness. 1590 Shakes. Mids. N. v. i. 12 The Poets eye in a fine frenzy rolling."
2 See the *OED*, "cool" 4.a. The line in question is cited as one of the examples.
3 The *OED* cites as one example for "imagination" 4.b. the words by Theseus in question.
4 Sir John Denham is an English poet (1615–1669).
5 Lakoff (1987) combats the traditional view of objectivism and advocates experiential realism, which characterizes meaning in terms of our collective biological capacities and our physical and social experiences as beings functioning in our environment.
6 See the *OED*, "amethyst," the etymology column.
7 See the *Random House Encyclopedia*, New Revised Edition, Random House, 1983; and the *Colombia Encyclopedia*, Third Edition, Colombia University Press, 1963.
8 The metaphorical expression "the sun" in Romeo's words "Juliet is the sun" (*Romeo and Juliet*, II. ii.), for example, has no referential function in that it does not refer to the central body of the solar system.
9 See *Macmillan English Dictionary*, "still ²."
10 There are cases in which the intensity of passionate thought is regarded as identical with that of the stormy wind besides rolling water, as in Hamlet's words to the players: "… in the very torrent, tempest, and, as I may say, whirlwind of your passion, you must acquire and beget a

    temperance that may give it smoothness." (*Hamlet*, III. ii.) There we can observe the cognitive process of mapping the concept WIND onto A MENTAL ACTIVITY. See Chapters II and III.

11 Lakoff (1987) claims that this conceptual metaphor is reflected in everyday expressions, such as "He was filled with anger" and "She couldn't contain her joy."

12 The existence of this biblical idea of a person as a receptacle was suggested by Hideki Watanabe (personal communication), who referred me to Psalm 23: 5 ("my cup runneth over") and Romans 9: 22–23 ("What if God, willing to shew his wrath, and to make his power known, endured with much longsuffering the vessels of wrath fitted to destruction / And that he might make known the riches of his glory on the vessels of mercy, which he had afore prepared unto glory"). The idea is also seen in many other biblical phrases: for instance "Upon the wicked he shall rain snares, fire and brimstone, and an horrible tempest: this shall be the portion of their cup" (Psalm 11: 6) and "he shall be a vessel unto honour, sanctified, and meet for the master's use, and prepared unto every good work" (II Timothy 2: 21). See also the *OED*, "vessel" n.1, 3.

13 One example of the metaphorical use of vessel is as follows: "For Jaquenetta — so is the weaker vessel called — which I apprehended with the aforesaid swain, I keep her as a vessel of thy law's fury…" (Shakespeare, *Love's Labour's Lost*, I. i. 261–263).

14 The BODY and the MIND making up a double container are also illustrated by examples like "sadness inside of *me*" and "sadness in *my heart*," the former of which realizes the OUTER CONTAINER, and the latter of which the INNER ONE.

15 Nomura (1996), through a close study of Japanese in such domains as SOUND, LANGUAGE, THOUGHTS and FEELINGS, provides a discussion about contrast between Japanese and English, stating that what he calls "the fluid metaphor" is prevalently used in the former, while "the individuum metaphor" is used in the latter. His comment on the domain of THOUGHT is: "It is quite common for Japanese to metaphorize THOUGHTS as a <fluid> welling up inside one's mind, whereas it seems more common for English to metaphorize THOUGHTS as <individuum> coming from outside" (p. 69). He suggests a strong correlation between the ubiquity of the fluid metaphor in Japanese and general characteristics of Japanese grammar and culture. I do not take a position against his claim that the Japanese language and culture possess some distinguishing characteristics, and that metaphors vary in degree of universality, some being nearly universal, others being culture-specific. However, my survey on the poetic use of English in this chapter has revealed that there is a coherent and predominant way of understanding mental activities in terms of modes of water seen in many English expressions, and that the mapping of the concept A FLOW OF WATER onto A MENTAL ACTIVITY is far from temporary or culture-specific: there are strong emotional motivations common to us all behind that mapping. See also Chapters II and III.

16 Wordsworth expanded the "Advertisement" of *Lyrical Ballads* (1798) into the "Preface" (1800), and he revised it in 1802. This quotation is from the edition of 1802.

CHAPTER II
Emotion and Four Elements

2.1 Introduction

Using Lakoff's cognitive linguistic approach (Lakoff and Johnson 1980, 1999; Lakoff 1987, 1993), striking studies on metaphors of emotion have been carried out by Kövecses (1986, 1990, 2000, etc). The outset of his studies was a joint research project with Lakoff on the concept ANGER published in 1986. This detailed study on the mapping between the source domain A HOT FLUID IN A CONTAINER and the target domain ANGER can also be found in Lakoff (1987).

As for emotion in general, Kövecses (1990, 2000) proposes various source domains that characterize emotion metaphorically. In 1990 he also presented a definite idea on the prototype of emotion. While his presentation of a range of metaphors is insightful, there is room for the further study of emotion prototype. The aim of this chapter is to attempt to clarify the attributes of emotion prototype and to identify specific emotions close to the prototype, discussing the significance of each source domain, or the lack thereof, on the metaphorical understanding of various types of emotion. I will give a brief overview of Kövecses' idea of prevalent metaphors of emotion and the emotion prototype, focusing on problems with his view, which I would like to solve through analyses of data collected from the British National Corpus (hereafter BNC).

2.2 Kövecses' (1990, 2000) view of prevalent metaphors of emotion and the emotion prototype

Kövecses presents groups of metaphors used for understanding EMOTION, in which the major source domains are A CONTAINER, NATURAL FORCES, AN OPPONENT, AN INANIMATE OBJECT, A LIVING ORGANISM, and so on (1990: Chs. 9–10). According to him, the most general and powerful metaphor among this group is the CONTAINER metaphor: it provides us with a more or less complete description of the concept of emotion by itself, whereas the other metaphors taken together yield a picture similar to the one provided by the CONTAINER metaphor (ibid., p.182). He illustrates "THE EMOTIONS ARE FLUIDS IN A CONTAINER" metaphor with examples like "She was *filled* with emotion," "I feel *empty*," "He *poured out* his feelings to her," and "He *bottled up* his emotions." He presents a detailed portrait of this metaphor by specifying correspondences between the source and the target domains (see Table 2.1), and based on this he offers a cognitive model representing a prototype of emotion consisting of five stages: "0: State of emotional calm," "1: Cause," "2: Existence of emotion," "3: Attempt at control," "4: Loss of control," "5: Action," and "0: State of emotional calm" again. The emotion that he regards as closest to the prototype is anger: it has a five-stage model in which the stages are the same as in the emotion prototype (ibid. Ch. 11).

Source: A FLUID IN A CONTAINER	Target: EMOTION
There is a fluid in the container that is cold and calm.	There is a lack of emotion.
Some external event (i.e. a heat source) produces heat and agitation in a container.	Emotion exists.
The fluid begins to rise, the temperature of the fluid increases and there is more and more agitation inside the container.	The intensity of emotion increases.
The heat produces steam and pressure is building up.	There is a great deal of emotional pressure.
The pressure is dangerous because it can lead to an explosion.	Emotional pressure is dangerous because it can lead to uncontrolled action.
There is a limiting point beyond which the pressure cannot increase without causing an explosion.	The intensity of emotion cannot increase indefinitely without leading to an uncontrolled response on the part of the self.
A certain amount of counterforce is applied that can prevent or delay the explosion.	An attempt is made to control the emotion.
It requires a great deal of counterforce to counteract the pressure.	Emotion is difficult to control.
When the increasing force becomes stronger than the counterforce, there is an explosion.	Loss of emotional control results in an uncontrolled response.
The container becomes dysfunctional, parts of it go up in the air, and what was inside comes out, which can cause harm to other objects or people around it.	There is possible damage to the self and to others.
The fluid is cool and calm again.	There is emotional calm again.

Table 2.1: Correspondences between thermodynamics of a fluid in a container and generation of emotion (Adapted from Kövecses 1990: 183)

In his more recent work (2000), Kövecses presents "EMOTION IS FORCE." It is a single underlying "master metaphor," and most of the well-known metaphors of emotion, such as FIRE, OPPONENT, NATURAL FORCE, are instantiation of the generic-level metaphor (p.61). He starts off the analyses of the specific-level metaphors with "EMOTION IS PRESSURE INSIDE A CONTAINER" (p.65), which, according to him, is "perhaps the best known and most studied metaphor for emotion." He puts emphasis on the CONTAINER metaphor in his argument on the metaphor for ANGER, too, stating that "the conceptual metaphor that seems to be the central one for anger is ANGER IS A HOT FLUID IN A CONTAINER. … The idea of the centrality of this metaphor in our folk theories of emotion in general was dealt with in some detail elsewhere (Kövecses 1990)" (Kövecses 2000: 22). As for the prototype of emotion, his argument in 2000 is less detailed than that in 1990, but does regard *anger* as one of prototypical emotion terms (pp. 3–4), showing a figure like Figure 2.1.

Figure 2.1: Prototypical vs. nonprototypical emotion terms by Kövecses (2000: 4) (The circle indicates that *anger*, *fear*, and *sadness* are better examples of emotion terms than *hope*, *pride*, *surprise*, and *lust*.)

2.3 A corpus study of emotion concepts

2.3.1 Queries to the FLUID IN A CONTAINER metaphor and the emotion prototype

Despite the vivid image of Kövecses' model in which the increasing force of boiling water and steam persuasively represents intensification of emotion, questions arises as to the centrality of the CONTAINER metaphor as applied to EMOTION. The first query is whether TO HEAT A FLUID IN A CONTAINER is more appropriate than any other concept as a way to describe the uncontrollability of emotion. This concept is comprehensible in terms of our daily activity in the kitchen. The rise of the temperature of water or soup in pots and pans results from human manipulation: we can usually control the temperature by regulating the heat of a stove. There may be an alternative concept that is more equivalent in describing the overwhelming force of an uncontrollable emotion. Second, people may also associate AN INTENSE EMOTION with THE COLD OR A

FALL IN TEMPERATURE. If they do have a "*cold*" feeling, should it be placed on the periphery of the category EMOTION, far from the emotion prototype? I also have a doubt about prototypical emotions. Kövecses' model is certainly consistent with our intuitive grasp of anger. Our bodily experience of feeling the blood turn hot when we become angry facilitates our acceptance of his view. This consistency, however, does not lead to the conclusion that ANGER is one of the prototypical emotions. On the contrary, there is a possibility that this emotion may have influenced his choice of the basic model for emotion metaphor. If some source other than A HEATED FLUID IN A CONTAINER is deduced from a detailed study of the first and the second problems, other specific emotions may possibly be identified as closer to the emotion prototype than ANGER.

2.3.2 Intuition vs. corpus data

The questions above relate to a methodological problem accompanying the traditional approach to metaphor from the cognitive linguistic point of view. Deignan (2005) points out that many cognitive linguists in research into metaphor have used intuitively generated data, i.e. data derived from the linguists' own internalized language experience (p.110), and shows that there is a discrepancy between products derived from intuition and those derived from factual evidence, i.e. the naturally-occurring expressions most frequently found in corpora (pp.95–96). She takes as her object of study Yu's (1995) seven realizations of the ANGER-AS-FIRE metaphor. Using the Bank of English concordances, Deignan's examination of the lexical items identified by Yu and their inflections reveals that, while two lexical items in Yu's examples ("These are *inflammatory* remarks" and "After the argument, Dave was *smoldering* for days") are frequent, others ("She was doing a slow *burn*," "He was breathing *fire*," "Your insincere apology has added *fuel to the fire*," "Boy, am I *burned up*," and "*Smoke* was pouring out of his ears") are either rare or absent in the corpus. She states that the ANGER-AS-FIRE metaphor has a number of lexicalization not mentioned by Yu, showing that *ignite* and its derivatives occur 332 times in the U.S. section of the Bank of English, of which 228 citations are metaphorical.

Deignan's argument gives useful suggestions for studies related to the prototype of concepts. In considering the prototypical attributes of a category, researchers can use the frequency with which the word for the category collocates with the words for the potential attributes of the prototype as a measuring stick. The following sections will show analyses of the attributes of the emotion prototype and an investigation into the specific emotions close to the prototype, based on the data from the BNC.

2.3.3 Metaphorical expressions for the uncontrollability of emotion

For several years I have studied the metaphor of emotion in literary texts as well as in everyday language use, and proposed in Omori (2007a, b) that one of the major metaphorical source domains utilized for understanding EMOTION is NATURAL PHENOMENA. This proposal owes much to the "EMOTIONS ARE NATURAL FORCES" metaphor presented by Kövecses (1990:162–163, 2000:71–72). He specifies his source domain NATURAL FORCES by listing the subordinate concepts STORMS, WAVES, FLOODS, and FIRE, illustrating these with examples like "There were *stormy* emotions when the news of the disaster reached the town," "Emotions *swept over* her," and "She was on *fire* with emotion." I have expanded his source domain into NATURAL PHENOMENA so that it can cover all the four elements comprehensively, i.e. AIR, WATER, FIRE, and EARTH, which have been traditionally regarded as the fundamental constituents of the natural world. While Kövecses placed the NATURAL FORCE metaphor lower in rank than the CONTAINER metaphor, I regard my NATURAL PHENOMENA metaphor as a cognitive device of crucial importance for the comprehension of emotion.

In the various metaphorical expressions for EMOTION derived from this source, I have concentrated, to conduct a corpus search efficiently, on the conventional pattern of two nouns connected by the preposition *of*, such as "*flood of joy.*" The first nominal in this pattern represents a concept derived from the source domain NATURAL PHENOMENA, and the second from the target domain EMOTION. This type of expression, which I would like to call "N *of* E," is an explicit linguistic realization of the metaphorical mapping.[1]

It needs close attention to extract metaphors from the results of the corpus search for "[nominal] *of* [nominal]." Only the examples in which the two nominals have vehicle-tenor relations should be picked up. The criteria of the vehicle-tenor relations is that the two nominals should belong to different conceptual domains, and that the first nominal should have a predicative role for specification of the second nominal: that is, the first nominal should be a description of the second nominal, as in the case of "*sea of emotion*" (in which "sea" is a description of "emotion;" in other words, emotion is considered to be the sea), or should be a derivative of a verb of which the second nominal is the subject, as in the case of "*upsurge of emotion*" (in which emotion is considered to surge up). Actually many search results do not meet these criteria. For example, "demonstrations" in "He hates demonstrations of emotion" is a derivative of the verb "demonstrate," of which "emotion" is the object. The same holds for "the voluntary control of emotion." I have counted those examples out.

The results of the corpus search for "[source-domain nominal] + *of* + *emotion* / *emotions* / *feeling* / *feelings*" indicate that the extracted metaphorical phrases are derived from various source domains including NATURAL PHENOMENA. I have identified six source domains from which more than ten citations are derived. Table 2.2 shows these major source domains and some examples. Metaphors derived from NATURAL PHENOMENA are outstanding in number, which indicates the predominance of the metaphor of the type "N of E."

Source	No. of citations	Examples
NATURAL PHENOMENA	102	"wave of emotion," "volcano of emotion," "crosswinds of emotion"
SUBSTANCES or SMALL OBJECTS	41	"mixture of emotions," "jumble of emotions," "residue of feeling"
A CONTAINER	38	"depth of emotion," "depth of feeling," "recesses of feeling"
A MOVING OBJECT or A VEHICLE	17	"switchback of emotion," "swings of emotions," "transfers of feeling"
A LIVING ORGANISM	14	"revival of feeling," "maggots of feeling," "bud of feeling"
TEXTILE or THREADS	13	"tangle of emotions," "tapestries of emotion," "texture of feelings"

Table 2.2: Number of occurrences of metaphorical expressions of the type "[source-domain nominal] of emotion(s) / feeling(s)" derived from the major source domains

Now let us look at the metaphors for EMOTION in general seen in the citations of metaphor in the type "N of E" retrieved from the BNC. Table 2.3 shows the number of occurrences of the type "N of E" with the words *emotion* or *feeling* or their plurals in the "E" slot (For further details, see Appendices 2.1 and 2.2). In this study, I have classified the occurrences into four domains subordinate to the source domain NATURAL PHENOMENA, i.e. AIR, WATER, FIRE, and EARTH. As a result, citations grouped into the domain WATER exceed all others in number (76 out of 102 citations), in which vehicles associated with various geographic forms of water like SEA, RIVER, and SPRING are included. The 76 citations are further classified based on the various forms of water as shown in Table 2.4.

Source	"emotion(s)"	"feeling(s)"	Total	Examples
AIR	7	2	9	"crosswinds of emotion," "outbursts of feelings"
WATER	45	31	76	"wave of emotion," "surge of emotion," "current of feeling"
FIRE	6	1	7	"flash of emotion," "inflamed rush of feeling"
EARTH	2	8	10	"volcano of emotion," "caverns of feeling"

Table 2.3: Number of occurrences of metaphorical expressions of the type "*N of E*" from the four different source sub-domains with the words "emotion(s)" or "feeling(s)" in the "*E*" slot

Geographic form of water	Vehicles related with water collocating with "of emotion(s)"	Vehicles related with water collocating with "of feeling(s)"	Total
SEA	ebb and flow, maelstrom, sea, surge (3), surges, swirl, tidal wave, tide (4), upsurge, upsurging, vortex (2), wave (6), waves (3), welter (2), whirlpool	groundswell, maelstrom, surges, tide (3), tides, upsurge (2), wave (4), waves, waves and currents, whirlpools	45
RIVER	rush (5), torrent (2), torrents (2)	current (3), currents (2), flood, flow, rush (2), stream, torrent, undercurrent	21
SPRING	outpouring (2), spring, welling-up, wells	outpouring	6
WATER IN A CONTAINER	cocktail, tubs	boiling tumult	3
OTHERS	—	drop	1

Table 2.4: Geographic forms of water expressed in the metaphor of the type "*N of E*" with the words "emotion(s)" or "feeling(s)" in the "*E*" slot

Table 2.4 shows that 45 citations, 59% of all the citations of the type "[words for water] *of emotion(s) / feeling(s),*" have lexical items associated with the SEA, whose scale is the largest in the natural world. Interestingly, the smaller the form of water is, the fewer the number of citations. It is evident that words indicating massive forms of water are preferable as a vehicle in metaphors of emotion, where uncontrollability is highlighted. The metaphorical expressions that use vehicles related to the SEA, e.g. "*surge,*" "*tide,*" "*tidal wave,*" and "*maelstrom,*" literally depict the motion of seawater as an energy far beyond human control. Words related to the flow of the RIVER, 28% of the total, rank second in expressing the uncontrollability of emotion. Vehicles like "*rush,*" "*torrent*" and "*flood*" which belong to the domain also connote in their literal meanings the enormous energy of water that occasionally causes immense damage to human lives. The number of metaphors derived from the sources SEA and RIVER (66 hits altogether) exceeds any number of citations derived from the major sources but NATURAL PHENOMENA shown in Table 2.2. These metaphors often collocate with expressions that describe the human effort to resist and control the fierce attack of water, such as "struggle" in (1), or they describe the failure of the effort, as in the case of "irresistible" in (2) and "unable to deal with…" in (3). (The parenthetical notes after each example refer to the BNC filename and sentence number.) The citations with vehicles belonging to WATER IN A CONTAINER, on the other hand, count only three, one of which refers to BOILING WATER. In summary, the most plausible source concept for characterizing the uncontrollability of emotion is A HUGE MASS OF MOVING WATER IN THE NATURAL WORLD.[2]

(1) She stopped again, *struggling with the torrent of emotions* she'd unleashed. (JY3 2752)
(2) I want my home, she thought, and was appalled by her childishness; but the *tide of emotion* was *irresistible, surging through her like great waves.* (F99 2651)
(3) He ran a hand through his hair, *unable to deal with the sudden wave of emotion* the conversation had brought with it. (JYB 3423)

2.3.4 A cognitive model and its theoretical implications

A wide ranging observation of emotion metaphors derived from MOVING WATER IN THE NATURAL WORLD enables me to assume a cognitive model which consists of the following correspondences between the source and the target domains.

Source: MOVING WATER IN THE NATURAL WORLD	Target: EMOTION	Example
A spell of dry weather makes a river waterless.	A shortage of stimulus causes lack of emotion.	drought of emotion
Water comes naturally to the surface from under the ground.	Emotion appears.	spring of emotion
A natural flow of water makes river.	Emotion becomes active.	currents of feelings
Some geographic cause prevents water from moving and makes it stagnate.	Some disappointing situation makes emotion inactive.	stagnant pool of emotion
When the volume of water in the river becomes too large, the water inundates.	When emotion becomes too active, it deviates from the norm and leads to abnormal behavior.	flood of feelings
The river finally flows into the sea.	Emotion enlarges.	sea of emotion
Seawater ebbs and flows alternately.	A specific emotion dominates a person intermittently and repeatedly.	ebb and flow of emotion
Seawater surges up.	The intensity of emotion increases.	surge of emotion
High waves beat upon the shore and sweep the region.	Intense emotion makes a person lose his or her reason.	tidal wave of emotion
When seawater swirls, it has a tremendous power against which people would never be able to struggle and would be swallowed up if caught in it.	When emotion is introverted and intensified in a confusing way, one is unable to control it; on the contrary he or she is controlled by it.	maelstrom of emotions

Table 2.5: Correspondences between moving water in the natural world and emotion[3]

The correspondences shown in Table 2.5 are motivated by structure of human experience. Water sprung up in a mountain increases in volume during its long travel to the sea, and its powerful flow is occasionally dangerous: failure to control it may cause a disastrous flood. The power of seawater is far beyond human biological capacities. Swimming in high waves may make people drown. Television images of storm surges and tidal waves sweeping everything, such as the tsunami that devastated the coastal areas around the Indian Ocean in 2004 and the tragic news of Tohoku Disaster in 2011, reinforce anew our bodily-based knowledge about water. Thus, the conceptualization of water in the natural world arises out of embodiment and is manifested in metaphor.

This cognitive model based on the embodied conceptualization of A HUGE MASS OF MOVING WATER IN THE NATURAL WORLD suggests that the concept is cross-culturally significant. The concept is closely involved with cultures of people who live in the water-rich environment. We Japanese also have wealth of words for expressing emotion in terms of A HUGE MASS OF MOVING WATER, such as "*kanjo-no-izumi*" (i.e. spring of emotion), "*kanjo-no-nami*" (i.e. wave of emotion), "*kanjo-no-ushio*" (i.e. tide of emotion), "*kanjo-no-uzu*" (i.e. whirlpool of emotion), "*wakideru-kanjo*" (i.e. springing emotion), "*namidatsu-kanjo*" (i.e. surging emotion), "*kanjo-ni-nagasareru*" (i.e. to be swept by emotion), and "*kanjo-ni-oboreru*" (i.e. to be drowned in emotion). Japanese people, who live on the islands surrounded by the sea, are well aware of both the blessings and the dangers of natural water. Japanese emotion metaphors derived from the source A HUGE MASS OF MOVING WATER IN THE NATURAL WORLD are naturally based on our embodiment of the concept NATURAL WATER.

2.3.5 "Temperature" of emotion

This section observes citations in the BNC expressing emotion as having some temperature. The result of my search for EMOTION words in general contains 14 citations with the collocate "*cold*," i.e. 13 hits of "*cold feeling*" and one hit of "*cold feelings*." On the other hand, my corpus data includes only one hit of "*hot emotion*," one "*hot feeling*," one "*boiling emotions*" and one "*boiling tumult of feeling*." It unexpectedly reveals that EMOTION in general is more frequently perceived as COLD than HOT. This result is, however, consistent with the search shown in Table 2.3: of all the metaphorical expressions of the type "*N of E*" with the words "emotion(s)" or "feeling(s)" in the "*E*" slot, the citations derived from the source FIRE account for less than seven percent (7 out of 102 hits). But here a hasty conclusion that EMOTION is *typically* perceived as COLD should be avoided. There are 18 tokens of "*warm feeling(s)*" and 12 tokens of "*warm*" followed by "feeling(s)" with occurrences of other modifying words between the two. However, this research does not lead to the idea that A "HOT" OR "BOILING" FLUID corresponds to the prototypical INTENSIFICATION OF EMOTION. It is also noteworthy that the emotion terms modified by "*warm*" generally have positive meanings, like "*warm feeling of happiness*" (FPM 1582), "*warm, satisfying feelings*" (ALH 1595), and "*warm, friendly feeling*" (HP6 1215). These search results are out of line with Kövecses' view that the emotion prototype is characterized in terms of A HEATED FLUID IN A CONTAINER and that one of the specific emotions closest to the prototype is ANGER.

When you perceive your feelings as COLD, what subcategory are they classified under? In the following citation "*cold feeling*" collocates with "dread."

(4) Memories of blood-red wine and cruelly glinting shards of glass came back to haunt her. It had been wickedly symbolic, stage-managed to stir in her *a cold feeling of dread*. (HA6 1921–1922)

In searching the BNC for the keyword "*cold*" occurring with nouns for specific emotions, I found collocates describing FEAR, such as "fear" (31 hits), "terror" (7 hits), and "horror" (6 hits). Phrases like "*cold chill of fear*" (JXV 1633) and "*icy fear*" (CDA 2522, and three other hits) also exemplify the association between COLDNESS and FEAR. Here are some of the citations in which "cold" collocates with a word for FEAR.

(5) As he dressed for dinner in his room, Dorian remembered what he had seen and *cold fear* ran through him like a knife. (GUS 943)
(6) If you let it, fear will hurl you into a sick, *cold terror*. (G35 641)
(7) And it came to him, with a *cold steely horror* chilling the bloodstream as if from a lethal injection.... (AT4 1693)

In these examples, COLD FEAR is regarded as what runs through the body (5), as morbid (6), or as making the blood cold (7). In Examples (5) and (7) you can also see the association between FEAR, COLDNESS, and A KNIFE. A similar example is "*the cold knives of fear*" (JXV 2837), where the three concepts are fully realized. The interrelationship of the concepts is probably based on our knowledge of the physiological effects of an attack with the weapon: that to stab a knife into our bodies brings about bleeding, loss of body temperature, and possibly death.

Worth noting is that "cold" can also collocate with words representing ANGER. In my data, 15 tokens of "fury," 15 tokens of "anger," and five tokens of "rage" occur with "*cold*." For comparison, I searched for "hot" collocating with words for ANGER. The result was that seven tokens of "rage" and six tokens of "anger" occurred with "*hot*." This shows that the association between ANGER and COLDNESS is far from exceptional but as common as or fairly comparable with the association between ANGER and HEAT.

The characteristic of COLD ANGER is exemplified in the following citations.

(8) Now that he had moved nearer Fran could see that there was a muscle ticking along the hard line of his jaw and that his eyes were glittering with something more than mere mockery, and she went cold. He wasn't just angry, he was furious, a *cold, icy fury*, which made answering shivers trickle along her spine. (JXV 615–616)
(9) 'Are you frightened, Englishman?' the Lieutenant laughed. Sharpe felt the anger then; the *cold anger* that seemed to slow the passage of time itself and make everything appear so very distinctly. (CMP 1605–1606)
(10) His *cold rage* thickened his accent, but the revolver in his hand remained steady. (CKE 243)

Example (8) shows Fran's perception that the emotion arising in the man stepping up to her is beyond mockery or mere anger. Example (9) describes a single combat between two men. The "*cold*" anger felt by the man provoked by his opponent is depicted as what makes him unusually sensitive to everything around him, even the passage of time. The man's rage in Example (10) is too fierce for him to pronounce his words clearly, but does not lead to the firing of his gun. The COLD ANGER in each example is of a tremendously high degree of intensity, and still does not accompany a violent action. These examples show that the very emotion ANGER that Kövecses placed the closest to the emotion prototype is sometimes perceived as COLD, not HOT, and that RISE IN TEMPERATURE OF A FLUID is not an almighty source for INTENSIFICATION OF EMOTION.

It should be noted that COLD ANGER and COLD FEAR are mentioned by Kövecses (2005), too, though the two are regarded as exceptions or unusual varieties of emotion. He construes COLD ANGER as "a particular kind of anger, say, when the angry person is meditating, in a self-controlled way, on a retribution that far outweighs the offense" (p. 288), and explains that "the notion of cold anger is based on conceptualizing a part of anger (retribution) as a rational act by the angry person. It is this rational, as opposed to emotional, decision that is conceptualized as being 'cold'" (ibid.). Kövecses concludes that in this case the "RATIONAL IS COLD" metaphor is applied to a part of the cultural model of anger, and claims that, despite the fact that the instance of cold anger seemingly contradicts the metaphorical conceptualization of anger as A HOT FLUID IN A CONTAINER, the conflict is more apparent than real (p.289). The persons who experience the feeling of cold anger in Examples (8) – (10), however, cannot be seen as following the dictates of *pure* reason as opposed to emotion. Their senses may be keenly honed as in the case of the person in Example (9) and this emotional state may enable them to advance reasoning, but our observation of the contexts surrounding "*cold anger / fury / rage*" above reveals that COLD ANGER is not purely rational but is also an intense emotion, which should not be placed outside of, or at the periphery of, the category of EMOTION. As for COLD FEAR contradicting his HOT FLUID IN A CONTAINER metaphor, Kövecses claims that "we conceive of the simple but highly generic metaphors that are based on tight correlations in experience (such as "INTENSITY IS HEAT") as powerful conceptual devices that can override local embodiment in other parts of the conceptual system (in "FEAR IS COLD")" (p. 289). His view is not consistent with the factual evidence in my corpus data. The presence of my examples is too strong to be overridden or regarded as trivial.

2.4 Attributes of emotion prototype and prototypical emotions

The studies above have revealed that in the metaphorical mapping on to THE UNCONTROLLABILITY OF EMOTION a cogent prototypical source is A HUGE MASS OF MOVING WATER IN THE NATURAL WORLD, and that the "temperature" of an intense emotion is not always perceived as HOT but sometimes as COLD. This section is an attempt to assess specific emotions in terms of the closeness to the emotion prototype.

As shown in Table 2.3, the most prominent source sub-domain utilized in the "N of E" type metaphors that use the words "emotion(s)" or "feeling(s)" in the "E" slot is WATER, and lexical items derived from this sub-domain account for 74.5% of all the metaphors of this type. The proportions of lexemes from the other sub-domains, i.e. AIR, FIRE, and EARTH are 8.8%, 6.9%, and 9.8%, respectively. This distribution makes up the attributes of the emotion prototype. In order to make a comparison, I carried out a similar corpus search for nine specific emotions, the result of which is shown in Table 2.6. Among the nine specific emotion concepts, PLEASURE, SADNESS, and ANGER have rich synonyms. In this corpus research, I adopted three keywords for the respective concepts: "pleasure," "happiness" and "joy" for PLEASURE, "sadness," "sorrow" and "grief" for SADNESS, and "anger," "resentment" and "fury" for ANGER.

In Table 2.6, the source domain NATURAL PHENOMENA is classified into the four elements, and the proportion of the citations grouped into the sub-domain most frequently used is indicated in terms of percentage. Figure 2.2 contrasts the distribution of source sub-domains utilized for understanding the emotion in general with the nine specific emotion domains. In this figure the specific emotions are placed in order based on the proportion of the citations from the source sub-domain WATER.

Target domain	Hits of "of E"	No. of meta-phors	Source sub-domain			
			WATER	AIR	FIRE	EARTH
EMOTION	1,003	102	76 (74.5%)	9 (8.8%)	7 (6.9%)	10 (9.8%)
PLEASURE	937	75	46 (61.3%)	9	17	3
SADNESS	325	27	15 (55.6%)	7	1	4
ANGER	542	117	47 (40.2%)	28	40	2
HOPE	503	125	4	4	116 (92.8%)	1
DESPAIR	264	39	4	6	1	28 (71.8%)
DESIRE	304	35	22 (62.9%)	4	7	2
RELIEF	708	39	28 (71.8%)	3	4	4
ANXIETY	431	18	13 (72.2%)	3	1	1
FEAR	401	40	22 (55.0%)	13	5	0

Table 2.6: The tendency of mapping in the "N of E" metaphor for emotion in general and the specific emotions

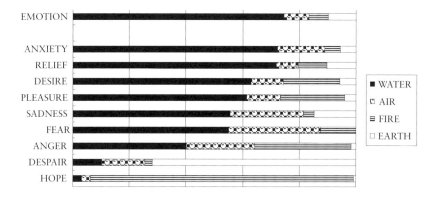

Figure 2.2: Distribution of source sub-domains for the emotion in general and the nine specific emotions

The emotions for which the domain WATER is frequently used as a source are ANXIETY, RELIEF, DESIRE, PLEASURE, SADNESS and FEAR. The proportion of the citations from the source WATER is above 70% in relation to ANXIETY and RELIEF, and above 60% in relation to DESIRE and PLEASURE. These specific emotions can be assessed as close to the emotion prototype. Also, more than 50% of the citations expressing SADNESS and FEAR are from the source WATER. The emotion FEAR, which can be associated with COLDNESS (as observed in the previous section), is never far off the emotion prototype.

ANGER, on the other hand, is somewhat distant from the prototype. The citations derived from the source WATER account for only 40.2%, and the proportion of the citations from FIRE (ex. "*a flame of anger*") closes in on the proportion of the citations from WATER, making up 34.2%. The emotions that are extremely far from the prototype are DESPAIR and HOPE. When it comes to DESPAIR and HOPE, metaphorical expressions derived from the source WATER are either uncommon or very rare. Each of them is absolutely unique in the distribution of their source sub-domains. In fact, many of the metaphors expressing DESPAIR (71.8%) are derived from EARTH, as in "*a quagmire of despair*," "*a deep chasm of despair*," and "*pits of despair*." In the metaphor for HOPE the source FIRE is overwhelmingly prevalent (92.8%) and such stereotypical expressions as "*a bright flame of hope*," "*a sudden flare of hope*," "*a light of hope*" and "*glimmers of hope*," serve as common examples.

The difference between DESIRE and HOPE is also worth notice, for the two are generally regarded as synonymous: they are grouped under the same category in most thesauri. The careful observation, however, reveals that they are utterly different. While the former has an attribute of emotion prototype in that the most frequent metaphorical source is WATER, the latter does not. The emotion concept similar to DESIRE is PLEASURE: the distributions of source sub-domains in these two concepts are surprisingly alike.

When the concepts close to the emotion prototype are metaphorically expressed by means of the source WATER, what kinds of vehicles are used? Table 2.7 is a classification of vehicles related with WATER that collocate with "of anxiety," "of relief," "of desire," and "of pleasure" in terms of geographic forms of water.

Geographic form of water	Vehicles related with water collocating with:			
	"of anxiety"	"of relief"	"of desire"	"of pleasure"
SEA	surge (2), upsurge, waves (2)	surge (9), surges, tide (2), wave (5), waves	sea, surge (3), tidal wave, tide, wave (3), waves (3), whirlpool	sea, surge (4), tide (2), wave (4), waves (4), whirlpool
RIVER	flood, current, rush, undercurrent (3)	flood (2), flow, rush (3), wash	flood, floods, flow, river, rivers, rush	flood (2), rills, stream
LAKE OR POND	ripples	ripple, ripples	—	ripple, ripples
SPRING	—	gush	swell	springs, spurt (5)
WATER IN A CONTAINER	—	—	water bottles	—
OTHERS	dollop	—	infusion	trickles

Table 2.7: Geographic forms of water expressed in the metaphor of the type "*N of E*" depicting emotions close to the prototype

The result of Table 2.7 demonstrates a tendency similar to the distribution of geographic forms of water expressed in the metaphor "[words for water] *of emotion(s) / feeling(s)*" shown in Table 2.4. These four specific emotions also prefer vehicles associated with large-scale forms of water like the sea and the rivers, where the motion of water is energetic and beyond human control. All of them, i.e. ANXIETY, RELIEF caused by the sudden resolution of ANXIETY, DESIRE, and PLEASURE caused by the achievement of DESIRE, can be characterized as emotions that are actively moving and hard to control with the power of reason.

2.5 Conclusion

This chapter took a brief look at Kövecses' argument on emotion metaphor, and proposed an alternative to his idea of the prototype of emotion. While he utilized the concept of water restricted within a container, I took notice of the boundless expanses of water in the natural world, and for my research into attributes of the emotion prototype I retrieved from the BNC metaphorical expressions containing both source and target-domain lexemes in the conventional form of two nominals connected by the preposition "of." As for the problems brought up at the beginning of this chapter, this study reached the following conclusions. (i) A source concept more suitable than TO HEAT A FLUID IN A CONTAINER for characterizing the uncontrollability of emotion is A HUGE MASS OF MOVING WATER IN THE NATURAL WORLD. According to the corpus analysis of the vehicles related to water, the smaller the geographic form of water is, the fewer the number of citations. (ii) Intense emotions are often felt to be COLD, the cases of which are no less represented than those felt to be HOT. COLD feelings of fear and anger are not to be placed on the periphery of the category EMOTION. (iii) The corpus data of the conventional metaphor "*N of E*" disproves the conjecture that ANGER is one of the prototypical emotions. According to the distribution of the four source sub-domains, the specific emotions closest to the prototype are ANXIETY and RELIEF, and DESIRE and PLEASURE are runners-up. DESIRE is remarkably similar to PLEASURE, and is quite different from HOPE, as against my expectation or descriptions given by many thesauri. HOPE is farthest from the emotion prototype in that the frequency of the source WATER is extremely low. DESPAIR and ANGER, next to HOPE, are peripheral in the category EMOTION. Each of these three shows its distinctive individuality in terms of the distribution of source sub-domains. Thus, corpus data produces unexpected discoveries about the position of specific emotions in terms of prototypicality, which are distinct from and sometimes inconsistent with the intuition of the researcher.

Notes

1 Cruse (1986) and Deignan (2005) mention conventional metaphors that have a structure that includes a slot where target-domain words are filled. Cruse points out that the meaning of the word "mouth" in phrases like "the mouth of the river" or "the mouth of the bottle" is highly context-bound: it is delivered by metaphorical interpretation. However, an unmodified use of the word "mouth" —as in "At school, we are doing a project on mouths" — is unlikely to be interpreted as a metaphor. Deignan presents the result of a corpus search, in which the verb "starve," when used metaphorically to refer to suffering because of the lack of something other than food, appears in one of the following three structures: "*starv** + *of* + noun" (ex. "starved of weapons"), "noun + - + *starved*" (ex. "investment-starved"), and "*starv** + *for* + noun" (ex. "starving for publicity").
2 I have also found in the BNC notable metaphorical expressions of emotion by means of vehicles describing uncontrollable natural phenomena related to elements other than water, such as "crosswinds of emotion," "inflamed rush of feeling," and "eruption of feeling," where we see violent movements of air, fire and earth on a large scale.
3 Among the examples shown in Table 2.5, "drought of emotion" and "stagnant pool of emotion" are retrieved from Google (http://www.google.co.jp/).

Appendix

Appendix 2.1

BNC citations of metaphorical expressions of the Type "N of E" from the four different source sub-domains with the words "emotion(s)" in the "E" slot

Source	No.	Filename	BNC citations
AIR	1	CAW 1411	But after the first 8½ lines these **crosswinds of emotion** are harmonized, and the poem concludes with a dignified and controlled recognition of the fact of death.
	2	A7L 1056	The culmination of the drama, an **explosion of emotions** during a thunderstorm, has parallels in other Rank-financed movies of the time, when the lid comes off and all the emotions that have been barely repressed throughout the film come pouring out as if from some Pandora's box.
	3	CKD 1401	Hari could not breathe, she felt lost in **a flurry of emotions**.
	4	AB3 1171	It's just one of those things this society has suppressed, along with any other strong or extreme **outburst of emotion**.
	5	BNP 1177	Though the Young Vic's small theatre-in-the-round is hardly the best place for a tense domestic drama, this tightly-controlled production keeps the dread steadily rising and nicely paces the **outbursts of emotion** against the background of rumbling resentment.
	6	H97 3776	That possibility had caused a **scurry of emotion** inside her, that, for the moment, Lisa had dared not examine too closely.
	7	H8S 3900	And in the **storm of emotion** that threatened to overwhelm her there was only room for one thought.
WATER	1	K49 108	The team served us with a final **cocktail of emotions**: happy, poignant and even philosophical.
	2	GVJ 79	The **ebb and flow of emotion** should therefore be carefully controlled.
	3	HA5 2129	Once inside, she slid the bolt, leaning thankfully against the door, a **maelstrom of emotions** fighting for supremacy.
	4	CU0 447	THOSE OF US who are convinced there is no longer room for sentiment at the hard edge of professional sport would have found it difficult to comprehend the **outpouring of emotion** that followed the exclusion of Geoff Marsh from the Australian tam for the final Test against India.
	5	KRU 33	No hint at the airport of the **outpouring of emotion** that was to come.

6	JY2 235	With a **rush of emotion** she couldn't put a name to Luce realised that her first instinctive feeling about him had been absolutely right.
7	JY4 2550	Her and Fernando, loving, making love as if for the very first time, with urgency and excitement and a fevered **rush of emotions**.
8	GVT 885	A sudden **rush of emotions** — jealousy and envy, mingled with satisfaction at observing them unbeknown — made him forget his uncomfortable situation for a moment.
9	JXV 2118	It had been three days since she'd seen Luke, three days that she'd spent trying to get him out of her system, but she couldn't deny the sudden **rush of emotion** at the thought of seeing him again.
10	JXV 3147	It was hard to stop the sudden **rush of emotion** just the mention of his name could provoke, but she did her best.
11	H9H 854	'If you want it to,' he answered simply, a rock of reasonableness that Belinda found rather reassuring in the **sea of emotion** between brother and sister.
12	HA5 1762	His name trembled on her lips once more, no longer a name but an endearment, a paean to the deep **spring of emotion** which was gushing through her, banishing logical thought, obliterating words like 'giving' and 'taking', replacing them with 'sharing'.
13	HGE 2338	As she cuddled him, seeing his tiny face, his perfect little hands, a great **surge of emotion** swept through her.
14	GUE 3360	'What don't I?' he mocked, the husky caress in his voice shooting a hectic **surge of emotion** right through her body.
15	JY2 455	It was a moment or two before she was able to control the wild **surge of emotion** and say with commendable aplomb, 'Good morning, Signor Lorenzo.
16	GUE 1877	She caught her breath, her palms damp just thinking about the powerful **surges of emotion** she'd felt in his arms.
17	GUE 404	Something strange happened inside her, a **swirl of emotion**, heightening awareness to a sharp, almost painful degree …
18	A4B 225	IF THERE had been unity, it would have been simple enough: in purely rugby terms the All Blacks are unbeatable, by Wales at any rate, so only a surge of hwyl, a **tide of emotion**, could hope to stop them.
19	JY8 4248	Desperately she swallowed back a **tide of emotion**.
20	F99 2651	I want my home, she thought, and was appalled by her childishness; but the **tide of emotion** was irresistible, surging through her like great waves.
21	ALL 1386	Someone started singing 'God Save the King' and soon everybody was joining in, thousands of strong hearts and lungs, shipyard workers, foundry men, train drivers, some still on strike, were swept away by the **tide of emotion**.
22	B19 652	Staggering over my own threshold again released a **torrent of emotions**.

23	JY3 2752	She stopped again, struggling with the **torrent of emotions** she'd unleashed.
24	GoN 1529	**Torrents of emotion.**
25	JXX 1743	It was five long years since any man — this man — had intimately touched her like this; five years in which she'd held at bay these deep **torrents of emotion**, which would not now be denied.
26	CK6 2105	And Bell also brought **tubs of emotion** to Erasure — the longing of the astonishing 'Oh L'Amour', the raging of 'Respect', the sheer Swedishness of 'Take A Chance On Me'.
27	JYB 1230	But what had caused that violent **upsurge of emotion**?
28	HA4 1051	To love one's neighbour, she thought as she trudged resolutely up the Finchley Road, must surely often be an effort of the will rather than a pleasurable **upsurging of emotion**.
29	JXX 1749	As he moved slowly at first his mouth sought first her breasts and then her lips, his breathing ragged as the pulsating, rhythmic movement quickened, echoing the rising heat in her blood, both of them caught up in a swirling **vortex of emotions**.
30	GUE 2419	She closed her eyes and arched blindly against him, let him guide her into another kind of darkness, where that unknown **vortex of emotion**, that powerful pull of attraction between them swirled and hypnotised, and this time the stars behind her eyelids were brilliant but softly incandescent, fireworks of intense delight, bursting in her head ...
31	BMR 1237	By then our approaching orgasms had synchronized to form a freak **wave of emotion** which threatened to wipe our personalities clean.
32	EC8 504	He 'felt a surge of patriotic emotion within him' but almost at once he 'incontinently began to analyse his **wave of emotion** and to wonder how much of it was due to the romantic beauty of his surroundings'.
33	BLW 1405	The role of step-parents can be hard, especially if the problems have not been foreseen and the marriage has taken place on a powerful **wave of emotion** and little else.
34	JYB 3423	He ran a hand through his hair, unable to deal with the sudden **wave of emotion** the conversation had brought with it.
35	JY2 3772	She heard the indrawn breath hiss sharply through his teeth, and felt the **wave of emotion** that washed over him.
36	CAH 276	Then about four days later it was pointed out to me that a real earthquake actually hit Germany last week, and she wasn't being poetic at all, and I actually felt cheated of the **wave of emotion** I had felt towards her.
37	H8S 366	And the **tidal wave of emotion** had left her drained for days.

	38	HoK 745	No story conveys a better impression of the unity of the Mediterranean world in the sixth century B.C. **Waves of emotion** spread from Asia Minor to Spain as soon as a new protagonist — Persia — disturbed the existing equilibrium of friendships, political alliances and commercial interests.
	39	GVJ 1752	Music is emotion, and musical forms, however free, must move in **waves of emotion**.
	40	GVJ 1741	We must not only abide by a precise form, but also build up the right **waves of emotion** to give it full human significance.
	41	CDS 846	Later, I asked myself whether in my extremity I, the helpless, had been seeking, as the hymn said, the help of God, and that in the act of seeking it, I had been granted it (he who seeks God, said Pascal, has already found him); or whether this spontaneous **welling-up of emotion** from the depths of my being was no more than the expression of a statement to myself.
	42	JY8 3159	Her eyes were enormous **wells of emotion**.
	43	H9L 2470	For a moment, as he bent over her, she looked up at him, her parted lips soft and full, and, as had happened in the night, she felt a **welter of emotion** rising, swamping her heart.
	44	AS5 204	Nothing could have prepared him, however, for the complex **welter of emotions** which followed Emma's death in 1912 after years of virtual estrangement.
	45	H8J 379	Claudia wished she could stop shaking; the touch of his hard body against hers had started up a **whirlpool of emotion** that left her wanting to run until she had put miles between them.
FIRE	1	HGM 3018	She raised her eyes to his face, but he could see no **flash of emotion** there, nothing of the slightly vulnerable girl who'd tried to hide her hurt under an efficient exterior.
	2	EEL 724	I really have never felt even a **flicker of emotion** when I sang the National Anthem.
	3	HTL 1674	Just for a moment I thought I saw a **flicker of emotion** in her eyes, but it was probably a trick of the light.
	4	CBG 9206	RETURNING to Anfield tomorrow means a great deal to Kenny Dalglish, but I'll be surprised if the players see a **flicker of emotion** in those tense last moments in the dressing room.
	5	GUE 1702	There was no **flicker of emotion** in the dark eyes.
	6	G1S 2864	Without any sign of hurry, or the slightest **flicker of emotion**, he took hold of her arm and removed it, just as the exploring fingers were about to reach their objective.
EARTH	1	EWH 782	For a week, while the ship was stored and watered and fresh livestock taken aboard, Sara lived in a strange **no-man's-land of emotion** in which she alternated between boiling excitement at what lay ahead and abject dolours at the thought of leaving Ireland.
	2	CDX 1120	What **volcano of emotion** must have been boiling inside that youngster under his teasing and laughing, under his occasionally expressionless face?

Appendix 2.2

BNC citations of metaphorical expressions of the Type "*N of E*" from the four different source sub-domains with the words "feeling(s)" in the "*E*" slot

Source	No.	Filename	BNC citations
AIR	1	B11 590	All across Canada there had been **outbursts of feelings** against the way radio broadcasting had been handled, and one of these certainly came from the Moose Jaw area.
	2	B30 298	However, the **ventilation of feelings** about the overdose, especially those experienced by the partner or other family members, should be encouraged early in therapy, otherwise they may impede progress.
WATER	1	HTP 896	The way in which some modern political leaders exploit envy for their own purposes, and the way it is built into some party programmes, positively suggest that this is a powerful **current of feeling** which can be readily and effectively exploited.
	2	HTP 887	In an age of secularization, in which religious myths have been ruthlessly unmasked and in which parricidal revolt and protest has been directed as much against God as against other father-surrogates, it is not surprising that a regressive **current of feeling**, comparable to that which sustained the Neolithic goddess-cults, no longer finds an obvious religious expression.
	3	EDE 128	However, these immediately familiar accusations against the moral failure of the British people touched on a much wider **current of feeling** in 1950s Britain which found a crystallising focus in the problems of the younger generation.
	4	HA4 969	A rather strange collection of men and women, thought Rupert with an anthropologist's detachment, none of whom really know each other but between whom **waves and currents of feeling** are already beginning to pass.
	5	HTP 881	Furthermore, of the two opposite **currents of feeling**, the positive, needing one is probably the older and more fundamental.
	6	HUN 191	So that makes the ego pro-social, and in Future of an Illusion, we saw Freud arguing, that there were fundamental pro-social **currents of feeling** in the ego, in terms of the ego's wish fulfilment for, for example, a benevolent god, a divine justice and things like this.
	7	G01 3318	He felt as if every last **drop of feeling** had been sucked out of him.
	8	ADE 112	To return to my burglary, I remember experiencing a whole **flood of feelings**.
	9	HH3 6200	Surely there was a **flow of feeling** here from people to people?

10	K5J 1426	There is a fascinating **groundswell of feeling** on the avant-garde led by Martin Margiela with his elaborately deconstructed and reconstructed flea-market treasures for a fashion that is fundamentally different from the designerisms of the Eighties.
11	GoT 684	To come to terms with the **maelstrom of feelings** aroused would mean accepting what most have been taught are 'wrong' feelings for a 'nice' person to have.
12	A5E 86	His elegiac tempo for the largo of the Cello Sonata allows him a sustained **outpouring of feeling**.
13	APM 322	Franca, looking at him, felt the old familiar **rush of feeling** as if her body advanced and entered his body.
14	HHA 2508	Fen moved closer, to stand at her shoulder, and his words were almost lost to her in the **rush of feeling** his nearness engendered.
15	CDC 440	There is clearly a self which needs to be repudiated, an ever-changing, superficial, grasping, possessive thing, the **stream of feelings**, thoughts and desires, which insists on taking over the direction of life.
16	KRH 4661	And so with Joyce we might talk, say, of the manageable stories of Dubliners and the still acceptable mixture of poignant retrospect and startling **surges of feeling** that mark the portrait of the artist as a young man.
17	JNB 290	It's gotta start somewhere, there's a motion, a **tide of feeling** going across the country on council from council, it won't be long before people like me are M P's and others around you that are M P's are in the [unclear]
18	EFA 345	Then, it had produced the **tide of feeling** which landed France in Vietnam.
19	Go4 1266	A vast **tide of feeling**.
20	ECG 598	I clipped into the top peg and swung around in **tides of feelings** below the bulge.
21	GUM 581	She was accustomed to it now, the **torrent of feeling**.
22	H8W 684	The quicksand in question was the **boiling tumult of feeling** and unrest in post-war Vietnam, brought about by the confusion caused by the split within the country.
23	ABH 1289	There is an **undercurrent of feeling** all across Asia, even in the rich parts, that this is a white man's war, a new outbreak of old-fashioned colonialism.
24	BML 795	The latter reality, behind the 'surface' reality, is readily experienced, being entered when we are 'transported' by a particular musical experience, by a breath-taking piece of prose or poetry, or by just having an **upsurge of feeling** of being right with the world.
25	HH8 1837	What did finesse have to do with that wild **upsurge of feeling** which had almost overwhelmed her?
26	H9G 1934	Did you get what you wanted?' and a **wave of feeling** that the day had been good came with the words.
27	AN8 563	He stood blinking against the effect of the lights on his eyes and felt the apprehension disappear under a new **wave of feeling** — anger.
28	H85 2806	A sudden **wave of feeling** for the clever, perfectionist girl washed over him.

	29	HGD 2292	She was unprepared for the **wave of feeling** that hit her; a great empty feeling — loss, grief, bitterness.
	30	GoT 83	I cry to release huge **waves of feelings** which can build up, especially when I cannot or dare not put feelings into words.
	31	CBN 799	It is easy to sympathise with his parents as these **whirlpools of feeling** kept arising out of nowhere.
FIRE	1	JY4 3876	It was all there, the passion and the glory and inflamed **rush of feeling** that she knew she would always have for him.
EARTH	1	ARG 1225	O lamps of fire! In whose splendours The deep **caverns of feeling**, Once obscure and blind, Now give forth, so rarely, So exquisitely, Both warmth and light to their Beloved.
	2	A6B 1623	These '**depths of feeling**' again look back to Eliot's 1920 'canalizations of something again simple, terrible and unknown', but now are linked directly to 'l'âme primitive'.
	3	K4Y 1309	Jez Hall's tenor sax sound is lighter and warmer than Bobby's providing just enough contrast in their many solos but also doubling mellower than before but still with a crying, keening sounding that taps enormous **depths of feeling**.
	4	A6B 2169	The matter of the drama continues to be eclectic as Eliot pokes beneath the glossy city surface to hidden **depths of feeling**, and as so often looks to Buddhism as well as Christianity.
	5	BML 658	The young reader is not likely to gain much insight into mature emotional behaviour or into **depths of feeling** and their expression from reading Enid Blyton's stories.
	6	AoP 1850	He has memorialised their encounter and its temporary effect upon his deeper self, the **depths of feeling** he had for her, in his significantly titled poem 'Destiny' (Flowers for Hitler):
	7	A6B 1617	After wondering why out of a lifetime 'certain images recur, charged with emotion, rather than others', Eliot sees these as symbolic, but of what we cannot tell, for they come to represent the **depths of feeling** into which we cannot peer.
	8	GUE 796	After last night's brief encounter, after that raw **eruption of feeling** he'd provoked inside her, had this little scene been engineered deliberately?

CHAPTER III
Conventional Metaphors for Antonymous Emotion Concepts

3.1 Introduction

How do we understand and conceptualize emotions? Studies on metaphor using cognitive linguistic approaches (Lakoff and Johnson 1980, 1999, Lakoff 1987, Kövecses 1986, 1990, 2000, 2008b, etc.) have tried to answer this question through analyses of examples formed by researchers' introspection or elicited from informants. Kövecses (2000, 2008b) argues that most of the well-known metaphors of emotion are instantiations of a single underlying "master metaphor": EMOTION IS FORCE. He proposes various specific-level metaphors under this general-level metaphor: EMOTION IS INTERNAL PRESSURE INSIDE A CONTAINER, EMOTION IS AN OPPONENT, EMOTION IS A WILD ANIMAL, EMOTION IS A SOCIAL FORCE, and EMOTION IS A NATURAL FORCE.

Recent studies on metaphor include attempts to refine cognitive theories from the perspective of corpus methodology (Deignan 2005, Stefanowitsch and Gries eds. 2006, Omori 2008, etc.). Deignan (2005) proves that there is a discrepancy between data generated by researchers' intuition and those derived from naturally-occurring expressions most frequently found in corpora. Omori (2008) analyzed a number of citations of conventional metaphors, containing both source- and target-domain lexemes, retrieved from the BNC.[1] The results of the corpus search revealed that one of the major metaphorical source domains utilized for understanding EMOTION IS NATURAL PHENOMENA, and the prevalent source domain in conventional metaphors for emotion is A HUGE MASS OF MOVING WATER IN THE NATURAL WORLD. Following up on this research, this chapter attempts to analyze conventional metaphors describing the specific emotions of PLEASURE, SADNESS, HOPE, FEAR and DESPAIR retrieved from the BNC using the same method, and to further clarify the systematic nature of the mappings which construct these metaphors.

3.2 Retrieving metaphors for emotions from the corpus

In Omori (2008), I concentrated — in order to conduct an efficient corpus search — on conventional metaphors with the pattern of two nouns connected by the preposition *of* (e.g., *surge of emotion* and *bud of feeling*). The results of the corpus search for "[source-domain nominal] + *of* + *emotion / emotions / feeling / feelings*" indicated that the extracted metaphorical phrases are derived from various source domains including NATURAL PHENOMENA. I identified six source domains from which more than ten citations are derived. See Table 2.2 in Chapter II for the list and the number of occurrences of the major source domains. The table shows that metaphors derived from NATURAL PHENOMENA are numerically predominant.

Table 2.3 in Chapter II indicates the result of the corpus search for occurrences of the type "[nominal from NATURAL PHENOMENA] + *of* + [nominal from EMOTION]" ("*N of E*"). The table shows the number of occurrences of the type "*N of E*" with the word *emotion* or *feeling* or their plurals in the "E" slot. In this study, I classified the occurrences into four domains subordinate to the source domain NATURAL PHENOMENA; i.e., AIR, WATER, FIRE, and EARTH. Citations grouped into the sub-domain WATER (74.5%) far exceed those of EARTH, AIR and FIRE (9.8%, 8.8% and 6.9%, respectively).

The following sections focus on the conceptualization of specific emotions through the examination of corpus data of "*N of E*" type metaphors. Here five emotion concepts are scrutinized: PLEASURE, SADNESS, HOPE, FEAR, and DESPAIR. Each of the metaphorical mappings onto these diverse concepts is presumed to exhibit a certain bias. In other words, it is highly likely that each emotion individually utilizes a specific domain, or some of its aspects, as a typical source. If that is the case, then each emotion concept is to be characterized not only by aspects of source domains utilized in metaphoric mappings onto the concept, but also by the lack of aspects which are involved in the mappings onto other concepts.

3.3 Pleasure and sadness

3.3.1 The antonymous relationships between PLEASURE and SADNESS

The emotion concepts PLEASURE and SADNESS are generally understood as opposite to each other. The antonymous relationship is sometimes linguistically illustrated through juxtaposition, typically in the form of antithetic couplet.

The BNC includes examples in which lexemes realizing the two emotion concepts are put side by side and surrounded by words which refer to other conflicting pairs of concepts, as follows (The parenthetical notes after each example refer to the BNC filename and sentence number):

(1) She is the all-powerful source of satisfaction and frustration, *happiness and sadness*, love and hate. (BNF 334)
(2) The station was truly a gateway through which people passed in endless profusion on a variety of missions — a place of motion and emotion, arrival and departure, *joy and sorrow*, parting and reunion. (AR0 124)

The literature concerning conceptual metaphor has also long contrasted the two emotions in terms of orientation: HAPPY IS UP, whereas SAD IS DOWN (Lakoff and Johnson 1980, etc.). It follows that there must be a similar contrast in mappings from NATURAL PHENOMENA onto these emotion concepts, which I will discuss in the following sections.

3.3.2 The search results

Analyses were performed on the metaphorical citations retrieved from the BNC of the type "*N of E*" with the words related to PLEASURE or SADNESS in the "E" slot, taking into account the conflicting tendencies of the mappings onto the two conceptual domains. As thesauri show, these concepts are rich in synonyms. In this corpus search I adopted five keywords for the respective concepts: *pleasure, happiness, satisfaction, delight,* and *joy* for PLEASURE; and *sadness, depression, melancholy, sorrow,* and *grief* for SADNESS. Tables 3.1 and 3.2 show the search results. The occurrences are classified into the four elements: AIR, WATER, FIRE, and EARTH (For further details, see Appendices 3.1 and 3.2). The parenthesized numbers after some of the words in the columns "'*N of E*' Type Metaphors" indicate frequency of the words.

Source	"N of E" Type Metaphors		N	Total
AIR	burst, flurry, storms, tempest	of pleasure	4	16 (16.2%)
	air (4), atmosphere, haze	of satisfaction	6	
	aura, burst	of happiness	2	
	aura, haze	of delight	2	
	explosion, flurry	of joy	2	
WATER	flood (2), rills, sea, springs, spurt (5), stream, surge (4), tide (2), trickles, wave (4), waves (4), whirlpool	of pleasure	27	50 (50.5%)
	surge, tide	of satisfaction	2	
	ocean heave, springs, surge (2), swell	of happiness	5	
	fountain, fountains, river, surge, waves	of delight	5	
	cup (2), flood, flow, spring (2), surge (4), uprush	of joy	11	
FIRE	flash, glimmer (3), glint, glow (3)	of pleasure	8	29 (29.3%)
	beam, flare, flicker, gleam (2), glimmer (2), glint, glow (4)	of satisfaction	12	
	glimmer, glow (3)	of happiness	4	
	—	of delight	0	
	afterglow, glow, light, radiance, spark	of joy	5	
EARTH	volcanic eruption	of pleasure	1	4 (4.0%)
	—	of satisfaction	0	
	—	of happiness	0	
	gardens, meadows	of delight	2	
	gardens	of joy	1	

Table 3.1: Number of occurrences of metaphors of the type "N of E" from the four different source sub-domains with the word related to PLEASURE in the "E" Slot

Source	"N of E" Type Metaphors		N	Total
AIR	air (3), aura (3)	of sadness	6	12 (30.0%)
	air, cloud	of depression	2	
	air (2), miasma	of melancholy	3	
	clouds	of sorrow	1	
	—	of grief	0	
WATER	pools, undercurrent, undertow, wave (2), waves	of sadness	6	23 (57.5%)
	sea, surge, wave (4)	of depression	6	
	surge, undertow	of melancholy	2	
	cup, frost, jet, sea (3)	of sorrow	6	
	surge (2), whirlpool	of grief	3	
FIRE	glimmer	of sadness	1	1 (2.5%)
	—	of depression	0	
	—	of melancholy	0	
	—	of sorrow	0	
	—	of grief	0	
EARTH	—	of sadness	0	4 (10.0%)
	—	of depression	0	
	—	of melancholy	0	
	—	of sorrow	0	
	canyon, chasms, deserts, stone	of grief	4	

Table 3.2: Number of occurrences of metaphors of the type "N of E" from the four different source sub-domains with the word related to SADNESS in the "E" Slot

3.3.3 Commonalities and disparities between PLEASURE and SADNESS

One of the marked tendencies common to the metaphors for PLEASURE and those for SADNESS is the weight of the domain WATER as the major source of the metaphorical mappings, a phenomenon similar to the mappings onto EMOTION in general (see Table 2.3 in Chapter II). Lexical items like *wave* and *surge*, indicating massive forms of moving water with enormous energy, are preferred as a vehicle in metaphors for PLEASURE as well as SADNESS, depicting a sudden powerful increase of the intensity of these emotions. Here are some of the citations in which a lexeme from WATER collocates with a word for one of these emotions.

(3) *In that instant*, Juliet felt a *surge of happiness* that *filled* her chest and almost *engulfed* her.   (JY0 4314)
(4) *[F]or one sweet moment*, she felt *a flood of joy sweep* through her.
                                                                                            (JYE 3843)
(5) He had been *hit* by a new *wave of depression*.   (A7H 1242)
(6) The odd thing was that, after he had entered the paint shop, he had felt as if a heavy *wave of sadness* had *suddenly* been *lifted* from out of him.
                                                                                            (CAB 2527)

The verbs in these examples, i.e., *fill*, *engulf*, *sweep*, *hit*, and *lift*, all emphasize the phenomenal strength of these emotions. The phrase *in that instant* in Example (3), *for one sweet moment* in (4), and *suddenly* in (6) indicate their sudden occurrences. These collocates, coupled with a word connoting the enormous power of water, show the overwhelming manifestations of pleasure and sadness.

Another trait of mapping shared by the metaphors for these two emotions is the use of vehicles derived from the source AIR like *air of satisfaction* (JY3 267) and *aura of sadness* (JYA 5009), indicating a continuity of emotion with no sudden changes.

Despite these commonalities, the corpus data show many citations that describe the conflicting properties of the targets PLEASURE and SADNESS. The conflicts are as follows:

— PLEASURE **burns with a bright flame, whereas** SADNESS **does not.**

Vehicles derived from the domain FIRE rank second in expressing PLEASURE. The corpus citations contain words describing a burning fire emitting a bright light, e.g., *glow of happiness* (JY4 3461, JYE 1691, K34 197), *flare of satisfaction* (H9L 1660), *flash of pleasure* (GUX 627), and *spark of joy* (G15 3414). Here we can see a clear source-target correspondence: flaming fire gives light and heat, the motive power of living beings; and correspondently, pleasure makes us vigorous and lively.

In contrast, the citations realizing metaphoric mappings onto SADNESS rarely utilize the domain FIRE as a source, with a single exception in which the word *glimmer* is used for a faint unsteady light: "Henri paused briefly under an archway, a *glimmer of sadness* pulsing within him" (FSR 4). The absence of vehicles from the FIRE domain in the metaphors for SADNESS seems to be caused by our understanding that SADNESS disheartens us and puts us in darkness, quite the opposite to the traits associated with PLEASURE.

— PLEASURE **explodes, whereas** SADNESS **does not.**

— PLEASURE spurts out, whereas SADNESS does not.
— PLEASURE erupts, whereas SADNESS does not.

A sudden occurrence of the strong emotion of pleasure is often depicted by words referring to a sudden outburst related to the domains AIR (*burst* and *explosion*), WATER (*spurt*, *spring* and *fountains*), or EARTH (*volcanic eruption*). Outbursts in the natural world correspond to a sudden, unexpected and irresistible increase of emotion, as emphasized in the citations below:

(7) The *explosion of joy* that had *suddenly burst* through her at the thought of seeing him, at the thought of being with him, for a moment *had overcome her sense*. (H97 4018)

(8) The world seemed to *tilt and spin and fold itself inside out* in a *volcanic eruption of pleasure*. (GUE 3476)

Metaphors expressing SADNESS, on the contrary, do not use such vehicles. Sad feelings do not seem to be emotions that pop out vigorously.

— PLEASURE blows violently, whereas SADNESS does not.

The intense and uncontrollable emotion of PLEASURE is also expressible by vehicles derived from the domain AIR, indicating strong gusts of wind, as exemplified in the citations containing the phrases *flurry of pleasure* (A15 591), *flurry of joy* (HH5 1770), *storms of pleasure* (B1C 1776), and *tempest of pleasure* (BoR 177). Again, these vehicles are absent in the corpus citations of "N of E" metaphors for SADNESS.

— SADNESS runs as an undercurrent, whereas PLEASURE does not.
— SADNESS stagnates, whereas PLEASURE does not.

The vehicles of SADNESS metaphors of the type "N of E" include *undercurrent* and *undertow*, meaning a current of water below the surface and moving in a different direction from any surface current.

(9) Joe was trying to be bright and cheerful, but there was a deep *undercurrent of sadness*, and later, when he had gone back to his office, Dana said: 'I think he's terribly lonely.' (AC6 1290)

Example (9) shows a contrast between a surface current of water represented by Joe's effort to look bright and cheerful, and a deep undercurrent which is his true emotion of sadness and loneliness. The corpus data also contain a citation with a vehicle referring to stagnant water, i.e., *pools of sadness* (HJ4 1675). As we will see in Section 3.4, the vehicles *undercurrent*, *undertow*, and *pools* are also used in metaphors for FEAR and DESPAIR. These metaphors indicate that negative emotions like sadness, fear, and despair are sometimes hidden, suppressed or forced to be inactive. Metaphors describing positive emotions like PLEASURE do not utilize those vehicles. The corpus data is impressively consistent and these well-known lyrics by the Beatles demonstrate the explicit contrast between the two emotions: "*Pools of sorrow, waves of joy* are drifting through my opened mind, possessing and caressing me" ("Across the Universe" by John Lennon / Paul McCartney).

— PLEASURE **is a fertile land, whereas** SADNESS **is an arid land.**

There is still another contrast between PLEASURE and SADNESS seen in the mappings onto those emotions from the domain EARTH. A positive aspect of the EARTH, fertility, is typically involved in the mapping onto PLEASURE, as exemplified by vehicles like *gardens* and *meadows*, referring to land that nurtures plants and animals.

(10) The world of the imagination is limitless and it is here that the mind must be freed, but it must also be given the spur of inspiration.... The mind must be made to expand endlessly, its expansion is a sure emotional pleasure. In this expansion lies the freedom that comes with it; for this journey and enlargement of the mind is also part of man's endless quest for growth and self-fulfilment. All our lives, we shall know that behind the veils of the transcendent is a world of freedom waiting for us, with its *meadows of delight*. (B1F 791–795)

Example (10) depicts the human ability to inspire the imagination as free mental expansion in the endless world. Here the expansion is regarded as emotional pleasure, and the delight felt with the sense of freedom is likened to meadows, a comfortable area for living beings.

Metaphors of sadness, in contrast, utilize vehicles like *deserts*, *canyon*, *chasms*, and *stone*, indicating soil geologically or geographically resistant to the existence of life.

(11) And after his death it seemed to her that she had walked in darkness like an automaton through a deep and narrow *canyon of grief* in which all her energies, all her physical strength, had been husbanded to get through each day. (C8T 2104)

Example (11) describes the sadness of a woman who has been bereaved of her husband. Her mental state is compared to a deep and narrow canyon, a place that is uncomfortable to stay in and hard to get out of once one steps into it. The geography is in sharp contrast to that of the endless meadows utilized as a vehicle of the metaphor for delight in Example (10).

A similar contrast is observed in the following citation.

(12) We carry the memory of childhood like a photo in a locket, fierce and possessive for pain or calm; everybody's past is inviolate, separate, sacrosanct, our heads are different countries with no maps or dictionaries, people walk vast *deserts of grief* or inhabit walled *gardens of joy*.

(BP8 1379)

One of the properties of the earth is that of supporting living beings in their physical health, and their health depends on its fertility. In Example (12) the fertile land indicated by the vehicle *gardens* corresponds to PLEASURE, which keeps and enhances one's mental health, and the arid land indicated by *deserts* corresponds to SADNESS, which weakens or impairs one's mental health.

3.4 Hope, fear, and despair

3.4.1 The HOPE-FEAR relationships and HOPE-DESPAIR relationships

The emotion concepts HOPE and DESPAIR are also generally understood to be an antonymous pair. This view is reflected in dictionary definitions: *Concise Oxford English Dictionary*, for example, defines *despair* as "the complete loss or absence of hope." The BNC also includes citations that contrast HOPE with DESPAIR, such as the following:

(13) Such violence *saps hope* and resilience out of a community, and *induces despair*. (HHW 533)

(14) It is time we *stopped talking of despair* and *started living in hope*.

(HU9 361)

(15) The school represents 'the *triumph of hope over despair*, of faith over doubt'. (K2F 818)

Dictionary definitions of the headword *fear*, on the other hand, are irrelevant to the concept HOPE, as exemplified by the following definition: "an unpleasant emotion caused by the threat of danger, pain, or harm" (*Concise Oxford*

English Dictionary). Some corpus citations, however, suggest that FEAR is also regarded as conflicting with the concept HOPE:

(16) With such a lot riding on the snip of a scissor, it's not surprising that the breast beneath the hairdresser's gown is heaving with unrealistic expectations and *conflicting emotions of hope and fear*. (A7N 705)

(17) Yet Lupus, awaiting a royal summons, was *torn between hope and fear*: attendance (and to ignore an invitation was dangerous) threatened new burdens, yet being with the king (though to appear uninvited was unthinkable) offered the prospect of benefits. (HPT 814)

(18) I was rowed downstream to Croisset; in my soul, *hope struggled with fear*, while the ancient oarsman struggled with the current. (G1A 2153)

(19) *Hope and fear were tripping over each other* inside her. (H97 4060)

(20) The words, 'Let's get this country moving again,' and 'We stand on the edge of a New Frontier,' were actually spoken by Kennedy, while 32 years later Bill Clinton promised to 'lift up the American people,' and of, '*a victory of hope over fear*... instead of four more tired old years, four new years.' (CEK 1703)

Example (16) explicitly shows that HOPE and FEAR are in conflict with each other. The person depicted in Example (17) is in a state of uncertainty, as he is unable to choose between the two opposing emotions. The pair of emotions are sometimes regarded as doing battle with each other: *hope* fights against *fear* as described in Example (18); *hope* and *fear* try to catch each other's foot and attempt to make the other fall over as shown in (19); and finally one side defeats the other as depicted in (20).

Both of the two pairs of emotion concepts, i.e., HOPE and DESPAIR, and HOPE and FEAR, are therefore to be deemed as antonymous. But the type of antonymy at work appears to be different for each of the pairs. Consider the following citations:

(21) The law lords in their ruling talk of the agony of mind the men must have suffered as they *alternated* between *hope* and *despair*. (KM3 230)

(22) They would have responded primarily to Jesus's message, which by its very nature, elicited emotions of, *simultaneously*, *fear* and *hope*. (EDY 1355)

Since DESPAIR means sheer lack of HOPE, the two concepts cannot be present together, though they can arise *alternately* in the mind, as seen in Example (21). In other words, despair vanishes from a person's mind at the moment when he or she feels hope, and vice versa. FEAR, on the contrary, can arise *simultaneously* with HOPE, as exemplified in (22). The two emotions are opposite to each other in that HOPE means an expectation that something *good* will or may happen, while FEAR is an expectation that something *bad* will or may happen; however, it *is* possible that the two expectations come into existence at the same time.

3.4.2 The search results

Tables 3.3 through 3.5 show the results of a corpus search for metaphors of the type "N of E" with *hope*, *fear*, and *despair* respectively in the "E" slot. In the tables the occurrences are classified into four source sub-domains, i.e., AIR, WATER, FIRE, and EARTH (For further details, see Appendices 3.3 through 3.5).

Source	"N of E" Type Metaphors		N	Percentage
AIR	atmosphere, cloud, outburst, storm	of hope	4	3.2%
WATER	cup, surge (2), rush		4	3.2%
FIRE	beacon (8), candle, flame (5), flames, flare, flash (3), flicker (6), gleam (5), gleams, glimmer (43), glimmers (7), glint, light (2), radiance, ray (24), rays (3), spark (4)		116	92.8%
EARTH	grounds		1	0.8%

Table 3.3: Number of occurrences of metaphors of the type "N of E" from the four different source sub-domains with the word *hope* in the "E" slot

Source	"N of E" Type Metaphors		N	Percentage
AIR	air, atmosphere (3), aura, smell (2), stench (4), tang, void	of fear	13	31.7%
WATER	cup, flood, jet, ripple (2), sap, spring, spurt, surge (3), trickle (2), tricklings, undercurrent, undertow, uprush, wave (4), waves (2)		23	56.1%
FIRE	flicker (5)		5	12.2%
EARTH	—		0	0%

Table 3.4: Number of occurrences of metaphors of the type "N of E" from the four different source sub-domains with the word *fear* in the "E" slot

Source	"N of E" Type Metaphors		N	Percentage
AIR	atmosphere, fog, gust, haze, miasma, vacuum	of despair	6	15.4%
WATER	backwash, pools, tide, undercurrent		4	10.3%
FIRE	ashes		1	2.6%
EARTH	brink, chasm, depths (15), edge (6), pit, pits (2), quagmire, verge		28	71.8%

Table 3.5: Number of occurrences of metaphors of the type "N of E" from the four different source sub-domains with the word *despair* in the "E" slot

3.4.3 Commonalities and disparities among HOPE, FEAR and DESPAIR

The corpus search results do not simply show the commonalities of HOPE, FEAR, and DESPAIR; we can also discern significant disparities among them. Like the metaphors for PLEASURE and SADNESS, terms which refer to massive forms of moving water with enormous energy are commonly used as the vehicles of metaphors for HOPE, FEAR, and DESPAIR, such as *surge of hope* (CBN 1330, JXV 1574), *surge of fear* (APU 1003, CCW 90, EFV 1590), and *tide of despair* (HNJ 3148), all describing a powerful increase in the intensity of these emotions. With regard to the source AIR, the vehicle *atmosphere* is commonly used, indicating the continuity of the emotions: *atmosphere of hope* (KRU 84), *atmosphere of fear* (CRT 547, EWG 955, K97 10498), and *atmosphere of despair* (K54 2479). These commonalities, however, are of less significance than the distinct differences among the three emotion concepts in terms of the major source sub-domains. As shown in the three tables above, the source FIRE is overwhelmingly prevalent in the metaphor for HOPE. In contrast, many of the metaphors for FEAR are derived from WATER, and the most frequent source for DESPAIR is EARTH. When compared to EMOTION in general, for which the domain WATER is the most frequently used as a source (cf. Table 2.3), FEAR is assessed as close to the emotion prototype, whereas HOPE and DESPAIR are absolutely unique in the distribution of their source sub-domains and extremely far from the prototype (see Chapter II for a detailed discussion on the emotion prototype and the position of specific emotions in terms of prototypicality).

3.4.4 The distinctive traits of HOPE, FEAR and DESPAIR

These three emotion concepts can thus be metaphorically characterized as follows: typical HOPE is a flaming fire; typical FEAR is flowing water, and typical DESPAIR is the barren or dangerous earth. The following is a detailed observation of these concepts:

— Typical HOPE is a flaming fire.

The great majority of the metaphors expressing HOPE are derived from the domain FIRE (92.8%), containing vehicles which refer to flame or light. Metaphors for FEAR, on the other hand, do not use vehicles related with FIRE, except for five occurrences of *flicker of fear* (G3G 2867, etc.). The emotion FEAR is never compared to fierce flames or bright light. Metaphors for DESPAIR seldom contain vehicles related to FIRE, either. There is only one occurrence of a vehicle associated with FIRE, cited below, which does not refer to fire itself but to ashes.

(23) Optimism must always be tinged with anxiety for it not to become braggartism, and there were enough instances in the past, mainly at Olympic Games where British *flames of hope* had turned to *ashes of despair*, for a note of caution to be sounded. (BMM 1642)

In this example we can see structural correspondences, that is, a mapping from *flames* onto *hope*, and from *ashes* (i.e. what is left behind after a fire is extinguished) onto *despair* (i.e. what is left behind after hope fades).

The scarcity of mappings from FIRE onto FEAR or DESPAIR is consistent with the existence of citations in which fear and despair are likened to darkness. There are occurrences of *fear* with the collocate *dark* in the corpus: *dark fear* (HH9 3144), *dark fears* (GUF 3643), *dark, irrational fears* (FAJ 618), *dark chamber of doubt and fear* (APM 1429), etc. Similarly, the corpus includes citations in which *despair* collocates with *dark*: *dark night of despair* (B1J 1775), *dark thoughts of despair* (B1X 1118), '*dark shadow of death' and of despair* (CDV 1564), *the wordless cry of frustration and despair that was the dark side of the collective human soul* (GW2 3580), etc. Just as darkness disturbs one's regular activities, so do the emotions of fear and despair disturb one's mental activities. The following citation shows that one can be *lost* in a state of despair:

(24) The angels tell the shepherds and wise men — "Do not be afraid". Do not be lost in the deep *darkness of despair and hopelessness*. Have *hope*. The *light* has come among us. The appearing of God's glory is here. A child has been born who will be greatly titled. He is our *hope*. (C8J 366–372)

In this example *hope* and *despair* are systematically described in terms of *light* and *darkness* respectively. It is also noteworthy that the rhythm of the alliterative phrase *deep darkness of despair* rings as if the connection between DESPAIR and DARKNESS was innate and natural.

This paucity of mapping from FIRE onto FEAR or DESPAIR is also related to our perception of these emotions as COLD. There are many citations in which *fear* collocates with *cold*: *cold fear* (CK0 810, FSJ1154, GUD 1087, etc.), *cold shiver of solitary-place fear* (G13 618), *cold tremors of fear* (GUF 3414), *cold sap of fear* (GV2 2779), etc. (cf. Section 2.3.5 in Chapter II). Similarly, *despair* and *cold* can collocate: *cold shiver of despair* (HH3 14850), *grief and deep despair were a cold wind whose power he could no longer fight against...* (FP3 265), *the look of their faces turned us cold with despair* (F99 3156), etc. Both *fear* and *despair* are also used together with *chill*: *chill of fear* (FSF 2656, G3E 784, H7W 311, etc.), *cold chill of fear* (JXV 1633), *chill of despair* (FSF 1852).

The 116 citations which instantiate the mapping from FIRE onto HOPE include not only those which contain vehicles referring to a fierce flame (e.g., *a bright flame of hope* (JYC 2393) and *a sudden flare of hope* (JYD 3727)), but also those in which *glimmer* or its plural is used (50 hits), describing a dim hope just like a faint unsteady light. The corpus data also includes six occurrences of *flicker of hope* (ABR 559, etc.), and those in which *flame* is modified by adjectives like *small* or *tiny* (*a small flame of hope* (C85 1177), *a tiny flame of hope* (JY2 3129)). Tiny flickering flames in the darkness enable us to walk forward; correspondingly, a little bit of hope can give us a hint of how to step forward toward the solution to a serious problem and the conquest of difficulties. A typical example is as follows:

(25) Firms in the capital are still pessimistic about the future, according to a survey by the London Society of Chartered Accountants. The survey, of 300 London firms, showed that the level of consultancy, investment and other business activities is dwindling and that many firms think that insolvency work has passed its peak. Staff levels have reached a low ebb and many firms are not expecting salaries to keep pace with inflation in the immediate future. There are a few *glimmers of hope*, however, since fewer firms are having trouble collecting fees and all but the larger firms are optimistic about increasing their client base. (CBW 666–669)

Another noteworthy expression is *beacon of hope* which occurs eight times in the corpus, as exemplified in the following citations:

(26) Aye, the production may have been poor, but the crude gameplay shone out like a *beacon of hope* for us downtrodden folk. (C87 2131)
(27) Considering the Statue of Liberty has been a *beacon of hope* for generations of newly-arrived immigrants, it's appropriate that Mario arrived in

New York with his parents 30 years ago. (CBE 885)

Just as a beacon shining in darkness serves as a guide for ships or aircraft, hope, symbolized by the gameplay in Example (26) and the Statue of Liberty in (27), guides people (downtrodden folk in (26) and newly-arrived immigrants in (27)) through difficulties onto a path to an enjoyable and fruitful life.

— Typical FEAR is flowing water.

WATER is the most prominent source sub-domain utilized in the "N of E" type metaphors with *fear* in the "E" slot. The citations derived from WATER account for 56.1%, many of which contain vehicles referring to the strong flow of water, as exemplified in *flood of fear* (HTM 60), *surge of fear* (APU 1003, CCW 90, EFV 1590) and *wave of fear* (A2J 277, CE7 1011, F99 1548, HGK 2505). A distinctive trait of metaphors for FEAR is that many of them describe the emotion as if it is a tide rising and ebbing in the human body, as illustrated by the following citations:

(28) Only now that he was safe did he feel a little *black jet of fear rising in his chest*, a gobbet of bile that filled his mouth, washing his teeth in acid.
(FP7 3666)
(29) As the bell rang again, insistently, urgently, she headed for the door, pulling the dressing-gown around her, feeling a *cold spring of fear welling up inside*. (H97 1956)
(30) A *ripple of fear* passed *down his spine*. (G04 3521)
(31) "Unfortunately I've managed to acquire neither," he said finally, straightening to his daunting height and sending a *trickle of fear down her spine* by tugging at the buttons on his shirt, apparently with every intention of undressing right there in front of her. (JY3 392)

These descriptions are related to such idiomatic phrases as "a chill runs up [*or* down] one's spine," and "to send a shiver up [*or* down] one's spine," which also describe the emotion of fear. These expressions all remind us of the uncomfortable feeling which runs through our bodies at the moment when we feel fear.

— Typical DESPAIR is the barren or dangerous earth.

EARTH is the dominant source in the "N of E" type metaphors expressing DESPAIR (71.8%). This is in stark contrast to the search results for "N + *of hope*" and "N + *of fear*": the mapping from EARTH onto HOPE was very rare (0.8%), and the mapping from EARTH onto FEAR absent. Many citations of metaphors for DESPAIR contain vehicles like *brink* and *verge*, referring to the extreme edge of land on which you face the danger of falling, or vehicles related to particular geographical features which could jeopardize life and make it difficult to escape, such as *depths*, *quagmire*, *pit(s)*, and *chasm*, as shown in the examples below:

(32) When you're ill and have sunk to the *depths of despair*, *black* thoughts enter your mind. (B1X 1407)
(33) She felt as though she were treading on thin ice and any false move might plunge her once more into the *dark depths of despair*. (JYE 4440)
(34) She stumbled away, broken and on the *verge of despair*. (JXU 2533)
(35) As the rest of Europe and the world progresses, are we to *be left in a quagmire of despair* at the end of another parliamentary Session, another era and another century? (HHW 534)
(36) Owen could hardly bear to look at her, so much was she at the mercy of the music, *plunging* with it into *pits of despair*, rising with it to heights of exaltation that were almost unbearable. (HTX 2674)
(37) It destroyed him and for a time he *was engulfed by a deep chasm of despair*, drinking heavily, taking amphetamines and LSD — and he was in his sixteenth year of smoking marijuana. (AP0 960)

All of the citations emphasize how the emotion has a harmful influence on one's mental health by using those vehicles which connote danger or a crisis. Examples (32) and (33) present a metaphorical image of the bottom of the sea or a lake. In these examples *despair* co-occurs with the adjective *black* or *dark*, reinforcing the description of despair as darkness. The alliterative phrases *depths of despair* in (32) and *dark depths of despair* in (33) are similar to (24) in that their rhythm emphasizes the strong associative relationship between despair and the bottom of water. Example (34) gives the image of a verge which makes a woman stumble and exposes her to danger. In Example (35) despair is caused by the situation in which a country is left behind as the rest of the world progresses, a desperate feeling that is compared to a swampy place that is difficult to wade over. In Examples (36) and (37) the vehicles refer to a deep hole in the ground that would be fatal if fallen into.

3.4.5 Synonymous relationships between FEAR and DESPAIR

Although dictionaries or thesauri in general do not treat the two emotion concepts as related to each other, FEAR is actually close to DESPAIR in that they are both opposite to HOPE. The synonymous relationships between the two emo-

CHAPTER III   CONVENTIONAL METAPHORS FOR ANTONYMOUS EMOTION CONCEPTS   71

tions are shown in the following metaphorical characterizations of them:

— FEAR is unpleasant air, and DESPAIR is injurious air.

Vehicles related to smell (i.e., *smell*, *stench* and *tang*) are noticeable in the citations that realize a metaphorical mapping from AIR onto FEAR. Strong smells make people uncomfortable, and cause them intense discomfort if they continue to experience the sensation. Similarly, continuous feelings of fear make people suffer discomfort. See, for example, the following citation:

(38) As the next day or two dragged by, fear became Cassie's almost *constant companion*. She smelled the *tang of fear* in her nostrils and the taste of it in her mouth. It *moved with her* silently from room to room, breathing softly against the back of her neck. It *accompanied* her to bed at night and filled her dreams with dread and her sleep with sudden awakenings.
(G1S 2499–2502)

In this example, Cassie suffers from constant fear, and feels it day and night as if it is a strong smell. The emotion of fear is what surrounds her and follows her about wherever she may be, traits that correspond closely with the qualities of air.

Some vehicles that are derived from the domain of AIR and used for mapping onto DESPAIR also evoke unpleasant kinds of gas. The vehicles in *fog of despair* (H7H 2501) and *haze of despair* (HH1 891) refer to types of water vapor that are opaque and thus impossible to see through. In addition, the vehicle in *miasma of despair* (G1L 1770) is related to a mass of air that is dirty, unpleasant and unhealthy. These vehicles remind us of the properties of despair, i.e., that it prevents us from seeing into the future and damages our mental health.

Moreover, the concepts FEAR and DESPAIR use vehicles like *void* and *vacuum*, referring to a space that is empty of air. See, for example, the following citation:

(39) Our form-teacher in her twin-set and pearls was round-faced and always smiling as the Iron Maiden of Nuremberg. Each day I met the furnace of her hate. She'd call me out of class, interrogate, then send me back in tears — or I'd break down and cry, then be sent out — to her…Trapped in a *vacuum of despair*, that term, I thought dramatically of *suicide* but lacked the means.
(FS5 101–114)

The person in this example underwent terrible tortures in her school days. She was fiercely hated by her form-teacher and received a sharp reproach from her every day. The despair caused by such tortures shares the highly destructive nature of a vacuum. Like a vacuum, despair suffocates people and causes them agony that possibly leads to death, as demonstrated by her desire to commit suicide.

— FEAR is a liquid with an unpleasant taste, and DESPAIR is a liquid that causes death.

The discomfort caused by the emotion of FEAR and the destructive nature of DESPAIR are also seen in the citation below, where vehicles derived from the domain WATER are utilized:

(40) I drank *fears like wormwood*, yea, made myself drunken with bitterness; for my ever-shaping and distrustful mind still mingled gall-drops, till out of the cup of hope I almost *poisoned* myself with *despair*.
(ADA 745)

Here both of the negative emotions are described in terms of a bitter cup. The liquid in the cup associated with FEAR tastes bitter, and that associated with DESPAIR is poisonous. The descriptions are highly evocative of the well-known words of Jesus in foreboding danger and death, "Are ye able to drink of the *cup* that I shall drink of …?" (Matthew 20.22.), "Father, if thou be willing, remove this *cup* from me …" (Luke 22.42.), and "Put up thy sword into the sheath: the *cup* which my Father hath given me, shall I not drink it?" (John 18.11.).

The bitter taste of FEAR and the poisonous nature of DESPAIR are also depicted in citations (41) and (42) respectively. They also make use of vehicles related to liquid. The liquid depicted in (41) is extremely unpleasant in taste, while *cocktail of despair*, described in (42), is characterized as causing death.

(41) Fran swallowed hard, feeling the *bitter taste of fear burning her throat* as she stared into the man's cold, flat eyes, wishing she could find her voice to tell him what he could do with his threats. (JXV 342)
(42) Prince Charles has accused the planners, architects and developers who designed our sprawling housing estates of mixing a *lethal cocktail of despair*. (J1M 2923)

— FEAR and DESPAIR run as an undercurrent. DESPAIR stagnates.

Like the emotion of SADNESS observed above, some metaphors describing FEAR and DESPAIR make use of vehicles related to an abnormal flow of water. Such expressions as *undercurrent of fear* (HWA 430), *undertow of fear* (FP0 3073) and *undercurrent of despair* (GWo 563) indicate that these negative emotions are hidden or inconspicuous. These vehicles also have the connotation of danger. People drown if they get carried away by an undercurrent or undertow.

A word referring to receding waves is also used as a vehicle for describing DESPAIR, as exemplified by *backwash of despair* (AoN 228). In addition, despair is sometimes suppressed and forced to be inactive like stagnant pools, as exemplified in (43).

(43) The irises had seemed to dilate into *black pools of despair*. (G3E 1319)
(44) She could feel no personal flavour but a *dirty undertow of fear*.
(FPo 3073)

It is also worth noting that the source-domain nouns in Examples (43) and (44) are modified by the adjectives *black* and *dirty* respectively, suggestive of darkness and opaqueness. These descriptions are consistent with the metaphors like *black jet of fear*, *dark depths of despair*, and *fog of despair* that were observed above.

3.5 Conclusion

In this chapter we have concentrated on the properties of antonymous emotion concepts through detailed analyses of conventional metaphors of the type "N of E" retrieved from the BNC. The main points of our discussion are as follows:

— Some specific emotions are similar to the emotion prototype, while others are different from it. The prototype of the category EMOTION is typically characterized in terms of the source domain WATER. The search results for citations describing the five specific emotions indicate that PLEASURE, SADNESS, and FEAR are close to the emotion prototype, for which the prevalent source domain is WATER. In contrast, HOPE and DESPAIR are further from the prototype in that citations derived from WATER are uncommon.
— The peculiarities of HOPE and DESPAIR are typically characterized in terms of their dominant source domains, i.e., FIRE and EARTH respectively.
— The relationships between a conflicting pair of emotion concepts can be characterized in terms of whether or not a particular aspect of a source domain, or the domain itself, is used in metaphorical mappings. The antonymous relationships between PLEASURE and SADNESS are demonstrable, for example, by the presence and absence of citations derived from the source domain FIRE.
— An unexpected relationship of antonymy between two emotion concepts is

acknowledged through identification of the presence and absence of source domain words in corpus citations. Unlike *despair*, *fear* is not clearly defined as antonymous with *hope* in dictionaries in general. Corpus evidence nevertheless shows that FEAR is also in conflict with HOPE in that citations describing the emotion of fear seldom contain vehicles derived from the domain FIRE, the dominant source utilized for understanding HOPE, and that *fear* is often modified by the adjectives *dark* and *cold*, that convey connotations opposite to that of *fire*.

— An unexpected relationship of synonymy between two emotion concepts is acknowledged through the examination of source domain words in corpus citations. FEAR and DESPAIR turned out to be closely related to each other in that both of them are describable by means of vehicles from the domains AIR and WATER referring to what is unpleasant and injurious to one's health.

The fourth and fifth points in particular imply the great advantages that the corpus methodology has over the introspective methodology adopted in traditional studies of metaphor. Much of the conceptual metaphor literature has based its arguments on the presence, *not* the absence, of particular source domains. Researchers can demonstrate the presence of a particular source domain and of the mapping from the source onto a target domain through assuming it by their intuitions and presenting some linguistic evidence to justify the assumption. The absence of a source domain, or scarcity of mapping, on the other hand, is verifiable only by an exhaustive observation of data extracted from a large corpus. Corpus analysis also reveals semantic relationships between concepts that are not clearly specified in dictionary definitions. The concepts FEAR and DESPAIR, in fact, are close to each other in that fear is the anxiety that something bad will or may happen, and despair comes when the anxiety turns into reality and there is no expectation at all of getting out of the bad situation. The relationship seems obvious with hindsight, but is hard to notice by unsupported intuition. Thus, proper use of corpus data brings important insights, and the corpus methodology makes a valuable contribution to cognitive linguistic theories on metaphor.

Notes
1 Chapter II of this book is a revised version of Omori (2008).

Appendix

Appendix 3.1

BNC citations of metaphorical expressions of the Type "N of E" from the four different source sub-domains with the words related to PLEASURE in the "E" slot

Source	No.	Filename	BNC citations
AIR	1	H8F 3650	She didn't feel pain, only a small **burst of pleasure** that intensified as he then licked her reddened skin.
	2	A15 591	A **flurry of pleasure** as my favourite, stacked nuts, came to the rescue and then the sling was just a few feet away.
	3	B1C 1776	**storms of pleasure**, bliss:
	4	B0R 177	I formed a Party, dashed to London at eleven o'clock at night, and for three days lived in all the **tempest of Pleasure** …
	1	F9R 2132	Oh, I think we ought to except our hostess,' she added with a curious **air of satisfaction**, 'Rosette knows how to keep a clear head, a remarkably clear head.'
	2	FEE 3200	That's more like it, "with a rich **air of satisfaction**, as if I were her masterwork" No, don't take it off just yet "It brightens the room."
	3	HNJ 3014	'Knew it would help,' said Iris with an **air of satisfaction** as she heaved a sofa back into place.
	4	JY3 267	Lucy leaned back with an **air of satisfaction**, then dimpled a grin at Virginia, adding apologetically, 'Could you possibly pour me another cup of tea?'
	5	ED6 227	At the conclusion of one-and-a-half days devoted to recording sessions for a new ASV release, to include clarinet concertos by Gerald Finzi and Sir Charles Villiers Stanford, one sensed a tangible **atmosphere of satisfaction** upon entering London's Henry Wood Hall.
	6	H9G 2425	She didn't any longer need Derek absolutely here and now for her to feel the throb in her blood of full summer throwing its **haze of satisfaction** over everything that came to her senses.
	1	BN1 1350	But it did feel peaceful, as though, even shielded against him, she could feel the **aura of happiness** that surrounded him….
	2	CR6 3037	She looked at Margaret with a question in her eyes and when she nodded felt a **burst of happiness** like she had never felt before.
	1	B1F 1199	Every moment then has significance and an **aura of delight** surrounds everything and it is as if he had found a rare wellbeing and joy.

	2	APW 2682	The assembled crowd rejoiced at this unexpected joy, and Luch stood quietly unnoticed by the steps as they all turned away to where Abbot Kenneth stood in a perfect **haze of delight**.
	1	H97 4018	The **explosion of joy** that had suddenly burst through her at the thought of seeing him, at the thought of being with him, for a moment had overcome her senses.
	2	HH5 1770	We were left in the guesthouse, drinking chilled white wine, whilst the sisters welcomed Lady Francesca and Sir Robert Clinton in a **flurry of joy** at seeing their old pupil and protg.
WATER	1	HGE 3053	He said huskily, 'Let me, McAllister,' and began to unbutton her blouse, 'I want to stroke you, McAllister, and not your clothes,' and she made no effort to stop him, and when he bent his head to kiss the breasts he had fondled with his hands the cry which she gave was one of pleasure, not fear, for now it was Dr Neil loving her so carefully that the **flood of pleasure** was almost on her from that alone.
	2	JYD 3488	With a hoarse cry she went into violent climax, her body possessed by the pulse that roared in her ears, her heart, her stomach, her thighs and made her limbs spasm and twist in ecstasy beneath him — no longer human, no longer conscious, no longer caring about anything except the dark **flood of pleasure** that rushed through her and shook her till she rattled and writhed to a hot, pulsing oblivion on his body.
	3	FS8 2901	There was just the touch he gave, disembodied, little **rills of pleasure** that seemed to be arriving from nowhere.
	4	HGM 2030	Nothing else was allowed to matter as her pent-up feelings were released, leaving her rocking on a **sea of pleasure** of such width and depth that she was totally out of control and overwhelmed.
	5	ANY 818	And it was nice to have someone else caress your body, and release the **springs of pleasure** hidden within it, instead of having to do the job yourself.
	6	AMC 1684	I had not been to such a party since before Leslie went to North Africa, and talking to Ika and his friends on a balcony canopied by a starry sky, I felt a **spurt of pleasure**, quickly followed by a surge of guilt: Leslie was dead, and I was alive, and capable of enjoying some temporary diversion.
	7	GUX 1327	He did not know what had possessed him the night before, yet, gradually, the sweetness she gave him began to dissolve his confusion; his vivid **spurt of pleasure** returned to him and he looked across at her and asked, 'Will you be coming to the passeggiata next Saturday?'
	8	HA9 495	Kelly would feel the same way, she realised, experiencing a little **spurt of pleasure** at the prospect of seeing her friend soon ...
	9	HA9 2180	But even as she began to shake her head, she heard her own voice accepting the invitation, felt a ridiculous little **spurt of pleasure** that he even wanted to be with her.

10	JY5 1931	'You again,' she said darkly, deliberately injecting hostility into her voice, at the same time resolutely squashing the ridiculous little **spurt of pleasure** she had felt on seeing him.
11	A06 824	Far example, madam, my life; my life, madam is a perpetual **stream of pleasure**, that glides through such a variety of entertainments, I believe the wisest of our ancestors never had the least conception of any of 'em.
12	FP1 618	The sky had now stripped back to blue as he entered slowly and with a **surge of pleasure** into the cut of Buttermere.
13	H8J 1372	'Not yet,' he said thickly, and fire ran through her veins as his hands cupped her breasts, making her gasp at the **surge of pleasure** his fingers evoked.
14	HGJ 1464	First the relief, then the **surge of pleasure**, then the peace: then the niggle of dissatisfaction growing into active discontent, into a sense of loss, of desperation, of craving — and then the fix.
15	JXT 2744	She felt an almost silly **surge of pleasure** rushing through her.
16	H7H 1596	When the band stopped they were both on a **tide of pleasure**; yet, she stepped away from him as though evading her share in the pleasure.
17	HGM 2021	Wave after wave of sensation ran through her until she thought she might drown in a **tide of pleasure** as his tongue and hands explored the soft silkiness of her body, his lips always returning, though, to meet her lips, like a humming-bird seeking nectar.
18	H94 3176	Small but dangerously exciting **trickles of pleasure** were still winging their way through her virtually defenceless body.
19	APM 1165	Franca turned, bracing herself against the old unthinking uninformed **wave of pleasure** which, urging her towards him, almost lifted her off her feet.
20	EWC 2194	Hazel sat nibbling and biting, the rich, full taste of the cultivated roots filling him with a **wave of pleasure**.
21	J17 2433	A **wave of pleasure**?
22	JY3 3830	She shuddered, half laughing, the joy reaching her heart and enveloping her in such a **wave of pleasure** that she felt weak-kneed.
23	G3S 568	Sitting there on the bucket amid the mixed aromas of pig and barley meal and coffee I could almost feel the **waves of pleasure** beating on me.
24	H8F 3196	And Julius was making it even more difficult, because the silken-smooth touch of his fingers was already producing mind-numbing **waves of pleasure**.
25	JY8 1143	It closed possessively on the aroused peak, sending delicious **waves of pleasure** shuddering through her.
26	JYD 2476	He lowered his dark head, his mouth claiming hers in a fierce, hot kiss as his hand stroked her breast, sending shock **waves of pleasure** through her.
27	H8F 3676	She shuddered as convulsively as he did, and became lost in the same giant **whirlpool of pleasure**.

1	JY5 3333	She knew a quick **surge of satisfaction** when the door flew open, but there was no time to revel in pride at her own achievement as she took in the scene beyond the door.
2	HA5 3176	In the heady fire of consummation Gina knew that the aching loneliness which had dogged her throughout her life was finally ended, her own desire rising to match Rune's as their mutual need drowned them in the remorselessly rising **tide of satisfaction**.
1	FP1 732	He felt as if he were in a trance, speaking the words of someone else; the pressure of this rare **ocean heave of happiness** had re-baptised him, and the words came from out of the air.
2	BoU 1604	I often used to wonder whether we should carry these new **springs of happiness** away with us when we emerged.
3	HHC 1971	Carrie felt a sudden **surge of happiness**.
4	JYo 4314	In that instant, Juliet felt a **surge of happiness** that filled her chest and almost engulfed her.
5	JYA 4548	Slowly the entire village followed them, moving with great dignity and a great **swell of happiness**.
1	AEo 2118	I trembled so much I broke the vase I had been dusting, and I felt a sweet **fountain of delight** flow up through me.
2	B3H 973	Such a well placed and well managed woodland would bring 'never failing **fountains of delight**' to the inhabitants.
3	ARG 1047	They feast on the abundance of your house; you give them drink from your **river of delight**.
4	HNJ 3081	It was what she had been hoping and longing for but there was no **surge of delight**, only a strong but strangely detached sense of relief that the worst of his ordeal was over.
5	FEE 49	Then this would never have happened, or if it had (I couldn't bring myself to unwish an experience which still washed over me with **waves of delight** when I remembered it) at least Toby would have known what he was doing, his eyes would have been open.
1	ACG 1719	The rabbi explains the custom by saying that Israel's **cup of joy** cannot be full if her triumph involves suffering, even for her enemies.
2	FXR 1066	Masters in this hall, my jug **cup of joy** overflows.
3	JYE 3843	Before she could escape she was in his arms and, for one sweet moment, she felt a **flood of joy** sweep through her.
4	CA3 1643	The elegance of his own style, the willingness of the assistants, the feeling that an endless **flow of joy** emanated from this eccentric and astute little man, the jade-green charm of the suit that was eventually chosen, the reserve, the luxury, the civilization of that day came back to her now as she stood gazing at iron scaffolding, aware of drunks in the square opposite and the depression that had undermined the world, and her, since the buoyancy of that radiant and particular day.

CHAPTER III CONVENTIONAL METAPHORS FOR ANTONYMOUS EMOTION CONCEPTS   79

	5	FUB 100	She drew both father and child to the top of the sea, and when she saw them a **spring of joy** burst in her heart and the power of speech returned to her.
	6	G10 1010	But the knowledge had lain beneath his thoughts, a warm, secret **spring of joy**.
	7	FS0 3	I love the fresh smell in the air when everything seems to be coming to life again and I felt a natural **surge of joy**, as if in a few weeks' time John would be coming home from his first trip away just as he should have done the previous April.
	8	GWG 1857	With a **surge of joy** Rain knew that Oliver's insensitivity was no longer her responsibility, that she could walk out of the door and not worry that he had upset people who might, by association, be cross with her.
	9	J17 2428	A **surge of joy**?
	10	J17 2430	SERAFIN: Not a **surge of joy**.
	11	HH1 523	For a breathless instant, made dizzy by the fierce **uprush of joy** sweeping through her, Isabel could not think beyond the fact that he had come.
FIRE	1	GUX 627	With a good heavy hot iron, it would stop belling out here and there, she thought, and she experienced a **flash of pleasure** at the quickness and deftness of her work.
	2	C8D 3079	I'm glad he's getting something out of life, a **glimmer of pleasure** among all the drudgery.
	3	G1W 1150	Dexter detected a **glimmer of pleasure**, as if the man felt instinctive sympathy for Lancaster and took personal satisfaction in thwarting the police.
	4	G2V 1549	'I've got something to tell you, Mum,' I opened, expecting massive surprise and a **glimmer of pleasure**.
	5	HGF 2967	If she was reading this, her eyes would meet mine with a **glint of pleasure** and a steely challenge.
	6	FS1 203	Harry felt a **glow of pleasure** — not least because his darling Alice was making such an obvious success of her career.
	7	H8S 1479	She felt an absurd **glow of pleasure** that he had understood.
	8	HTR 2491	'That's right,' said Loretta, with a little **glow of pleasure**.
	1	CDA 1095	Nevertheless, Alexai Ybreska gazed upon the weed-festooned mound with a **beam of satisfaction**.
	2	H9L 1660	Her lips moved to plead, but no sound passed them, and she glimpsed the **flare of satisfaction** in Luke's smouldering eyes as they flickered to her mouth, which was like a crushed flower now, a red rose, brilliant and vulnerable.
	3	HA6 984	With a bright **flicker of satisfaction**, she watched him slide down into the water, his large body making a flurry of waves ripple the surface.
	4	HHB 3293	Doreen giggled as a strange **gleam of satisfaction** leapt into her eyes.
	5	H7H 278	There was melancholy in all his remembrances, hardly a **gleam of satisfaction**, even though he had ridden a few unexpected winners in his time.

	6	GoL 1794	Normally a cautious man, Kragan felt the **glimmer of satisfaction** spread within him.
	7	HGM 2654	There wasn't the faintest trace of pity in his face as he saw the defeated posture, just a **glimmer of satisfaction** that his own plans were starting to go well for a change.
	8	ANL 1016	A **glint of satisfaction** showed in Rivington's eyes.
	9	B1X 2714	Gallagher felt a warm **glow of satisfaction**.
	10	CEC 1454	Shamlou experienced a **glow of satisfaction**.
	11	GUD 1349	Jenny sat down, laughing even louder and eventually Antony, a pleasant **glow of satisfaction** in his mind, sat down laughing also.
	12	JYE 786	Sophie felt a **glow of satisfaction** as she bent down to open her case.
	1	KA2 329	They gazed at him with blue-black fly filled eyes, and a small **glimmer of happiness** grew on their faces.
	2	JY4 3461	He looked fantastic and had actually acquired quite a suntan — or was it just a **glow of happiness**?
	3	JYE 1691	Or was it, Sophie wondered, the **glow of happiness**?
	4	K34 197	But most women would prefer not to trust to that special '**glow of happiness**' to give them sparkle on their special day.
	1	APU 2327	'That's better,' his grandmother approved when Richard returned, still pink-cheeked and with the **afterglow of joy** in his eyes.
	2	BoB 181	As Judy Joliffe gazed at him, she felt a **glow of joy** surge through her.
	3	CA5 1836	The light that belongs to you is the **light of joy**.
	4	ARG 1806	As we praise God for all our circumstances, seeing them in the light of his presence and love, then we become literally 'thankful persons', transfused by a new **radiance of joy** and thanksgiving.
	5	G15 3414	Blanche could imagine her weeping with her son over his confession but, like Marek, she was a little puzzled that Tatyana had not shown even a **spark of joy** at the revenge he had taken.
EARTH	1	GUE 3476	The world seemed to tilt and spin and fold itself inside out in a **volcanic eruption of pleasure** …
	1	B1F 448	In this state, the mind rests in its **gardens of delight**.
	2	B1F 795	All our lives, we shall know that behind the veils of the transcendent is a world of freedom waiting for us, with its **meadows of delight**.
	1	BP8 1379	We carry the memory of childhood like a photo in a locket, fierce and possessive for pain or calm; everybody's past is inviolate, separate, sacrosanct, our heads are different countries with no maps or dictionaries, people walk vast deserts of grief or inhabit walled **gardens of joy**.

Appendix 3.2

BNC citations of metaphorical expressions of the Type "N of E" from the four different source sub-domains with the words related to SADNESS in the "E" slot

Source	No.	Filename	BNC citations
AIR	1	CJH 316	The village and coastline have an **air of sadness** because of the many ruined crofts facing the water, but there is hospitality for the many visitors.
	2	FR9 1809	No doubt an **air of sadness** will pervade our match with old rivals Hellingborough today.
	3	K91 1113	They had that **air of sadness** that comes over one when a funeral passes by, and I overheard one say: 'It's no longer an army!
	4	H0C 1055	Even with the bustle of oil activity, Scapa was a lonely place with an **aura of sadness**, forever haunted by its sad history of scuttled and torpedoed ships; each time I passed the Royal Oak buoy on our way into Scapa Pier I was reminded of this history.
	5	H7W 3701	Still thinking about the woman and her **aura of sadness**, Polly started.
	6	JYA 5009	She felt an **aura of sadness** around her like a pall.
	1	BMP 547	'You feel a place is dead if there's no school in it — there's an **air of depression** somehow'.
	2	C8L 449	With hindsight, I know I should have seen the warning signals in the man himself, which I missed through inexperience, but the result was that a **cloud of depression**, a sense of failure, settled over me, and also over the whole team.
	1	A0D 9	He was leaning against the rail smoking a cigarette and staring with an **air of melancholy** towards the distant island.
	2	APC 1647	Although a spacious courtyard made the small rooms light, and I was well served by a bed, table and chair of Van Gogh simplicity, I could not deny that an **air of melancholy** hung over the place.
	3	C9U 1355	But this tone soon dissolves into a **miasma of melancholy**.
	1	ARG 396	We have to admit that happiness has no integrity unless it has burst through the **clouds of sorrow**.
WATER	1	HJ4 1675	It's a laugh a minute, with little **pools of sadness** under foot.
	2	AC6 1290	Joe was trying to be bright and cheerful, but there was a deep **undercurrent of sadness**, and later, when he had gone back to his office, Dana said: 'I think he's terribly lonely.'
	3	F9U 452	Both books display Minton's effervescent gaiety, but, even before his illustrations became overlaid with a period nostalgia an **undertow of sadness** could be discerned beneath their cheerful manner.

4	CAB 2527	The odd thing was that, after he had entered the paint shop, he had felt as if a heavy **wave of sadness** had suddenly been lifted from out of him.
5	HXU 1694	He later admitted that that evening "a **wave of sadness**" swept over him and he seriously considered withdrawing.
6	ECT 3509	I think it was a kind of defence mechanism, my way of warding off those **waves of sadness**.
1	FU2 987	Dadda, voyaging day by day farther out on his black **sea of depression**, made his one contribution to the talk.
2	G1S 1477	She felt a great **surge of depression** and a feeling of imminent disaster as though she were very old and death was not far away.
3	A6X 1750	In the midst of this unrelenting **wave of depression**, I found myself, dressed in a borrowed dinner jacket, on the M11 headed for Cambridge, where I was about to make my first (and last) appearance as an after-dinner speaker.
4	A7H 1242	He had been hit by a new **wave of depression**.
5	FS1 1896	He felt a sudden deep **wave of depression**, coupled with uncertainty.
6	HHB 2281	The thought sent a **wave of depression** over her.
1	CJF 403	But this had been followed by a sense of personal outrage, an emptiness and then a **surge of melancholy**, not strong enough to be called grief but keener than mere regret, which had surprised him by its intensity.
2	CAG 1903	In an absorbing, epic quest for the self, the humour, occasional nostalgia and vibrancy of the novel's language fail to deflect from an **undertow of melancholy** and the sense of irrecoverable loss.
1	HGF 529	Abandoned to drink from her **cup of sorrow**, the asylum superintendents would have marked the baby as 'an accidental addition which wholly unbalances the tottering mind'.
2	B1F 332	There is little great poetry that has not come from the **frost of sorrow**, and this is the supreme compensation that the creative man has this faculty of distilling from the very substance of sorrow, a beauty that transforms the world into paradise.
3	CH2 10860	TEARS ON **JET OF SORROW**
4	ANX 2238	Paradise in the **Sea of Sorrow**: Our Minamata Disease by Michiko Ishimure, translated from Japanese by Livia Monnet Yamaguchi Publishing House, pp 365, 5000 yen/$35
5	ANX 2246	Paradise in the **Sea of Sorrow** appeared in Japanese in 1969, the first part of a trilogy.
6	ANX 2264	I do not know how easy it will be to find Paradise in the **Sea of Sorrow** outside Japan.
1	AoD 1492	The concrete was cold to his bottom, and he stared at the stairs down which Bunty had fallen, his throat and his face and his eyes seeming to swell up in a great hot **surge of grief**.

	2	H7E 1441	Once the initial **surge of grief** had passed the funeral was almost a celebration.
	3	ADE 61	For many Christian people who are caught up in the **whirlpool of grief**, the most difficult part may well be their realization that they are in fact feeling very distressed.
FIRE	1	FSR 4	Henri paused briefly under an archway, a **glimmer of sadness** pulsing within him.
EARTH	1	C8T 2104	And after his death it seemed to her that she had walked in darkness like an automaton through a deep and narrow **canyon of grief** in which all her energies, all her physical strength, had been husbanded to get through each day.
	2	BN1 2077	How each evening his thoughts festered and multiplied, decimating **chasms of grief** littered the shining path of sleep.
	3	BP8 1379	We carry the memory of childhood like a photo in a locket, fierce and possessive for pain or calm; everybody's past is inviolate, separate, sacrosanct, our heads are different countries with no maps or dictionaries, people walk vast **deserts of grief** or inhabit walled gardens of joy.
	4	GUG 803	Han Ch'in's death lay there in that silence; cold, heavy, unmentionable: a dark **stone of grief** in the guts of each that neither had managed to pass.

Appendix 3.3

BNC citations of metaphorical expressions of the Type "N of E" from the four different source sub-domains with the word *hope* in the "E" slot

Source	No.	Filename	BNC citations
AIR	1	KRU 84	The United Nations reception centres for Contra rebels to return and lay down their weapons, opened for business in an **atmosphere of hope** rather than anticipation.
	2	APM 618	Tears came again to Franca's eyes, strange tears, tears for everything, for herself as everything, tears out of the terrible **cloud of hope** and fear that hangs over all things.
	3	HY5 1545	The dream of a "new diplomacy" remained, in spite of the **outburst of hope** generated by the creation of the League of Nations, no more than a dream.
	4	FP6 2400	There are a few minutes, perhaps not more than three or four, when I exist in a bewildering **storm of hope**, joy, incomprehen-sion and dread, when they don't find the body at the bottom of the shaft.
WATER	1	ADA 745	I drank fears like wormwood, yea, made myself drunken with bitterness; for my ever-shaping and distrustful mind still mingled gall-drops, till out of the **cup of hope** I almost poisoned myself with despair …
	2	CBN 1330	Landscapes were empty and without meaning unless they could be related to an inner view, to a feeling of emptiness or apprehension, a sadness, a **surge of hope**, an ecstasy.
	3	JXV 1574	There was a thread of anger in the question, but Fran ignored it, just as she forced herself to ignore the sudden **surge of hope** that filled her heart.
	4	HH1 3306	A quick **rush of hope** surged through her, only to be instantly squashed when Isabel remembered the treacher-ous reality behind the truth.
FIRE	1	A2J 149	He ended by saying that the prospect of a Labour govern-ment was a **beacon of hope** for millions of striving and oppressed people throughout the world.
	2	ABL 3	Capella hangs low, pale, large, moist and trembling almost engulfed between two horn of the wood upon the headland, the frailest **beacon of hope**, still fluttering from the storm out of which the land is emerging.
	3	B71 1404	While other workers have published careful studies showing modest, often transitory, benefits of training for IQ, Heber's projects stood as a **beacon of hope** for dramatic and lasting benefits, and also as the defence against those who say that IQ has proved disappointingly hard to budge.
	4	BMC 2462	Perhaps it will provide a **beacon of hope** for future generations of pianists for whom it is not too late to swerve off their mat and sterile paths, to follow the lead of a genuine eccentric and a genuine musician?

CHAPTER III CONVENTIONAL METAPHORS FOR ANTONYMOUS EMOTION CONCEPTS 85

5	C87 2131	Aye, the production may have been poor, but the crude gameplay shone out like a **beacon of hope** for us downtrodden folk.
6	CBE 885	Considering the Statue of Liberty has been a **beacon of hope** for generations of newly-arrived immigrants, it's appropriate that Mario arrived in New York with his parents 30 years ago.
7	FTW 874	Overnight a highly suspect communist renegade was transformed into an eternally youthful dissident communist, a **beacon of hope** for a generation of young men and women rebelling against the anarchronistic irrelevance of an outmoded educational system and the serial alienation of a post-industrial society.
8	K5H 3622	While France stands shoulder to shoulder with Germany, and the two countries together account for half the EC output, the exchange rate mechanism will survive, representing a **beacon of hope** for federalists who still see a common currency as the bridge across which Europe must pass to a federal future, and a baleful threat for the sovereign Britishers, who see it as a black hole which could draw EC members inexorably into the same destiny.
9	B1J 1780	The **candle of hope** is to me a more satisfactory symbol than a sickly stanza.
10	AJD 395	For even in the darkest days of two-party Tory and Labour domination, the **flame of hope** burns brightly here,' he said.
11	C85 1177	A small **flame of hope** lit.
12	JY2 3129	A tiny **flame of hope** that Luce had never even acknowledged flickered and died as his words, and the facts behind them, hammered themselves into her brain.
13	JY5 3684	The tiny darting **flame of hope** died instantly as the door swung open, but was replaced by a rush of real and genuine gladness as she looked into her father's face.
14	JYC 2393	The news of the Seren had ignited a bright **flame of hope** which left her cold and utterly despondent when it shed no light at all on the mystery of her identity.
15	BMM 1642	Optimism must always be tinged with anxiety for it not to become braggartism, and there were enough instances in the past, mainly at Olympic Games where British **flames of hope** had turned to ashes of despair, for a note of caution to be sounded.
16	JYD 3727	'Can I take a message?' she said on a sudden **flare of hope**.
17	EDF 984	A **flash of hope** after the unexpected success at Bauge in 1421; but Cravant and, in particular, Verneuil put paid to hopes of a quick revival.
18	G0N 2893	The **flash of hope** in her eyes made him wish he could report a more substantial discovery than the meagre piece of intelligence he had to contribute.
19	JY4 3872	To her shock and horror his head swooped down and as his mouth claimed hers so impassionately a **flash of hope** surged in her heart like a spear of lightning out of a blackened sky.

20	ABR 559	A **flicker of hope** came when three West Indian wickets went down for 69, but then it was Haynes' turn to come good after a disappointing series.
21	CKD 84	His shoulders drooped, he expected nothing, but a small **flicker of hope** showed in the uptilting of his chin.
22	HH1 3944	A **flicker of hope** stirred to life, although it was accompanied by a shiver of horror, as Isabel saw the evil hidden once again behind the truth.
23	HH8 3914	The last tiny **flicker of hope** seemed to die inside her, and as it did all the lights in the grand chamber went out.
24	JXU 2196	Nothing could get out — or in, she registered with a **flicker of hope**.
25	K22 2171	The result was all wrong ... 6–2 on aggregate to Tranmere but there was a **flicker of hope** in the flames as United's cup run went up in smoke ...
26	A12 182	From the opening piteous pleas with shaking hands as the dancers sink to the floor in the depths of their sorrow, the choreographic pattern of the overall rhythm is seen to swell in size and intensity as the music does until there comes the **gleam of hope**, a quiet moment when a child-like figure dances in wonder at the ways in which she can explore not only the space in which she moves, but also the ways in which she shapes each part of her body into an ever flowing design.
27	CEX 2122	The **gleam of hope** vanished.
28	CR6 1276	He saw a **gleam of hope** appear in Roy's eyes.
29	G3S 2449	It was the number one awkward question but I discerned the faintest **gleam of hope**; he had spoken in the unmistakable harsh, glottal accent of my home town.
30	HRJ 784	The only **gleam of hope** the Prime Minister could offer was that the Cabinet had on the previous day agreed to ask the Bank of England whether an increase of cuts from 56 million to 76 million, including a ten per cent cut in unemployment benefits, would be enough to ensure an American loan.
31	CNK 40	**GLEAMS OF HOPE** AMIDST THE THE GLOOM OVER GALWAY AFTER DEC's DEPARTURE
32	A1S 190	It has suffered a severe blow to trading confidence and the only **glimmer of hope** for the shares appears to be the prospect of a takeover.
33	A34 77	By yesterday evening the largest lender, the Halifax, which held out a **glimmer of hope** earlier in the day that it could stick with its 13.5 per cent rate, acknowledged a rise was inevitable.
34	A98 137	While it approved some types of drug testing, the Supreme Court did leave the anti-testing forces a **glimmer of hope** for ultimate legal containment.
35	AHU 1502	NOTTINGHAM condemned Rosslyn Park to almost certain relegation while giving themselves a **glimmer of hope** of survival in League One with their first victory of the season, based on three tries by flanker Martin Pepper and 18 points from outside-half Guy Gregory.

36	AKM 585	West Ham's 4–0 victory over Norwich on Saturday had offered a **glimmer of hope** and scuppered the planned mass second-half walk-out by supporters in their continuing protest at the general running of the club.
37	AL6 55	Mrs Shephard said the unemployment figures were 'a **glimmer of hope**' but added that it would be foolish to build too much into one month's statistics.
38	BMD 2111	However, there is a **glimmer of hope**.
39	C8J 360	Those who have learnt to accept their difficulties without the **glimmer of hope** are set free.
40	CAP 434	Eventually came a **glimmer of hope**.
41	CAU 327	There is a **glimmer of hope** on the horizon.
42	CBD 560	A report suggesting a slight rise in house prices brought a further **glimmer of hope** for embattled homeowners yesterday.
43	CD2 868	Some **glimmer of hope** still remained; but the woman's voice dispelled it.
44	CEN 4239	But there is one **glimmer of hope** for Becky, who has just started school.
45	CEP 8102	Courier's only **glimmer of hope** came when he broke serve in the first game of the third set, but it was only a momentary lapse of concentration by the German, who so likes to win in front of his countrymen and women, as he broke back in the next game.
46	CH2 12362	The news gave a **glimmer of hope** that Michael Wainwright, 42, and Paul Ride, 33, might get an early release.
47	CH3 3278	Two Paul Eastwood penalties against one to Rudd gave Hull a **glimmer of hope**.
48	CH6 8564	If ever there was a tiny **glimmer of hope** that her marriage to Andy could be salvaged she's blown it now.
49	ECM 759	When doctors announced that there was a **glimmer of hope**, Raine organized a private ambulance to take him to the National Hospital for Nervous Diseases in Queen Square, central London where for several months he lay in a coma.
50	ED7 2365	This is life-affirming stuff, undoubtedly cynical and perhaps even bitter, but retaining some **glimmer of hope** and resolution in spite of all that.
51	EFA 699	Perhaps there was a **glimmer of hope** in 1949 when someone of the stature (rather than the disposition) of de Gaulle might have seized the burning brand; and four years later Mendès France could face the unacceptable although by then there was practically no alternative.
52	EFT 773	The last two verses give a **glimmer of hope**.
53	FPB 2518	Buzz recalled Elinor's swift rage and felt another **glimmer of hope**, but a thought occurred to her: If they insisted on treating Nell like a crazy person, she might actually end up like one.
54	H92 250	His dreams would have to wait, be returned intact to some cupboard deep in the recesses of his mind, whence they would arise, undaunted, at the next **glimmer of hope** in his career.

55	HH5 832	Nevertheless, I had a **glimmer of hope**.
56	HJ3 2790	However a **glimmer of hope** has appeared on the horizon.
57	HJ3 2890	A 44th minute goalmouth melee in which Colin Allister and Norman McGladdery were both denied was the nearest Bann came to giving themselves a **glimmer of hope**.
58	HJD 1500	After a few minutes, someone broke the silence in an attempt to offer a **glimmer of hope**.
59	J9L 74	Only the A E U have the courage to stand up against big brother, the T U C, warning against denying the unemployed a **glimmer of hope**.
60	JY5 3488	The cryptic little comment sparked off a tiny **glimmer of hope** deep within her — could he be trying to tell her that she'd proved distracting?
61	K1J 735	Doctors say there is now a **glimmer of hope** for the survival of the twelve-year-old Warrington bomb victim, Timothy Parry.
62	K1K 3756	One **glimmer of hope** though, tonight police say that someone who knows the couple claims to have seen them at a garden centre in herefordshire.
63	K1W 2762	And Felton's miscue off Neil Smith offered them a **glimmer of hope**.
64	K21 2704	There is now a **glimmer of hope** ... this is the first reasonable amount of water a pond in Blewberry has had for at least two years.
65	K25 1571	A **glimmer of hope** for Gloucester.
66	K4T 698	'We must win this week-end to have a **glimmer of hope** of catching them.
67	K55 2331	LIMESTONE CONTROVERSY: **GLIMMER OF HOPE**
68	K55 2332	British Steel on Thursday appeared to add a faint **glimmer of hope** into the controversy over a plan to switch thousands of tonnes of limestone dust from rail to road.
69	K59 1626	Mr Hayward detected a **glimmer of hope** in the fact that the rate of increase in liquidations had slowed down, with only a 3.5 per cent rise in the last three months of 1992.
70	K97 2567	There was one **glimmer of hope** for Mr Bush.
71	K97 3422	'After a week's work it was satisfying to win against Brighton but it was only a **glimmer of hope**.'
72	K97 16231	Perhaps the only **glimmer of hope** is that there has been no increase in the use of heroin, cocaine and crack just 1.2pc admit to trying them, the same as in 1990.
73	KAV 340	The judge knew this man of old: he was the pit-bull of the legal profession, attacking any weak spots with devastating precision, and seeing him ended the Judge's faint **glimmer of hope** that he might just get home in time for the football.
74	KS7 119	Paul Biddle squandered another chance for Milton on seventy one minutes as he put the ball wide from close range and then with ten minutes remaining, Fairmile offered themselves a **glimmer of hope** as Wayne Glossop fired home through a ruck of players.
75	AL6 480	'**Glimmers of hope**' after lowest jobless rise for two years

CHAPTER III CONVENTIONAL METAPHORS FOR ANTONYMOUS EMOTION CONCEPTS

76	AL6 485	A cautious Mrs Gillian Shephard, the new Employment Secretary, said yesterday that too much should not be read into one set of figures before adding that they and a series of other favourable statistics may offer '**glimmers of hope**' on the jobless front.
77	ARD 634	But, despite these **glimmers of hope**, this survey of the left's response to Distant Voices, Still Lives and A Very British Coup has, on the whole, demonstrated how much the mainstream operates a hegemony in the area of critical discourse.
78	CBE 2448	Amid the renewed **glimmers of hope** is the knowledge that this is the 19th attempt at a ceasefire.
79	CBW 669	There are a few **glimmers of hope**, however, since fewer firms are having trouble collecting fees and all but the larger firms are optimistic about increasing their client base.
80	GWJ 1284	The paper offers **glimmers of hope** in the fight against the disease, through the promotion of better understanding.
81	HWV 1422	Where are the **glimmers of hope**?
82	AKM 649	But Mr Coleman offered a **glint of hope** for Mr Bates, adding: 'This policy on ground-sharing was formed for very good reasons.
83	CKD 1097	'We'll survive, papa,' Emily said with a certainty that brought a **light of hope** into her father's eyes.
84	FRJ 163	The **light of hope** that had flickered in Tubby's eyes died and he shook his head wearily.
85	ARG 1804	But giving thanks to God, even in suffering, can be inspired by a **radiance of hope** that sees all things in the light of eternity.
86	B11 505	Out of this morass of doleful depression there came a bright **ray of hope** and a rhyming solace to the weary and dispirited housewives of the country in the person of Edna Jacques.
87	BMW 446	The sound of footsteps on the rickety staircase leading to her workroom made Theresa look up from her drawings, a small **ray of hope** that refused to be extinguished flickering to life.
88	BN4 958	Another **ray of hope** is the International Tropical Timber Organisation (ITTO) which was established in 1986.
89	CBT 2370	The only statutory **ray of hope** is the phrase 'except while being kept overnight on premises occupied by the person making the car available to them'.
90	CD6 1489	But the Red Or Dead catwalk show offered a **ray of hope**.
91	CE6 329	how she is like a '**ray of hope**' —
92	CF8 311	STRONGER-than-expected factory production revealed yesterday provided another **ray of hope** for Chancellor Norman Lamont as he put the final touches to the Budget.
93	CH2 13098	The **ray of hope** came as his grieving wife Jean, 60, left his bedside to attend her mother Winifred's funeral.
94	CNA 124	A decade ago the argon laser was hailed as a 'new **ray of hope** for portwine stains.'

95	CRB 329	Your review of Raymond Bonner's 'At the Hand of Man' (April 24th) is **a ray of hope** for those of us who live with dangerous wild animals.
96	EEF 1467	Gilpin (1987), like many liberal economists, regards it as contrary to consumer interests, whereas others describe it as 'a **ray of hope** in a dismal world '.
97	EFG 973	There was just one small **ray of hope**.
98	FPY 795	In seeking to equip and help both amateurs and professionals in their work as church musicians, they offer a **ray of hope** in what is, overall, a fairly sombre picture.
99	FTX 543	The only **ray of hope** which the BDDA perceived in the report was Dr Eichholz's call for "a close study of all methods of communication including phonetics linguistics, fingerspelling, finger-reading and gesture", coupled with a recommendation that "fingerspelling (the spelling and the reading of it) should be taught in schools at least in the final period of school life."
100	G12 737	Do you think it holds out a **ray of hope** among the problems which perplex us all so sorely today?'
101	H94 2515	The struggle to understand everything showed clearly on her face, and slowly, surely, she found a **ray of hope** in the mess, something to compensate for the painful discovery that she'd been ignorant of her own roots.
102	J18 1328	Such ideas as the use of more legumes or other nitrogen-fixers and the ingenious use of nitrogen-fixing bacteria in the floating fern, Azolla, in paddy fields in southern China offer a **ray of hope**.
103	JK2 261	Finally in eighteen thirty, there was yet another revolution in France, and that brought him a a **ray of hope**.
104	JYB 2997	There is one **ray of hope** — one member of the rescue team, himself an experienced caver, is a Casualty consultant from Suffolk who has volunteered to go down with the party to provide immediate medical assistance to the injured man.
105	K1B 2708	And you know what they say about every cloud having a silver lining — well could young Joey Beecham be United's **ray of hope**?
106	K1K 854	It's results will be published at the end of next year, when scientists and patients will find out if it's more than just a **ray of hope**.
107	K2G 79	**Ray of hope** on port wine stains
108	K5A 1203	For a few months, I entertained a **ray of hope** that after many, many years there was now less need for young men to face death in battle, but that hope has now died.
109	KRM 2117	There is one **ray of hope**, though.
110	CFH 454	'There are **rays of hope**, however.
111	CNA 125	Was this optimism justified, and what of more recent **rays of hope**?
112	HHW 13528	When the Secretary of State was enjoying himself for about 10 minutes claiming that a large number of us supported CND, he offered some **rays of hope** and sunshine that I had not seen for some months.

	113	CGL 1175	Other airfields that have a **spark of hope** on the horizon include: Ipswich, Leavesden and Hullavington, although there are many more airfields where the future looks bleak.
	114	CJJ 2234	For a moment, Yeremi felt a **spark of hope**.
	115	HJD 1631	A **spark of hope** was rekindled in him, as his eye traced the faint line and saw it formed a two-foot square.
	116	JYD 3216	Rachel looked at her and felt a **spark of hope**, knowing Damian did want, above and beyond all else, to make love to her.
EARTH	1	K4C 875	**Grounds of hope**

Appendix 3.4

BNC citations of metaphorical expressions of the Type "N of E" from the four different source sub-domains with the word *fear* in the "E" slot

Source	No.	Filename	BNC citations
AIR	1	HH3 1830	An **air of fear** has replaced the sense of purpose which marked the Sankara years.
	2	CRT 547	Assisted often by 'convict warders', who add to an **atmosphere of fear** and connive in the corruption which is endemic in many institutions.
	3	EWG 955	He never in fact produced the list (which in a speech the next day had been mysteriously reduced to 57) but his smear tactics worked in an **atmosphere of fear**.
	4	K97 10498	An **atmosphere of fear** had descended with many witnesses too afraid to come forward, she added.
	5	APD 1140	It was not long before the authorities began to harass the unions, and to maintain an **aura of fear** to keep their membership dormant.
	6	FB0 715	Until, under the mirror, after many a circle and feint, after many a playful retreat and renewed approach, Ivan at last cornered her, and even before he opened his mouth she felt the **smell of fear** from herself: her pores broke open, she stood there panting slightly, her hair rising on the back of her neck in terror, her heated skin covered in icy sweat: 'And when,' asked Ivan pleasantly, 'are you two going to make the announcement?
	7	FYV 205	His sheets have the white **smell of fear**.
	8	CEH 713	Added to the musty crypt smell there would be the stink of sweat and unchanged babies, all mingling with the **stench of fear**, because tonight everyone was more on edge than usual.
	9	HH5 1583	I caught the **stench of fear** from the cardinal.
	10	K95 1761	Fitzormonde was probably a brave man but Athelstan could almost taste the **stench of fear** which emanated from him.
	11	K95 2386	Nevertheless, he could almost smell the **stench of fear**: the house was too quiet.
	12	G1S 2500	She smelled the **tang of fear** in her nostrils and the taste of it in her mouth.
	13	FP3 1341	So near, so near was the freedom of the sky ... but across such a terrible **void of fear**.
WATER	1	GVL 2564	As Carradine bled his life out in the Dream, Yggdrasil tasted its first **cup of fear**.
	2	HTM 60	It brought back a **flood of fear** and an almost unbearable memory of loss, the body of the warrior Gyonval fighting with the wood, impaling itself on a sharp branch as if that might keep the soul from parting.

CHAPTER III CONVENTIONAL METAPHORS FOR ANTONYMOUS EMOTION CONCEPTS

3	FP7 3666	Only now that he was safe did he feel a little black **jet of fear** rising in his chest, a gobbet of bile that filled his mouth, washing his teeth in acid.
4	G04 3521	A **ripple of fear** passed down his spine.
5	GUG 2178	Tuan Ti Fo felt a small **ripple of fear** pass through him, yet calmed himself inwardly, a still, small voice chanting the chen yen to dispense with fear.
6	GV2 2779	She drew away from him, feeling the cold **sap of fear**.
7	H97 1956	As the bell rang again, insistently, urgently, she headed for the door, pulling the dressing-gown around her, feeling a cold **spring of fear** welling up inside.
8	CJF 230	That **spurt of fear** at the thought of the police had passed.
9	APU 1003	Martha stepped back off the verandah, feeling a **surge of fear** conditioned by the beatings of earlier years.
10	CCW 90	He raised his eyes to stare into my face, and I felt a **surge of fear**.
11	EFV 1590	Everywhere bells ring the alarm; a **surge of fear** sweeps over the countryside.
12	HJD 1698	Grant had to suppress the **trickle of fear** which ran through him, tightening his solar plexus and quickening his pulse, as he faced this dangerous man.
13	JY3 392	'Unfortunately I've managed to acquire neither,' he said finally, straightening to his daunting height and sending a **trickle of fear** down her spine by tugging at the buttons on his shirt, apparently with every intention of undressing right there in front of her.
14	C8T 1265	And then irritation began to give way to the first **tricklings of fear**.
15	HWA 430	But beneath it all, beneath the strange rituals that passed in this milieu for normality, there was an **undercurrent of fear**, of latent panic.
16	FP0 3073	She could feel no personal flavour but a dirty **undertow of fear**.
17	G0Y 1461	Most of the time one was all right — or at least as all right as one had ever been — and then out of the blue it struck, a hideous **uprush of fear**, of longing, of shame.
18	A2J 277	No, what I want to know is whether the US is gripped by a **wave of fear** of the Japanese.
19	CE7 1011	A sudden **wave of fear** that a new world war was in the making found expression not through the LNU — whose recruitment declined sharply during 1933 — but in some rather less disciplined eruptions of protest.
20	F99 1548	Suddenly a **wave of fear** washed over her mind and she became tinglingly aware, as if she hadn't realized it before, what danger they were in.
21	HGK 2505	Felipe stood in front of her like a lion-tamer, a whip in his hand with the thong coiled out of the way, and for a second Maggie felt a **wave of fear**.

	22	JXU 4208	With a lunge, he grabbed the bag from between her fingers and flung it across the parquet, where it landed with a thump before skidding to rest beneath a radiator, then before she could react to such a flare of violence he was reaching out for her, dragging her into his embrace, his lips ravening hungrily over her own with a fever of desire that sent shock **waves of fear** and desire quivering through her.
	23	JXV 3177	He didn't deserve it, yet she couldn't stop the cold sick **waves of fear** she felt at what might happen to him.
FIRE	1	G3G 2867	Despite robe and boots she moved with graceful speed, and without any **flicker of fear**.
	2	HA9 2025	She closed her eyes against the **flicker of fear** running through her veins.
	3	HH5 1153	Do you know, I saw a **flicker of fear** in those cunning eyes and realised why his Satanic Eminence needed us so much.
	4	JXY 2239	He didn't answer at first and there was something about the quality of his silence that caused a **flicker of fear** to touch her heart.
	5	JY0 3942	For a brief moment the old lady's gaze rested on her, and Juliet thought she glimpsed a **flicker of fear**.
EARTH	—	—	—

Appendix 3.5

BNC citations of metaphorical expressions of the Type "*N of E*" from the four different source sub-domains with the word *despair* in the "*E*" slot

Source	No.	Filename	BNC citations
AIR	1	K54 2479	Mr Kemp said the **atmosphere of despair** which swept the homes after the closure announcement on January 9 had now gone.
	2	H7H 2501	Nicandra's big hands hung by her sides, her world shifted place, all certainty lost and gone in a salty **fog of despair**.
	3	G0Y 3360	She felt a **gust of despair**.
	4	HH1 891	Through a **haze of despair** she noticed that the Sheriff was still frowning at her.
	5	G1L 1770	A **miasma of despair** rose from the cluster of black Workshops and Fenella felt it billow out and engulf them in its sick, cold desolation.
	6	FS5 112	Trapped in a **vacuum of despair**, that term, I thought dramatically of suicide but lacked the means.
WATER	1	A0N 228	It has happened in France, Cameron felt like saying, and then the thought of the gulf between France and Scotland came over him so dauntingly that he suffered a **backwash of despair**.
	2	G3E 1319	The irises had seemed to dilate into black **pools of despair**.
	3	HNJ 3148	Eleanor succumbed to another shuddering **tide of despair**.
	4	GW0 563	And yet, even though her father had talked to her like one adult to another, as if at last he was ready to acknowledge that she'd grown up and was making her own decisions, she'd sensed the **undercurrent of despair** in what he was saying.
FIRE	1	BMM 1642	Optimism must always be tinged with anxiety for it not to become braggartism, and there were enough instances in the past, mainly at Olympic Games where British flames of hope had turned to **ashes of despair**, for a note of caution to be sounded.
EARTH	1	CKD 88	Just when she had been on the **brink of despair**, one of her rich customers had given her a handsome order.
	2	AP0 960	It destroyed him and for a time he was engulfed by a deep **chasm of despair**, drinking heavily, taking amphetamines and LSD — and he was in his sixteenth year of smoking marijuana.
	3	ADE 199	Fifth, there is the period of acceptance, which can seem to be in stark contrast to the **depths of despair** of the previous stage.

4	B19 945	She had come to the Centre in the **depths of despair**, weeping, gnashing her teeth and venting her hatred upon the doctors who had told her, at the eleventh hour that she had cancer and nothing could be done.
5	B1X 1407	'When you're ill and have sunk to the **depths of despair**, black thoughts enter your mind.
6	B1X 1901	So relaxed now; yet only a short while ago he had been in the **depths of despair**.
7	CAR 1506	He said that although the public faces of the parents were brave, and they were trying to bear up, there were times when they sank to the **depths of despair**.
8	CDG 1037	Sometimes I was in the **depths of despair**, but the other inmates helped to carry me through prison.
9	CEJ 1104	This detail in the story shows that the son was driven to the **depths of despair**.
10	CU1 1370	Had the besweatered Pakistanis held their catches there is no knowing to what **depths of despair** England might have sunk that evening.
11	ECM 1709	With savage irony, when she was in the **depths of despair**, the tide of publicity turned against her.
12	EVC 1458	Small things would make her happy; one harsh word would send her into the **depths of despair**.
13	GWH 1177	My poor master was in the **depths of despair**.
14	HJ3 4835	One side feeds on the other's terror, dragging our community to new **depths of despair**.
15	HSL 509	It takes you and deposits you at the edge of a precipice and you can watch helplessly as you dangle and your hopes for survival are sinking into the **depths of despair**'.
16	J0W 2163	Once, Ken told John Lahr, he was in the **depths of despair**.
17	JYE 4440	She felt as though she were treading on thin ice and any false move might plunge her once more into the dark **depths of despair**.
18	A95 297	It is a dangerous moment, pregnant with hope teetering on the **edge of despair**.
19	A9E 436	It is a dangerous moment, pregnant with hope teetering on the **edge of despair**.
20	B1L 214	Driven to the **edge of despair** and traumatised by the prospect of a court-case that deeply injured his pride, he threw himself in front of an express train bound for Edinburgh.
21	B1X 615	I wanted to drive her to the very **edge of despair**.
22	CDV 320	One may say that the wise characters in The Lord of the Rings are often without hope and so near the **edge of despair**, but they do not succumb.
23	ECM 46	At times the loneliness of her position has brought her to the **edge of despair**, so much so that she has made a number of suicide attempts, some more half-hearted than others.
24	FT6 473	The service remains in a **pit of despair** compounded by underfunding and the closure of specialist resources such as Peper Harrow.

25	HTX 2674	Owen could hardly bear to look at her, so much was she at the mercy of the music, plunging with it into **pits of despair**, rising with it to heights of exaltation that were almost unbearable.
26	HTX 3937	Too strong-willed and forceful to remain easily in any slot into which a male-oriented Moslem society might force her, regarding marriage, certainly to a Moslem, as the ultimate form of prison, conducting life as a ceaseless battle for Home Rule and Independence, she sometimes found things too much for her and plunged into **pits of despair**, from which she would spring out again almost immediately with a soar and a vehemence which left Owen dazzled.
27	HHW 534	As the rest of Europe and the world progresses, are we to be left in a **quagmire of despair** at the end of another parliamentary Session, another era and another century?
28	JXU 2533	She stumbled away, broken and on the **verge of despair**.

CHAPTER IV
Emotions and Animal Metaphors

4.1 Introduction

Metaphors used for understanding EMOTIONS consist of conventional mappings from a series of source domains. A corpus study reported in Chapter II identified six major sources: NATURAL PHENOMENA, SUBSTANCES or SMALL OBJECTS, A CONTAINER, A MOVING OBJECT or A VEHICLE, A LIVING ORGANISM, and TEXTILE or THREADS (see Table 2.2 in Ch. II). This chapter concentrates on the domain ANIMALS, a sub-domain of A LIVING ORGANISM, and discusses correspondences between ANIMALS and EMOTIONS. Here I make a detailed observation of English idioms and poetic expressions, examining tendencies of animal vehicles used for specific emotions and arguing about the systematic nature of correspondences between the source and the target domains.

4.2 Animal idioms for emotions

4.2.1 Meaning of idioms and conceptual metaphors

Idioms are generally understood as "a group of words established by usage as having a meaning not deducible from those of the individual words" (*Concise Oxford English Dictionary*). Research in the semantic traditions regards meanings of idioms as "unpredictable from the syntactic and semantic properties of their constituents" (Lyons 1981: 145). This view of idioms entails an idea that the relation between the form and the meaning of an idiom is arbitrary and conventionally fixed. It follows from the idea that even a "figurative" idiom, which can be presumed from the meanings of its constituents to have originally had a metaphoric meaning, has lost its former metaphoricity and is now to be classified as a dead metaphor. Gibbs (1992, 1994, etc.), however, makes a contention contrary to this dead metaphor view, arguing that semantic interpretations of idioms are not arbitrarily determined. According to him, idioms are motivated by metaphorical mappings, and the figurative meaning of an idiom "cannot be reduced to simple literal paraphrases. People make sense of idiomatic speech precisely because of their ordinary metaphorical knowledge which provides part of the link between these phrases and their figurative interpretations" (Gibbs 1994: 268).

The metaphorical motivation for idiomatic meaning is investigated by experimental studies of Gibbs and his colleagues. Gibbs and O'Brien (1990) carried out a detailed examination of speakers' mental images of idioms. They asked their participants to describe their mental images of some idioms and to answer questions about the causes, intentionality, and manner of action in their mental images. The descriptions given by the participants contained rich details. For example, when they were given anger idioms such as *blow your stack*, *hit the ceiling* and *flip your lid*, the participants specifically imagined some force causing a container to release pressure in a violent manner. These responses are based on people's folk conceptions of heated fluid or vapor building up and escaping from containers with enormous pressure. They know that pressure (i.e., stress or frustration) causes the action, one has little control over the pressure once it builds up, its violent release is done unintentionally and once the release has taken place (i.e., once the ceiling has been hit, the lid flipped, the stack blown), it is difficult to reverse the action. The data show that our understanding of these anger idioms is motivated by a metaphorical mapping of the source domain HEATED FLUID IN A CONTAINER onto the target domain THE ANGER EMOTION.

Nayak and Gibbs (1990) also report highly suggestive experiments. One of the experiments (pp. 324–327) examined whether or not readers use their understanding of the temporal sequences inherent in emotion concepts when interpreting the appropriateness of idioms in varying discourse situations. Participants were asked to read pairs of stories and to judge the appropriateness of each final idiomatic phrase. They rated idioms embedded in conceptually congruent contexts higher than idioms read in conceptually incongruent stories. Consider, for example, the following pair of stories:

Text 1:
Mary was very tense about this evening's dinner party. The fact that Bob had not come home to help was making her fume. She was getting hotter with every passing minute. Dinner would not be ready before the guests arrived. As it got closer to five o'clock the pressure was really building up. Mary's tolerance was reaching its limits. When Bob strolled in at ten minutes to five whistling and smiling, Mary {blew her top / bit his head off}.

Text 2:
Mary was getting very grouchy about this evening's dinner party. She prowled around the house waiting for Bob to come home to help. She was growling under her breath about Bob's lateness. Her mood was becoming more savage with every passing minute. As it got closer to five o'clock Mary was ferociously angry with Bob. When Bob strolled in at 4:30 whistling and smiling, Mary {bit his head off / blew her top}.

Although both of these texts describe how Mary's anger accumulates with the passage of time, conventional expressions used to describe anger differ. Text 1 depicts Mary's increasing anger in terms of increasing pressure and heat. The use of phrases like *very tense*, *making her fume*, *getting hotter*, *the pressure was building up*, and *reaching its limits* is based on the conceptual metaphor ANGER IS HEATED FLUID IN A CONTAINER. On the other hand, the conventional expressions used in Text 2, i.e., *to prowl*, *to growl*, *to be savage*, and *ferociously* primarily describe animal behaviors and characteristics. Mary's anger is understood here according to the metaphor ANGRY BEHAVIOR IS ANIMAL BEHAVIOR.

The participants of the experiment gave high appropriateness ratings to *blew her top* in Text 1, and *bit his head off* in Text 2. *To blow one's top* and *to bite someone's head off* are both grammatically and semantically appropriate for the given scenario. The participants' judgments about the appropriateness of an idiom, however, exhibited a decided bias. The judgments were definitely influenced by coherence between the metaphorical information depicted in a discourse context and the conceptual metaphor reflected in the lexical makeup of an idiom.

These experiments show that interpretation of many idioms is not arbitrarily determined. People make sense of idioms precisely because the idioms are motivated by conceptual knowledge, which itself is constituted by metaphor. Holding this viewpoint, the next section will concentrate on emotion idioms including animal terms, investigating whether there are some correspondences between specific emotions and animal groups, and considering the metaphorical mappings which motivate those idioms.

4.2.2 Idioms including animal terms for emotions

Here is a report of an investigation on animal idioms describing human emotions by reference to dictionaries. Three dictionaries were closely scrutinized: *English Idioms* by James Main Dixon, *The Penguin Dictionary of English Idioms*, and *Kenkyusha's English-Japanese Dictionary for the General Reader*. There were 782 entries for idioms including animal terms in these three dictionaries. Some of them appear in all three dictionaries, while others are found in only one or two of them. Out of those 782 entries, I extracted idioms for human emotions as shown in Table 4.1.

Emotions	Idioms		N. of entries
PLEASURE AND HAPPINESS	tail(s) up, to look like the cat that ate [swallowed] the canary, in high [fine, full, good] feather, to be as happy as a lark, halcyon days, as happy as a clam	like a dog with two tails, to take wing(s), to crow over, as merry / chirpy / lively as a cricket,	10
SADNESS AND UNHAPPINESS	like a drowned mouse, It is a sad house where the hen crows louder than the cock		2
ANGER	to take the pet, to have kittens, to twist the lion's tail, to get one's monkey up, to be spitting feathers, with one's hackles up [rising], to take owl,	to have pups, like a bear with a sore head, as prickly as a hedgehog, to make the feathers / fur fly, to make someone's hackles rise, (as) mad as a wet hen, to go off at half cock	14
FEAR	to turn tail (and run), to say an ape's paternoster, a little mouse, to show the white feather, to be chicken / chicken-hearted,	to have one's tail between one's legs, (as) scared [weak, timid] as a rabbit, goose flesh / skin / pimples, to chicken out, to turn turtle	10
ANXIETY	to have butterflies in one's stomach / tummy		1

Table 4.1: Animal Idioms Describing Human Emotions in Three Dictionaries

As this table shows, the three dictionaries contain 10 entries of animal idioms describing PLEASURE AND HAPPINESS, two entries in relation to SADNESS AND UNHAPPINESS, 14 to ANGER, 10 to FEAR, and one to ANXIETY. Whereas idioms for PLEASURE AND HAPPINESS, ANGER, and FEAR count ten or more, idioms for SADNESS AND UNHAPPINESS and ANXIETY are scarce. ANXIETY can be regarded as an emotion related to FEAR, but the scarcity of animal idioms for SADNESS AND UNHAPPINESS deserves attention. The emotion of SADNESS AND UNHAPPINESS may be relatively difficult to associate with the concept ANIMAL. In this study, one animal idiom including the term *sad* was found in Kenkyusha's and Dixon's dictionaries, i.e., *a sad dog*. However, it is defined as "a merry fellow; a gay man; a man given to joking" (Dixon), a phrase used to talk about a person who is unrelated to the emotion of sadness.[1]

The next table presents a classification of vehicles in the animal idioms for human emotions, describing what parts or elements in the source domain of animals are mapped onto the target domain of emotions. Here, the source domain of animals are divided into classes (mammals, birds, and others [reptiles, arthropods and mollusks]), and the animal idioms are accordingly placed.

SD (ANIMALS)		TD (EMOTIONS)	PLEASURE AND HAPPINESS	SADNESS AND UNHAPPINESS	ANGER	FEAR	ANXIETY
MAMMAL	PET	(general)	—	—	to take the pet	—	—
		DOG	tails up, like a dog with two tails	—	to have pups	to turn tail (and run), to have one's tail between one's legs	—
		CAT	to look like the cat that swallowed the canary	—	to have kittens	—	—
	LARGE ANIMAL		—	—	like a bear with a sore head, to twist the lion's tail	to say an ape's paternoster	
	SMALL ANIMAL		—	like a drowned mouse	to get one's monkey up, as prickly as a hedgehog	as scared as a rabbit, a little mouse	—
BIRD	DOMESTIC FOWL		to crow over	It is a sad house where the hen crows louder than the cock	to make someone's hackles rise, with one's hackles up, as mad as a wet hen, to go off at half cock	goose flesh / skin / pimples, to show the white feather [2], to chicken out, to be chicken (-hearted)	—
	OTHERS		in high feather, to take wing(s), as happy as a lark, halcyon days	—	to make the feathers fly, to be spitting feathers, to take owl	—	—
REPTILE, ARTHROPOD (INSECT), MOLLUSK			as merry as a cricket, as happy as a clam	—	—	to turn turtle	to have butterflies in one's stomach / tummy

Table 4.2: Parts or Elements in the Source Domain of Animals Mapped onto the Target Domain of Emotions

The result of Table 4.2 demonstrates a tendency of animal idioms describing human emotions to include vehicles related to animals familiar to daily lives of human beings: pets like cats and dogs, domestic fowls like hens and geese, small mammals like rabbits, mice and monkeys, and other small creatures like turtles, crickets and butterflies.

Large animals, on the other hand, are not frequently adopted as vehicles of animal idioms. The vehicles referring to large animals, i.e., *bear*, *lion*, and *ape*, depict only negative emotions like ANGER and FEAR, and the idiom including the vehicle *lion*, "to twist the lion's tail," means specifically "to humiliate or provoke Great Britain" (*The Penguin Dictionary*). The specific meaning of this idiom comes from the lion as an emblem of English royalty, so that the use of the vehicle is to be regarded as somewhat different from other animal vehicles. Since anger is an intense emotion and sometimes accompanies an offensive movement toward others, I expected large carnivorous animals to be frequently chosen for depiction of this dangerous emotion. Contrary to my expectation, however, the only idiom for anger including a large animal term except "to twist the *lion*'s tail" is "like a *bear* with a sore head." All the other idioms for anger are related to small animals like pups, kittens, domestic fowls, and so on. The idioms "to have pups" and "to have kittens" may have originated from the behavior of mother dogs and mother cats cautious and aggressive in order to protect their young.

Idioms for PLEASURE AND HAPPINESS for the most part show animal behavior related to height or elevation. "Tails up" and "like a dog with two tails" evoke a dog lifting and wagging its tail with pleasure. "Take wings" and "in high feather" depict a bird flying high in the sky. High-pitched songs by larks and crickets are associated with "as happy as a lark" and "as merry as a cricket." "To crow over" is also derived from a cock making loud high sounds early in the morning. The concept of HEIGHT related to these animal behaviors is naturally mapped onto the domain of PLEASURE AND HAPPINESS. Generally, human beings adopt an erect posture and lift up a high-pitched voice when they are happy, while unhappiness forces them to droop their heads and to drop their voice. The concepts HAPPINESS and UP are experientially correlated with each other, and so are UNHAPPINESS and DOWN, and it is this correlation in our daily experience that motivates the metaphorical mappings in HAPPY IS UP and SAD IS DOWN (Lakoff and Johnson 1980, Lakoff 1987). Based on these metaphorical mappings, we seem to project animal behavior related to height onto human emotion of happiness.

It is also notable that most idioms originated in behavior of domestic fowls depict negative emotions such as SADNESS, ANGER and FEAR, with the exception of "to crow over." Hens and cocks, unlike other birds appearing in idioms for pleasure and happiness, cannot fly in the air. This trait may be a factor in the frequent use of domestic fowls as vehicles of idioms with negative meanings.

4.3 Animal metaphors in poetry

4.3.1 Sommer and Weiss (1996)

This section observes animal metaphors describing human emotions which appear in poetry and other literature. In this subsection, I consult *Metaphors Dictionary* by Sommer and Weiss (1996). This dictionary is a collection of more than 6,500 metaphors extracted from works by poets, novelists, prose writers, speech writers, journalists, scientists, philosophers, business people, actors, students and so on. The extractions are classified into thematic categories. Out of the categories, this study chose JOY (exhibiting 16 examples), HAPPINESS / UNHAPPINESS (13 examples), HOPE (28 examples), SORROW (13 examples), GRIEF (27 examples), ANGER (22 examples), FEAR (17 examples) and WORRY (14 examples), and observed all of the given examples. All the emotion categories except for ANGER contained examples where animal terms or words for animal behaviors are metaphorically used, all of which will be quoted below (boldface mine).

JOY
(1) I left the presence on the **wings** of elation — Louis Auchincloss, "Portrait of the Artist by Another," *Skinny Island*
(2) Joy is … the falling / or fallen pride of summer's **lark** / calling the leaves to hide him — William Bell, "to a Lady on Her Marriage"
(3) Come, on **wings** of joy we'll **fly** / To where my Bower hands on high — William Blake, "The Birds"
(4) The magical **bluebird** of joy and human satisfaction that may be seen **flitting** distantly through the branches of life — Christopher Morley, "What Men Live By"

The dictionary contains four examples of animal metaphor describing the emotion of joy. All of the four examples include vehicles related to birds. The word *fly* in Example (3), *flitting* in Example (4), and *wings* in Examples (1) and (3) depict characteristics of birds to fly high in the sky against the force of gravity. Moreover, *lark* in Example (2) and *bluebird* in Example (4) refer to songbirds which lift up a cheerful and high-pitched voice. In the last subsection I observed idioms for the emotion of PLEASURE AND HAPPINESS and pointed out that these idioms are related to animal behavior of flight and high singing voice, and that the expressions are based on the conceptual metaphor HAPPY IS UP. Similarly, the animal metaphors in Examples (1) through (4) adopt vehicles related to flying and singing birds precisely because those behaviors of birds are closely connected with the conceptual domain UP and therefore the meanings of these vehicles are readily mapped onto the domain of emotion JOY on the basis of bodily experience of human beings.

Idioms are fixed and conventional expressions, whereas the poetic texts are products yielded by flexible creativity of poets and writers. However, in both of the two types of expression the same kind of metaphorical mapping serves as the basis of description of joy. This finding supports the view of Lakoff and Turner (1989) that poetic language and ordinary language are based on the same modes of thought. Metaphoric links between conceptual domains originating in bodily experiences of human beings accelerate conventionalization and fixation of ordinary language, and at the same time stimulate poets to awaken their imagination and to create figurative expressions.

HOPE

(5) Mind a **beehive** of hopes buzzing and stinging — John Dos Passos, *U.S.A., The 42nd Parallel*
(6) On the **wings** of hope, of love, of joy, Miss Meadows sped back to the music hall — Katherine Mansfield, "the Singing Lesson"
(7) The **white bird** of hope flew out the window — Richard Selzer, "A Pint of Blood," *Letters to a Young Doctor*
(8) Richmond: True hope is swift, and flies with **swallow's wings** — William Shakespeare, *The Tragedy of King Richard the Third*, Act 5, scene 2, line 23

Sommer and Weiss offer four examples of animal metaphors describing HOPE, in one of which (Example (5)) a vehicle related to a bee is chosen, and in the other three of which (Examples (6) through (8)) vehicles related to birds are chosen.[3] Like metaphors for JOY, these vehicles refer to winged creatures. Especially in Example (8) the swiftness of the flight of a swallow is associated with hope. The color of the bird depicted in Example (7) is also noteworthy. White is the brightest color so that it is associated with positive behavior (Deignan 1995). These examples show that the characteristic of these flying animals and the bright color are concerned in the metaphorical mapping onto the positive emotion of hope.

It should be noted that the connection between hope and wings stems not only from a pleasant situation. Hope is occasionally perceived in adversity (ex., *a few glimmers of hope* in Example (25) in Chapter III), and then it can be ephemeral (as exemplified in *The gleam of hope vanished* (CEX 2122) and *The last tiny flicker of hope seemed to die inside her* (HH8 3914), both extracted from the BNC). The above example (7) also describes an unfavorable situation, in which a patient complains to a doctor. [4] In such a situation, even if a hope is raised it is unstable and easily vanishes. This temporariness of the emotion naturally corresponds to the elusiveness of winged creature referred to by the vehicle *bird* and the expression *flew out the window*.

SORROW

(9) Aethelwold [in response to Maccus's "In God's name, what hath worn thee down?"]: The **teeth** of Sorrow. I am Sorrow's bone — Enda St. Vincent Millay, *The King's Henchman*, Act 2
(10) Bolingbroke: Fell sorrow's **tooth** doth never rankle more / Than when he **bites**, but lanceth not the sore — William Shakespeare, *The Tragedy of King Richard the Second*, Act 1, scene 3, line 302
(11) Don't let the **dogs** of sorrow out — Sharon Sheehe Stark, "Overland" *Boulevard*, No. 12–13

The three examples for SORROW include vehicles related to the dog. The speaker (Aethelwold) in Example (9) compares himself to a "bone" bitten by "teeth of sorrow," so it is presumably a dog that owns the teeth and causes the speaker to suffer. The emotion of sorrow in Example (10) is also compared to some creature with teeth that bites the speaker (Bolingbroke), who is condemned to banishment from England. His Father, John of Gaunt, tries to comfort him, saying "For *gnarling sorrow* has less power to *bite* / The man that mocks at it and sets it light" (I. iii. 292–293, italics mine). Following this, Bolingbroke's lines which start with "O, who can hold a fire in his hand / By thinking on the frosty Caucasus?" and end with the words quoted in (10) are full of lamentation. Since his father's words *gnarling sorrow* evoke a growling dog, the creature referred to as *he* in Example (10), which "bites, but lanceth not the sore," must also be a dog. Example (11) explicitly compares sorrow to dogs. The metaphorical mapping of SORROW that brings us pain onto the concept of A DOG is based on our bodily experiences: a dog is familiar to human beings, and so is the sharp pain caused by a bite of a dog.[5]

FEAR

(12) Terror in the house does **roar**, / But Pity stands before the door — William Blake, "Fragment"
(13) Fear ... is a carrion **crow** — Ralph Waldo Emerson, "Compensation," *Essays: First Series*
(14) Now comes the evening of the mind. / Here are the **fireflies** twitching in the blood — Donald Justice, "The Evening of the Mind"
(15) Thou art a frighted **owl** / Blind with the light of life thou'ldst not forsake —

Trumbull Stickney, "Be Still. The Hanging Gardens Were a Dream" 6
(16) Fear is a slinking **cat** I find / Beneath the lilacs of my mind — Sophie Tunnell, "Fear"

Various vehicles are chosen in these animal metaphors for FEAR. They make a clear contrast with metaphors depicting positive concepts like JOY and HOPE. The word *roar* in Example (12) refers to a deep sound made by a savage beast, as opposed to high-pitched and cheerful voices of song birds like larks and bluebirds in the metaphors for JOY exemplified above. Unlike those diurnal birds depicted in metaphors for JOY and HOPE, fireflies in Example (14) and an owl in Example (15) are nocturnal creatures. A cat in Example (16) can also move around at night. Moreover, a crow in Example (13) is black, whereas the bird of hope in Example (7) is white.7 These animal vehicles are thus closely related with NIGHT and BLACK, the concepts which are naturally mapped onto the emotion of FEAR (cf. Section 3.4.4 in Chapter III), for human beings are diurnal and unable to see in the dark, so that we feel an instinctive fear of the darkness.

WORRY
(17) The last moments [before a trip] are earthquake and convulsion, and the feeling that you are a **snail** being pulled off your rock — Anne Morrow Lindbergh, Letter, September 7, 1929
(18) A **spider** of anxiety crawled up the back of my neck — Donna Tartt, *The Secret History*

Animal metaphors for the emotion of WORRY quoted by Sommer and Weiss are relatively scarce. Small invertebrate animals such as a snail and a spider are chosen as vehicles. As observed in Section 4.2.2, animal idioms describing anxiety were also rarely found: there was only one idiom in the three dictionaries: "to have butterflies in one's stomach / tummy." These invertebrate animals easily remind us of the emotion of worry. They are fragile because of their lack of backbones and their lives are full of perils. But it is their creeping or crawling motion that recalls "a chill that runs up your spine," and we have a fixed expression "creeping fear." These traits of the small and weak animals are thus naturally associated with the domain of WORRY, making those metaphors above fully persuasive.

4.3.2 FEAR and HOPE in the *OED*

As seen in Section 4.3.1, animal metaphors quoted by Sommer and Weiss (1996) show a clear contrast between vehicles for FEAR and those for HOPE and JOY. This result is in accordance with the corpus search shown in Section 3.4.1 in Chapter III, where we observed examples in which HOPE and FEAR are regarded as opposing emotions. This section makes use of the *Oxford English Dictionary* as a source of data, and observes the quotations in which the terms for those emotions are used together.

Century	The *OED* quotations		
17th	1621		Burton *Anat. Mel.* i. ii. iii. x, Thus between hope and fear, suspicions, angers..we bangle away our best days.
	1637		Milton *Comus* 411 An equal poise of hope and fear Does arbitrate the event.
	1656		Osborne *Adv. Son* v. §26 (1896) 124 Do not pre~engage Hope or Fear by a tedious expectation.
	1660		*Andromania* i. i. in Hazl. *Dodsley* XIV. 200 See the ambassadors entertain'd With such an evenness as should be us'd to men We neither fear nor love.
	1670		Milton *Hist. Eng.* vi. (1851) 262 For fear or hope of reward they attested what was not true.
	1676		Hale *Contempl.* ii. 212 Thou..may'st most justly expect from the children of Men our uttermost Love, and Fear.
	1679		T. Siden *Hist. Sevarites* 95 We began to hang between fear and pleasure.
	1685		Baxter *Paraphr. N.T.* Matt. xxv. 7 Self-love, and fear, will make them cry for Mercy, with some kind of Repentance, though they be unconverted.
	1687		Miege *Fr. Dict.* ii. s.v., His mind sticks betwixt Hope and Fear.
	a1698		J. Fraser *Mem.* (1738) vii. 239 Tho' in my sensitive Faculty I find not these Impressions of Joy and Fear, yet do I find them in my estimative appretiative Faculty.
	a1700		in *Cath. Rec. Soc. Publ.* (1911) IX. 336 She was both loved & fear'd by those yt had ye happines to be under her conduct.
18th	1711		M. Henry *Hope & Fear Balanced* 16 Then 'twill be Folly to curse your Stars (as some profanely speak).
	1714		R. Fiddes *Pract. Disc.* ii. 380 Those mysticks who would discard the passions of hope and fear.
	1716		Collier on *Chas. V*, III. vii. 62 The Landgrave+wrote to Granvelle.. begging an explicit declaration of what they had to fear or hope.
	a1716		South *Serm.* (1716) IV. 196 Hope and Fear are the two great Handles, by which the Will of Man is to be taken Hold of.
	1756		C. Smart tr. *Horace, Epist.* i. ii. (1826) II. 191 To him, that is a slave to desire or to fear, house and estate do just as much good as paintings to a sore-eyed person.
	1757		W. Wilkie *Epigoniad* vii. 192 Amaz'd we stood; in silence, each his mind To fear and hope alternately resign'd.
	1758		Johnson *Idler* No. 6 310 The true causes of her speed were fear and love.
	1759		Johnson *Rasselas* xxix. (1787) 85 The future [is the object] of hope and fear.

	1770	J. Love *Cricket* 5 Where, much divided between **Fear** and Glee, The Youth cries Rub; O Flee, you Ling'rer, Flee!
	1772	Test *Filial Duty* II. 88 Unagitated by alternate hope and fear, the heart is quiet.
	1775	Wesley *Calm Address* 12, I am unbiassed: I have nothing to hope or fear from either side.
	1788	V. Knox *Winter Even*. xlv, The alternate excitation of hope and fear is attended with considerable delight.
	1791	Burke *Let. Memb. Nat. Assembly* Wks. VI. 12 The shifting tides of fear and hope.
19th	1802–1812	Bentham *Ration. Judic. Evid.* (1827) V. 662 Hope and fear..run into one another and are undistinguishable.
	1809–1810	Coleridge *Friend* (1865) 161 The civilized man gives up those stimulants of hope and fear which constitute the chief charm of savage life.
	1814	Scott *Ld. of Isles* vi. xxxvi, He..greeted him 'twixt joy and fear, As being of superior sphere.
	1820	Shelley *Hope, Fear, & Doubt* 9 Nor did I hope to pass Untouched by suffering, through the rugged glen.
	1827	J. F. Cooper *Prairie* II. xiii. 217 His looks appeared to be strangely vacillating between hope and fear.
	1838	Thirlwall *Greece* xliii. V. 293 While the public mind was thus suspended between hope and fear.
	1850	McCosh *Div. Govt.* ii. ii. (1874) 212 The superstitious man vacillates.. between hope and fear, between self-confidence and despondency.
	1868	Morris *Earthly Par.* i. 254 In that wan place desert of hope and fear.
	1869	Lecky *Europ. Mor.* I. iii. 414 It struck alike the coarsest chords of hope and fear, and the finest chords of compassion.
	1871	R. W. Dale *Commandm.* x. 257 It was God who made us susceptible to hope and to fear.
	1878	Lecky *Eng. in 18th* C. II. ix. 540 The evil of all attempts to deflect the judgment by hope or fear.
	1884	W. H. Harris *Honey-Bee* 271 Apiculturists, like agriculturists, are subject to many and great alternations of hope and fear.
20th	1902	W. Watson *Coron. K. Edw*. VII iii, And changelessly the river sends his sigh Down leagues of hope and fear.

Table 4.3: Emotions contrasted with **fear** in the *OED* quotations
(hope 27/ love 4/ joy 2/ pleasure 1/ glee 1/ desire 1)

Table 4.3 shows the *OED* quotations in which *fear* collocates with a word referring to positive emotions, put in chronological order.[8] Those quotations numbered 37 in all, in 27 of which *fear* and *hope* co-occur. In these 27 examples, the two terms appear in the form "hope and fear," "fear and hope," "hope or fear" or "fear or hope." Chronologically, five examples in which *fear* collocates with *hope* appear in the 17th century, 10 examples in the 18th century, 11 examples in the 19th century, and one example in the 20th century. This collocational pattern is consistently found over approximately 300 years. It is noteworthy that in the *OED* the number of examples including *hope* and *despair* within the three word span are no more than 13, in nine of which *hope* is preposed, and in the rest *despair* is preposed. Contrary to the dictionary definitions, in which *despair* is regarded as "the complete loss or absence of *hope*" whereas *fear* is understood irrelevantly with hope as "an unpleasant emotion caused by the threat of danger, pain, or harm" (*The Concise Oxford English Dictionary*), these records of the language use reveal the fact that the emotions of HOPE and FEAR are diachronically recognized as antonymous.

4.3.3 Traditional metaphors of FEAR in the *OED*

In this section I report on a quotation search through the *OED* for *fear* co-occurring with an animal term. I found examples including *fear* and a word referring to or related to a bird.[9] These examples, all by eminent literati, are shown below in chronological sequence.

1596 Spenser *F.Q.* (ed.2) iii. xii. 12 [Fear] fast away did **fly**, As ashes pale of hew, and **wingyheeld** [1590 **winged heeld**].
1742 Gray *Eton* 62 These shall the fury Passions tear, The **vulturs** of the mind, Disdainful Anger, pallid Fear, And Shame.
1744 E. Moore [10] *Fables* vi. 90 Fear **wings** his **flight**; the marsh he sought, The snuffing dogs are set at fault.
1782 J. Scott *Poet. Wks.* 235 Pale fear, who un~pursued still **flies**.
1817 Southey *Life* (1850) IV. 233 Are they rendered absolutely helpless by fear, like a fascinated **bird**?
1847 Tennyson *Princess* iv. 359 Fear..**wing'd** Her transit to the throne, whereby she fell Delivering seal'd dispatches.
1920 A. Huxley *Leda* 15 The sky Was full of strange tumult suddenly — Beating of **mighty wings** and **shrill-voiced** fear.
1932 Kipling *Limits & Renewals* 47 A Fear leaped out of the **goose-fleshed** streets of London between the icy shop~fronts.

The metaphoric meaning of the word "vulturs" (vultures) in the quotation from Thomas Gray in 1742 is ambiguous in that it is placed side by side with various furious passions, such as anger, fear, and shame. However, in the rest of the examples words related to a bird are entirely used as a vehicle for the emotion of FEAR. Kipling in 1932 uses *goose-fleshed* as a description of streets of London probably covered by frost or snow, a surface looking uneven. The whole frozen city is compared to a bird feeling icy fear. This correspondence seems natural because of our daily experience of getting goose bumps when we feel fear. However, a more attentive consideration on this vehicle reveals that our condition of the skin when we feel fear is compared to that of a dead goose whose feathers are plucked away. *Goose-flesh* has an association with DEATH of the bird. From this word we probably imagine the emotion of fear which a goose itself must feel when it is caught and about to be killed. It is this imagination that makes the mapping of the skin condition of a goose onto the feeling of fear natural and convincing.

In many of the examples above the emotion of fear is compared to a bird flapping its wings and flying in the air. The quotation from Huxley in 1920 is particularly noteworthy. Here the emotion of fear is identified with a bird with mighty wings and shrill voice — probably a raptorial bird such as an eagle and a hawk. Similarly in the quotation from Tennyson in 1847 the emotion is described as what beats its wings and drives a person toward the throne. This description of fear evokes an eagle, the king of birds.

Bird idioms for the emotion of fear observed in Section 4.2.2 all include a word related to a domestic fowl, and have a metaphorical image that the bird itself feels fear. And so does the example of Kipling quoted above. On the other hand, the vehicles depicted in the most quotations from the *OED* refer to raptorial birds which make people feel fear by flapping their huge wings and giving shrilling screams. In the examples given by Sommer and Weiss (1996) as observed in Section 4.3.1 a carrion crow and an owl appeared. Making an observation of these examples together, we can presume that there is a close correspondence between FEAR and RAPTORIAL BIRDS in the tradition of English poetry.

According to Hideki Watanabe, a philologist and researcher on *Beowulf*, there is a poetic trope, generally called "beasts of battle" in Old English, which employs the names of "hrefn" (raven), "earn" (eagle), and "wulf" (wolf). These carnivorous animals appear in pairs or trios in eight OE poems. The old literary tradition declares that the eaters of carrion accompanied marching soldiers in hopes of getting corpses heaped in battlefields. The following quotation is a part of the news of the death of Beowulf brought to his troops by a messenger. He notifies imminent battles which will end in a miserable loss. The ominous symbols of "beasts of battle" describe the terrible situation into which the warriors are supposed to fall. Like the other literary quotations shown above, the dark color ("wonna") of a raven and its persistent cries ("fera reordian")[11] emphasize the horrors of the sight of the corpses devoured by the carnivorous bird.[12]

> nū se herewīsa hleahtor ālegde,
> gamen ond glēodrēam. Forðon sceall gār wesan
> monig morgenċeald mundum bewunden,
> hæfen on handa, nalles hearpan swēġ
> wīġend weċċean, ac se wonna **hrefn**
> fūs ofer fæġum fela reordian,
> **earne** secgan hū him æt æte spēow,
> þenden hē wið **wulf** wæl rēafode. (*Beowulf*, 3020–3027. Boldface mine.)

In the medieval period, dispositions and emotions were often personified in allegorical poems. A famous work, *Roman de la Rose*, includes a description of a personified character Drede, who dreads a bird's flight and a shadow. Here again a bird is depicted as what arouses the emotion of fear. The following quotation is from the Middle English translation by Chaucer.

> A **foulis** flight wol make hir [= Drede] flee,
> And eek a shadowe, if she it see.
> (Geoffrey Chaucer, *The Romaunt of the Rose*, 4231–4232. Boldface mine.)

The poetic metaphors for FEAR in the *OED* quotations observed above may possibly be based on this literary tradition of linking the emotion of FEAR to CARNIVOROUS BIRDS since the Old English period. As Tennyson is known for his knowledge of Old English poems — and he made a partial translation of *Beowulf* — the concept of "beasts of battle" is very likely to have lived through the history of literature.

The carnivorous birds chosen as vehicles for the emotion of FEAR are violent, of good physique, dark in color such as black and brown, with awful talons and beaks, and ghastly screeching as well. These traits present a remarkable contrast with those of song birds, which are chosen as vehicles for positive emotions such as JOY and HOPE, as seen in Section 4.3.1. Figure 4.1 shows the mapping of the antonymous relation between song birds and carnivorous birds onto the domain of EMOTION.

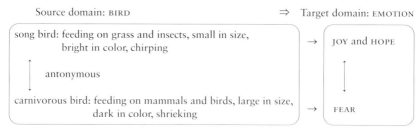

Figure 4.1: A mapping of the antonymous relation in the conceptual metaphor EMOTION IS A BIRD

4.3.4 Metaphoric coherence in texts

This chapter has investigated the systematic nature of animal metaphors through observation of idioms and poetic expressions. Finally, as a case study I observe examples of coherent metaphoric descriptions of emotion in literary works. The following is a poem by Emily Dickinson, who compares her mental state to a little hound. Here a series of actions peculiar to dogs are chosen as metaphoric vehicles (italics by the author, boldface mine):

> What shall I do — it **whimpers** so —
> This little **Hound** within the Heart
> All day and night with **bark** and **start** —
> And yet, it will **not go** —
> Would you *untie* it, were you me —
> Would it stop **whining** — if to Thee —
> I sent it — even now?
>
> It should **not tease** you —
> By your chair — or, on the mat —
> Or if it dare — to **climb your dizzy knee** —
> Or — sometimes at your side to **run** —
> When you were willing —
> Shall it come?
> Tell Carlo —
> He'll tell *me*!
>
> (Emily Dickinson, "What shall I do — it whimpers so — ." Boldface mine.)

The poet uses three verbs typically applied to dogs referring to ways of making noises. Each of them has a figurative sense used to talk about human voices and ways of speaking, [13] as shown in the table below:

Word	Literal sense (applied to dogs)	Metaphoric sense (applied to humans)
whimper	to make a series of low, weak crying noises	to say something with a quiet, continuous, unhappy sound in your voice
bark	to make a sharp explosive cry	to utter abruptly or aggressively
whine	to make a long, high-pitched complaining cry	to complain in a feeble or petulant way

Table 4.4: Verbs for a dog's cry used in Dickinson's poem titled "What shall I do — it whimpers so —

Those words in the poem are used for description of the "little Hound within the Heart," namely, the poet's own inner voice telling her thoughts and feelings. It is not explicitly shown whether the person referred to by the pronoun *you* is a man whom the poet loves, or her bosom friend, or possibly God. In any case, the poet is feeling terribly lonely because she cannot see him. Those three verbs all depict her "silent" complaint about her loneliness, which is sometimes feeble and continuous, and sometimes abrupt and aggressive.

Words referring to typical behaviors of dogs such as *start, not tease you, clime your ... knee,* and *at your side to run* are also used to describe changes in the poet's emotions. Figure 4.2 shows correspondences between the behaviors of a little hound and the mental states of the poet. A pet dog generally calls its master in a plaintive voice to attract his or her attention, and if it fails in drawing notice, it barks and moves about. When it is allowed to be at the side of its master, it cheerfully fawns on him or her. The poet consistently links these typical behaviors of a pet dog to aspects of her affection, namely, grieving over her misfortune of missing her love, earnestly wishing that she could see him, and imagining how satisfied she would be if she was beside him.

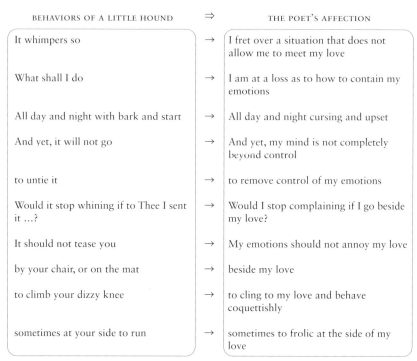

Figure 4.2: A metaphorical mapping from the domain of BEHAVIORS OF A LITTLE HOUND onto the domain of THE POET'S AFFECTION in the Dickinson's poem titled "What shall I do — it whimpers so —"

The following passage from Shakespeare also employs several canine terms but renders a different sentiment. It is lines of Helena, who is in love with Demetrius but curtly rejected by him. Coldly told that "I love thee not; therefore pursue me not," she desperately pleads with him as follows (boldface mine):

And even for that do I love you the more.
I am **your spaniel**; and, Demetrius,
The more you **beat** me, I will **fawn** on you.
Use me but as **your spaniel**; **spurn** me, **strike** me,
Neglect me, **lose** me; only **give me leave**,
Unworthy as I am, to **follow** you.
What worser place can I beg in your love
(And yet a place of high respect with me)
Than to be used as you use **your dog**?
  (William Shakespeare, *A Midsummer Night's Dream* II. i. 202–210. Boldface mine.)

Her words indicate her servility and at the same time her stubbornness. She calls herself "your spaniel" and "your dog," begging him to treat her like a dog. According to her, it does not matter if he pushes her away with his foot, strikes her, neglects her, or loses her. All she wants is to be allowed to follow him. These obsequious, and obstitute, words of hers completely weary him, and he treats her even more coldly, saying "Tempt not too much the hatred of my spirit, For I am sick when I do look on thee."

Her masochistic passion for him is similar to a dog's loyalty indeed. A pet dog such as a spaniel [14] fawns on its master no matter how many times it is beaten. Its peculiar behavior naturally corresponds to Helena's pitiful but persistent attempt to attract Demetrius' attention by demeaning herself.

Although it remains to be revealed whether Dickinson, in writing "What shall I do — it whimpers so — ," was allusive or making reference to *A Midsummer Night's Dream*, it is probable, and at least possible, that she was unconsciously influenced by the Shakespearean art of figurative expression. However, the feeling of love depicted by Dickinson makes a clear distinction to that of Helena. Each of these two texts makes use of a conceptual metaphor in which a strong feeling of affection is understood in terms of behaviors of a pet dog, and yet Helena's emotion is simply and thoroughly servile, whereas the affection described by Dickinson has various aspects: loneliness, puzzlement, complaint, uncontrollability, longing, clingingness and satisfaction, all of which are in correspondence with elements of the domain of a pet dog. Dickinson's poetic text exhibits extension and elaboration (cf. Lakoff and Turner 1989: 67) of an existing conceptual metaphor.

4.4 Conclusion

In this chapter, I observed idioms and literary expressions which metaphorically describe human emotions by means of animal vehicles. The detailed observations have revealed the systematic nature of metaphor: an antonymous relation in the source domain of animals is replicated in the target domain of emotions. I also took a close look at literary texts which coherently present animal metaphors, and made a comparison between two literary works. This case study revealed that the two different authors using the same conceptual metaphor exhibit different correspondences of the mapping, highlighting different aspects of a target domain.

The study reported on this chapter is not an exhaustive research into animal metaphors. Vehicles referring to various beasts and birds have been taken as examples, but metaphors depicting a horse, for example, are yet to be investigated. As the horse is another familiar domestic animal in the English culture, it is likely to be frequently chosen as vehicles describing human emotions, as seen in the wording of Shakespeare: "The king is come, deal mildly with his youth, / For young hot colts being rein'd do rage the more" (*King Richard II*, II. i. 69–70). More comprehensive collection of data and closer analyses of them remain to be done.

Notes

1 According to the *OED*, *sad* acquired a meaning of "deplorably bad" as an intensive qualifying terms of depreciation or censure at the end of the 17th century, and the idiom *sad dog* with a jocular tone came to be used at the beginning of the 18th century (the *OED* "sad" adj. 6).
2 This idiom stems from an old saying that a gamecock with a tail containing white feathers is weak at a cockfight (*Kenkyusha's English-Japanese Dictionary for the General Reader*). That is why I classified the source domain of this idiom under DOMESTIC FOWLS.
3 Sommer and Weiss (1996) offer one more example of an animal metaphor for hope, i.e., "Pistol: Hope is a curtal dog in some affairs" (William Shakespeare, *The Merry Wives of Windsor*, II. i. 112). Following Ford's line "Well, I hope it be not so," it means that Ford's word "hope" is as unreliable as a dog with a cocked tail and therefore less good for hunting (because of loss of balance). The word "hope" here is somewhat metalinguistic and not a sheer metaphoric vehicle, and thus unsuitable for an examination in this study. See Alexander Schmidt, *Shakespeare Lexicon and Quotation Dictionary*, vol. 1, Dover Publications, 1971; and The Arden Shakespeare CD-ROM.
4 Richad Selzer is a surgeon and author in the United States. *Letters to a Young Doctor*, published in 1982, is a collection of 23 stories, five of which take the form of letters in which an older physician gives advice to an imaginary young surgeon.
5 It is interesting that, while a dog's teeth and its behavior of biting are associated with the emotion of sorrow, a dog's tail lifting and wagging evokes the emotion of joy, as observed in Section 4.2.2.
6 Sommer and Weiss (1996) mistyped "Thou art" as "Thou are" (p. 173). Here I quote the passage from the original text (*The Poems of Thumbull Stickney*, edited by George Cabot Lodge, William Vaughn Moody and John Clierton Lodge, Mifflin, 1905).
7 One of the metaphoric quotations describing fear extracted by Sommer and Weiss (1996) is "For weeks she had lived in a black sea of nausea and fear" (Mavis Gallant, "Bernadette," *The New Yorker*, 1950–1960). Its vehicle does not refer to an animal, but is noteworthy in that the color of the sea is depicted as black.
8 The data in Table 4.3 have been compiled with the aid of Hideki Watanabe, the joint-researcher on the project supported by a Grant-in-Aid for Scientific Research from Japan Society for the Promotion of Science, Grant Number 19520422.
9 The relation between a word referring to a bird and a word related to a bird is called "endonymy" in lexical semantics. It is based on the notion of semantic encapsulation, and involves the incorporation of the meaning of one lexical item in the meaning of another. The term whose meaning is included in this way is called the endonym, and the containing term is called the exonym. Some examples of endonymous pairs are as follows (the endonym is given

first): animal: horse, horse: mare, horse: stable, hand: finger, hand: glove, foot: kick (Cruse 1986: 123). The word *bird* then can be characterized as endonym, and *wing* as exonym.
10 Edward Moore (1712–1757) is an English dramatist.
11 See Watanabe (1993) on "gellende gryre" (yelling horror), a phrase peculiar to Old English.
12 Other famous Old English examples where the beasts of battle appear are as follows: "Þæs se hlanca gefeah / **wulf** in walde, ond se wanna **hrefn**, / wælgifre fugel. Wistan begen / þæt him ða þeodguman þohton tilian / fylle on fægum; ac him fleah on last / **earn** ætes georn, urigfeðera, / salowigpada sang hildeleoð, / hyrnednebba" (Judith 205b–212a); "Hreopon herefugolas, hilde grædige, / deawigfeðere ofer drihtneum, / wonn wælceasega. **Wulfas** sungon / atol æfenleoð ætes on wenan, / carleasan deor, cwyldrof beodan / on laðra last leodmægnes fyl" (Exodus 162–167); and "For folca gedryht. Fyrdleoð agol / **wulf** on wealde, wælrune ne mað. / Urigfeðera **earn** sang ahof, / laðum on laste. Lungre scynde / ofer burg enta beaduþreata mæst, / hergum to hilde, swylce Huna cyning / ymbsittendra awer meahte / abannan to beadwe burgwigendra" (*Elene* 27–34).
13 Watanabe (2009, Section 5) observes words for a cat's cry and their metaphoric senses. See also Watanabe (2008).
14 *Lacon* by Charles Caleb Colton (1832), a collection of proverbs and aphorisms, also compares love to a spaniel as follows: "Love is an alchymist that can transmute poison into food – and a spaniel, that prefers even punishment from one hand, to caresses from another" (vol. 2, p. 212). See also Watanabe (2006) on a structure of figurative senses of terms referring to species of dogs.

CHAPTER V
Bestiality and Humanity through Animal Metaphors

But ask now the beasts, and they shall teach thee; and the fowls of the air,
and they shall tell thee:
Or speak to the earth, and it shall teach thee: and the fishes of
the sea shall declare unto thee.
Job, 12. 7–8.

5.1 Introduction

This chapter is an investigation of animal metaphors referring to quadrupeds. We make a definite identification of metaphoric meanings of names and phrases related to animals by making use of dictionaries, and give careful consideration to conceptual mappings in which physiological and behavioral qualities of animals are linked to personalities and characters of human beings as well as their behaviors, making reference to the concept of "the Great Chain of Being," a widespread cultural model providing a background to European literature and the history of ideas.

5.2 Generic terms for the animal and their metaphoric meanings

When an animal term is used as a metaphoric vehicle for a human character or behavior, what attributes are attached to the animal? The *OED* defines figurative senses of generic terms for the animal such as "animal," "beast," and "brute" as follows (underlines mine):

(1) Contemptuously or humorously for: a human being who is no better than a brute, or whose animal nature has <u>the ascendancy over his reason</u>; a mere animal.   (*OED* "animal" *n.* 3. a.)

(2) 'A brutal, savage man; a man acting in any manner <u>unworthy of a reasonable creature</u>.' J. In earlier usage, often connoting <u>stupidity</u> or <u>folly</u> (cf. Fr. *bête*); in modern phraseology opprobriously employed to express <u>disgust</u> or merely <u>aversion</u>. Now freq. in weaker sense.
 (*OED* "beast" *n.* 5. a.) [1]

(3) A man resembling a brute <u>in want of intelligence, cruelty, coarseness,</u>

sensuality, etc. Now (*colloq.*) often merely a strong term of reprobation or aversion, and sometimes extended to things. (*OED* "brute" *n.* 2.)

The adjectival forms and derivations of these terms are defined as follows:

(4) Of or pertaining to the functions of animals; or of those parts of the nature of man which he shares with the inferior animals. (Thus opposed to *intellectual* and *spiritual*). (*OED* "animal" *a.* 3.)

(5) Of human beings, their actions, and attributes: Brute-like, brutish; dull, senseless, stupid; unintelligent, unreasoning, uninstructed; sensual.
(*OED* "brute" *a.* 2.a.)

(6) 2. *transf.* Like a beast in its want of intelligence; 'below the dignity of reason or humanity' (J.); brutish, untaught, irrational; rude, barbarous.
3. *esp.* Like a beast in obeying and gratifying the animal instincts and sensual desires; debased, depraved, lustful, cruel, brutal, beastly, obscene.
(*OED* "bestial" *a.*)

(7) Pertaining to, resembling, or characteristic of the brutes:
a. in want of intelligence or in failure to use reason: dull, irrational, uncultured, stupid.
b. in want of control over the appetites and passions: passionate, sensual, furious. (*OED* "brutish" *a.* 2.)

(8) 1. *trans.* To degrade to the level of a brute; to make bestial, brutalize.
2. *intr.* To sink or lapse to the level of a brute; to become bestial or degraded. (*OED* "imbrute" *v.*)

These definitions above show our understanding that the animal is of lower grade (as in definition (8)) and inferior to human beings (as in definitions (4) and (6)), lacking of intelligence or ability to reason (as in definitions (1) through (7)), stupid (as in definitions (2), (5) and (7)), in want of control over violent emotions like sexual desire and fury (as in definitions (3), (5), (6) and (7)), in want of control over violent behavior and thus cruel and barbarous (as in definitions (3) and (6)), and an object of disgust and aversion (as in definition (2)).

This understanding of the animal is closely related to the concept of "the Great Chain of Being." This concept, whose constituents originating in Greek philosophy,[2] provided a background to European literature and the history of ideas, and now it still exists as a contemporary and unconscious cultural model indispensable to our understanding of ourselves, our world and our culture (cf. Lakoff and Turner 1989). In this model, forms of beings and their properties are placed on a vertical scale. Lovejoy (1936) argues about the Western history of ideas in terms of this concept, quoting literary texts that depict the configuration of the hierarchy, including the following lines by Pope. Here, beneath the human beings are, in order, beasts, birds, fish, insects, and microbes: [3]

(9) Vast chain of being! which from God began,
     Natures aethereal, human, angel, man,
     Beast, bird, fish, insect, what no eye can see,
     No glass can reach; from infinite to thee,
     From thee to nothing.
                              (Alexander Pope, *An Essay on Man*, Epistle I, 237–241.)

The concept of the Great Chain of Being has attracted the attention of cognitive studies on metaphor. Lakoff and Turner (1989) take it up in Chapter 4, characterizing each form of being as having all kinds of attributes that lower forms of being have, and lacking attributes possessed by higher forms of being. They introduce the notion of the Great Chain Metaphor, a conceptual complex made up of a metaphor, commonsense theory and a communicative principle,[4] and argue about animal metaphors making use of this notion. Following Lakoff and Turner, Kövecses (2002) indicates conceptual metaphors for understanding human beings through animals, such as HUMAN BEHAVIOR IS ANIMAL BEHAVIOR and PEOPLE ARE ANIMALS, stating that the main meaning focus of those metaphors is "objectionability" or "undesirability" (p. 125).

As stated above, the *OED* definitions of the metaphoric sense of generic terms referring to the animal describe that the animal is "lower" than the human (that is, *inferior* in definition (4), *debased*, *depraved* in definition (6), and *to degrade*, *to sink or lapse* in definition (8)). These descriptions are easily explicable by the cultural model of the Great Chain of Being. In this model, the animal is regarded as of lower level, lacking high-level properties that the human has. The metaphoric meanings of generic animal terms describing a person as unintelligent, irrational, stupid, and in want of control over violent emotions, as well as the meanings of "objectionable" and "undesirable" which reside in the HUMAN-AS-ANIMAL mapping pointed out by Kövecses, are all due to the cultural model which places the animal beneath the human in the conceptual hierarchy.

It should be noted that the "properties" of animals are not actually inherent in animals but what are understood in terms of human properties. For example, our folk understandings that "dogs are loyal" and "lions are courageous," are in fact metaphorical, for loyalty and courage are human character traits. As Lakoff and Turner (1989) put it, "human loyalty requires a moral sense and a capacity for reflective moral judgment. Human courage requires an awareness of danger, a moral judgment that places the importance of the act above the danger, and a conscious will to carry out the act under those circumstances." We know that dogs and lions lack such a moral sense and a capacity for moral judgment. They only behave the way they do out of instinct (p. 194).

Similarly, generic terms for the animal have connotative meanings of stupidity, sensuality, and cruelty because we make observations of the instinctive behaviors of animals for the purposes of ingestion, dispute for their territories and the opposite sex, reproduction, and avoidance of danger, and understand that they exhibit those behaviors as a result of lack of higher order properties like a moral sense, self-control, and intelligence, particular qualities of human beings. Thus animal metaphors describing the human such as "You beast!" and "He is a brute of a man" are related to twofold metaphoric mappings in which HUMANLY CHARACTERIZED ANIMAL PROPERTIES are linked to PHYSIOLOGICAL QUALITIES OF THE ANIMAL, and then the ANIMAL is linked to the HUMAN, as shown in Figure 5.1.

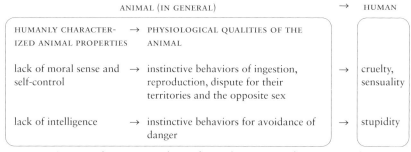

Figure 5.1: Conceptual mapping as a basis of metaphoric senses of generic animal terms

In the metaphoric mapping shown above, instinctive behaviors of the animals in general are negatively understood and mapped onto negative human properties. Does it also hold true for family names of animals like *canine* and *feline*? The OED and the *Merriam-Webster Dictionary* define the metaphoric meanings of the major Latinate family names of animals as shown in Table 5.1. These family names are classified as adjectives when used in their metaphorical senses.

Family Name	OED	Merriam-Webster Dictionary
canine	of appetite, hunger, etc.: Voracious, greedy, as that of a dog. *canine appetite, hunger*: the disease bulimy. *canine madness*: hydrophobia.	of or resembling that of a dog <canine loyalty>
feline	Resembling a cat in any respect, cat-like in character or quality.	resembling cat: as a. sleekly graceful, b. sly, treacherous, c. stealthy
bovine	Inert, sluggish; dull, stupid; cf. *bucolic*.	of, relating to, or resembling bovines and especially the ox or cow
equine	Of, pertaining to, or resembling a horse.	of, relating to, or resembling a horse or the horse family
ovine	Resembling a sheep; sheeplike, sheepish.	of, relating to, or resembling sheep
cervine	Of a deep tawny colour.	of, relating to, or resembling deer
murine	Resembling a mouse; of or belonging to the family *Muridæ* or the sub-family *Murinæ*.	—
simian	Characteristic of apes; resembling that of apes; ape-like, apish.	of, relating to, or resembling monkeys or apes

Table 5.1: The metaphoric meanings of the major family names of animals in the *OED* and the *Merriam-Webster Dictionary*

Whereas most of these definitions imply negative evaluations such as voraciousness, greed, slyness, treacherousness, sluggishness and stupidity, positive ones like loyalty and grace are unnoticed or neglected in the definition columns for the generic terms as shown in (1) through (8). In the next section, the focus of observation will be further narrowed down to metaphoric usage of terms for specific animals with special attention to these neglected aspects of positive and meliorative senses.

5.3 Specific terms for animals and their metaphoric meanings

When terms referring to specific animals like dogs, cats, cows and horses are metaphorically used, what connotations do they bear? Appendix 5.1 at the end of this chapter shows a search result of the *OED*, the *Merriam-Webster Dictionary* and the *Kenkyusha's English-Japanese Dictionary for the General Reader* for metaphoric meanings of specific terms for animals. This study covers generic names like *cat* and *dog*, terms for species like *wildcat* and *jackal*, gender-specific terms like *bitch* and *stag*, and age-specific terms like *kitten* and *puppy*. The observation on these dictionary definitions reveals correspondences between animal terms and their metaphoric evaluations as follows:

(10) animal terms belonging to the cat family: fierce, spiteful
(11) animal terms belonging to the dog family: despicable, ferocious, greedy, sexually aggressive
(12) animal terms belonging to the weasel family: cunning, sneaky, persistent
(13) animal terms belonging to the bear family: rough, unmannerly
(14) animal terms belonging to the cow family: coarse, foolish
(15) animal terms belonging to the swine family: sensual, degraded, coarse
(16) animal terms belonging to the horse family: stubborn, foolish
(17) animal terms belonging to the hare family: timid
(18) animal terms belonging to the mouse family: timid, contemptible

As can be seen in (10) through (18), metaphoric usage of animal terms mainly implies negative connotations. We understand physiological qualities of animals like ingestion, dispute, and reproduction in terms of human properties and evaluate them negatively, and then map those evaluations back onto the human domain once again, making use of them for description of negative emotions and behaviors of the human being. This thought pattern is clearly shown, for example, in Wilkinson's *Thesaurus of Traditional English Metaphors* (2002), which records various animal similes, most of which contain adjectives implying our negative evaluations of animals (see Appendix 5.2 at the end of this chapter). The conceptual mapping, which forms the background to these figurative meanings, is shown in Figure 5.2.

CHAPTER V BESTIALITY AND HUMANITY THROUGH ANIMAL METAPHORS   127

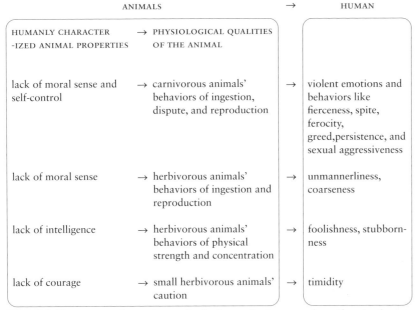

Figure 5.2: The conceptual mapping as a basis of metaphoric senses of specific animal terms

It is worth noting here that not all animal metaphors have negative meanings. The following definitions in the *OED* and the *Merriam-Webster Dictionary* imply positive evaluations.

(19) lion: Taken (in a good sense) as the type of one who is strong, courageous, or fiercely brave.   (OED)
(20) tiger: A person of very great activity, strength, or courage.   (OED)
(21) bulldog: Applied to persons: One that possesses the obstinate courage of the bulldog.[5]   (OED)
(22) fox: An attractive woman. U.S. slang.   (OED)
(23) sheep: In biblical and religious language, applied (as collective plural) to persons, in expressed or implied correlation with shepherd. With varying specific reference: said, e.g., of Israel, the Church, or mankind generally, viewed as under the guidance and protection of God, and as owing obedience to Him; of those who are led by Christ as the Good Shepherd (John x. 1–16); and of those who are under the charge of a spiritual pastor, or who are viewed as needing to be spiritually fed or directed. Hence occas. in sing.   (OED)
(24) lamb: One who is as meek, gentle, innocent, or weak as a lamb.   (OED)
(25) buck: A gay, dashing fellow; a dandy, fop, 'fast' man.   (OED)

(26) horse: an athlete whose performance is consistently strong and reliable
(*Merriam-Webster Dictionary*)
(27) thoroughbred: Applied to human beings or their attributes: sometimes implying characteristics like those of a thoroughbred horse, as gracefulness, energy, distinction, etc. / A well-born, well-bred, or thoroughly trained person. Also a first-rate motorcar, bicycle, or other vehicle.
(*OED*)
(28) bull: one that resembles a bull (as in brawny physique)
(*Merriam-Webster Dictionary*)
(29) eager beaver: a person who is extremely zealous about performing duties and volunteering for more (*Merriam-Webster Dictionary*)

The metaphoric meanings shown above imply that we admire and yearn towards figures, physical strength, and behaviors of these animals. The yearning arises from our general recognition that the physiological characteristics of these animals exceed the abilities of human beings. It is noteworthy that this recognition is quite contrary to the cultural values of the Great Chain of Being. Human beings regard the lion, for example, as a more prestigious and authoritative creature than themselves. The lion, praised as "the king of beasts," is a motif in the national emblem of Great Britain (cf. *OED* "lion" 5.c. *British Lion*). Richard I of England received the appellation "the Lion Hearted" (cf. *OED* "lion-heart" b).[6] Moreover, the biblical passages quoted below compare God and Jesus to the lion, where the animal is deified and evokes great awe in human beings:

(30) They shall walk after the LORD: he shall <u>roar like a lion</u>: when he shall roar, then the children shall tremble from the west. (Hosea, 10.11.)
(31) Thou huntest me as <u>a fierce lion</u>: and again thou shewest thyself marvellous upon me. (Job, 10.16.)
(32) And one of the elders saith unto me, Weep not: behold, <u>the Lion of the tribe of Juda</u>, the Root of David, hath prevailed to open the book, and to loose the seven seals thereof. (Revelation, 5.5.)

The sheep and the lamb appearing as a metaphoric vehicle in the Bible also exemplify a view that overturns the general ideas of animals based on the Great Chain of Being. They are docile in nature, lacking fighting instincts, thus suitable for a burnt offering (cf. Genesis Ch. 22). A prophecy of the Savior's Passion quoted in (33), as well as the reference in (34) and (35) to Jesus who sacrifices himself to God, liken the Messiah to the lamb and the sheep, assuming these animals to have a divine nature comparable to that of Jesus.

CHAPTER V BESTIALITY AND HUMANITY THROUGH ANIMAL METAPHORS 129

(33) He was oppressed, and he was afflicted, yet he opened not his mouth: he is brought as a lamb to the slaughter, and as a sheep before her shearers is dumb, so he openeth not his mouth. (Isaiah, 53.7.)
(34) The next day John seeth Jesus coming unto him, and saith, Behold the Lamb of God, which taketh away the sin of the world. (John, 1.29.)
(35) Forasmuch as ye know that ye were not redeemed with corruptible things, as silver and gold, from your vain conversation received by tradition from your fathers; But with the precious blood of Christ, as of a lamb without blemish and without spot: (I Peter, 1.18–19.)

The positive implications in the dictionary definitions of the metaphorically used animal terms shown in (19) through (29) also result from our view that these animals far surpass ordinary people in physiological qualities, again distinct from the cultural model of the Great Chain of Being. The conceptual mappings of these "outstanding" animals onto an excellent person are schematically expressed in Figure 5.3, where physiological qualities of the animals are characterized in terms of human properties and regarded as physically, esthetically, and religiously superior to the average human, and then applied to positive emotions, behaviors, and qualities of human beings.[7]

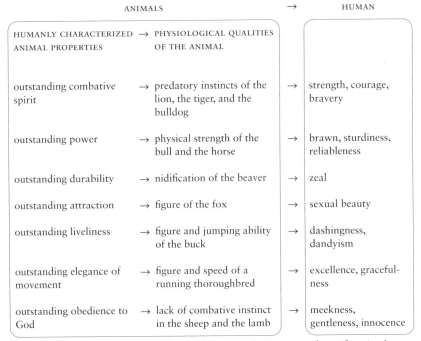

Figure 5.3: The conceptual mapping as a basis of metaphoric senses of specific animal terms indicative of positive evaluations

5.4 Metaphors evoking animal behaviors

Shakespeare's *The Taming of the Shrew* is well-known in Japan by the title *Jaja-uma Narashi (Breaking in an Unruly Horse)*.[8] The term *shrew* in the original title refers to a small mouse-like animal with a long pointed snout, with a figurative sense of "an ill-tempered scolding woman" (*Merriam-Webster Dictionary*). The character named Katherina, marked by her aggressively assertive personality, is quite suitable to be likened to this small animal, but an unruly horse is also an ideal vehicle for the strong woman, as Petruchio convincingly compares her to large snorty herbivorous animals, saying "My horse, my ox, my ass, my any thing" (*The Taming of the Shrew*, III. ii. 231).[9]

The title of the drama is also noteworthy for the use of the word *taming*. According to Palmatier's *Speaking of Animals: A Dictionary of Animal Metaphors* (1995), the verb *tame* developed in the 14th century to express the process of domesticating animals, but it soon acquired figurative senses, coming to apply to *cleaning* the land (i.e., *taming the wilderness*), *harnessing* natural energy, and *toning down* language (p. 382). The *OED* further states that the verb has acquired a metaphoric meaning of "to overcome the wildness or fierceness of (a man, animal, or thing); to subdue, subjugate, curb; to render gentle, tractable, or docile" ("tame" v1. 2). The term in the drama successfully express a gradual change of Katherina's behaviors, evoking an image of a wild herbivorous animal being gradually domesticated.

This section focuses on figurative uses of words referring to animal behaviors and human-animal relationships, with special reference to Palmatier (1995), who records not only animal names but plentiful expressions of animal behaviors and their metaphoric usages as well.[10] Descriptions of fighting between animals, being hunted by the human, being tamed and domesticated, and other behaviors peculiar to animals will be under consideration here.

Palmatier defines and describes metaphoric meanings of phrases referring to fighting between animals as follows:

(36) **make the fur fly**: To engage in a violent argument. …When people engage in a violent argument, the fur that flies is angry words, including insults, threats, and expletives. When a violent argument is expected to take place, it is predicted that *the fur will fly*.
(37) **go for the jugular**: To attack an opponent in his / her most vulnerable spot. …A person who has an *instinct for the jugular* is able to sense where an opponent's weakness lies and to attack it with deadly consequences.
(38) **lock horns**: To have an angry confrontation with someone. …People *horn in on* other people when they intrude on them or force themselves on them

without an invitation. As a result, the host and the unwanted guest may *lock horns* with each other, each willing to die for his/her rights.

"Making the fur fly" refers to a situation in a fight between animals, where clumps of their fur are often removed by teeth or claws. *Jugular* in "going for the jugular" means a jugular vein in the neck that carries blood from the head to the heart. According to Palmatier, it is a favorite point of attack for smaller animals, such as hyena, on larger animals, such as the gnu, which then slowly bleeds to death. "Locking horns" is a behavior of horned animals like bulls, goats, mountain sheep, and perhaps broadly including deer and elk, which use their horns as weapons, and engage in a battle when their territory or harem is "horned in on" by another male. These three concepts are mapped onto "a violent argument between people," "attacking an opponent's weakness with deadly consequences," and "an angry confrontation" respectively, making it possible to understand fierce battles between people in terms of a fighting between animals.

Notwithstanding their intense fighting instincts for survival, animals are easily hunted by human beings. Phrases referring to hunting often metaphorically express how humans themselves get into trouble:

(39) **open season**: To be a time when certain individuals, groups or institutions are out of favor and subject to criticism, attack, and/or ridicule. …At various times, members of certain professions (such as doctors, lawyers, and politicians) and certain large organizations (such as businesses, churches, and unions) come under fire for questionable practices. During these times it is *open season* on them: i.e., they are *fair game*, or legitimate targets for attack.

(40) **caught napping**: To be caught off guard or unprepared. …A person who is *caught napping* is either asleep on the job, unprepared for a sudden development, or unaware of a development that has already taken place. Result: dismissal.

(41) **smoke out**: To force someone to come out of hiding; to bring something suspicious into public view. …To *smoke* a criminal *out* of a hiding place is to either perform the same operation or to use tear gas or loud noise. Result: capture. To *smoke out* corruption is to publicize it through the mass media. Result: truth.

(42) **break cover**: To suddenly come out of hiding. …People who have committed a crime or have escaped from prison or jail also *take cover* or *hole up* in expectation of being hunted by the police. When the officers get too close, the criminals sometimes *break cover* in order to avoid capture or find a better hiding place.

(43) **bait**: A lure; to lure someone into a trap. ...People also *bait the hook*, set out *decoys*, and *bait the trap* for other people: i.e., they attempt to trick them into incriminating themselves or falling for a scam.
(44) **pitfall**: A hidden danger. ...A human *pitfall* is a problem that you don't recognize until you encounter it, such as contaminated soil on a building site. A *bottomless pit* is a need that can never be completely satisfied or a debt that can never be fully paid.
(45) **fenced in**: To be or feel restrained in your freedom of action. ...A person who is *fenced in* feels *cooped up* or restricted in his/her ability to accomplish something.

Once the "open season" comes and restrictions on the hunting of particular animals are lifted, the animal is "caught napping" when it is discovered sleeping in its hiding place, or "smoked out" of its den or hole. It "breaks cover" in a flurry of feathers or fur, desperately tries to escape, but unfortunately it is drawn into the range of a gun, net, or trap by a "bait," or caught into a "pitfall," and finally it is "fenced in," that is, restrained in its freedom of movement. These phrases consisting of a process of hunting animals are used to talk about troubles experienced by people, in which they are unfairly criticized, suddenly suffer disadvantage without expecting it, or their secrets are exposed. A person who has committed a crime and is chased by the police comes out of a hiding place in order to avoid capture. People are sometimes unaware of the dangers facing them and easily deceived, and then restricted in their ability to accomplish their purposes.

Phrases referring to animals caught and tamed by the human are metaphorically used to express how a human is obedient to another:

(46) **lead someone around by the nose**: To manipulate, dominate, or control someone. ...Men who are *led around by the nose* or *have a ring through their nose* are either *henpecked*, i.e., are under the control of a domineering wife, or are easily deceived.[11]
(47) **(have someone) eating out of your hand**: To have someone in your power or control. ...Wild animals that are enticed to *eat food out of your hand* are sometimes regarded as "tame," but mostly they are just hungry — and they can still *bite the hand that feeds them*. Animals in the wild can become dependent on humans for food, just as humans can become submissive to other humans who dominate them.
(48) **jump through hoops**: To be forced to perform meaningless tasks; to go out of your way to please someone. ...People *jump through hoops* when they do their best to cater to someone's wishes, or when they are made to do menial tasks as a test of their resolve, as in boot camp.

Once an animal is "led" by a rope attached to a brass ring passing through the cartilage between its nostrils, it gradually gets dependent on humans for its food, "eating it out of the human hand." If it is trained for the circus, it is made to "jump through hoops." These concepts are mapped onto the domain of the human and used to understand human behaviors of falling under the control of someone, obeying someone, and performing meaningless tasks to cater to someone's wishes.

FIGHTING metaphors shown in (36) through (38), HUNTING metaphors in (39) through (45), and TAMING metaphors in (46) through (48), applied to human behaviors and emotions, are all based on the negative evaluations of animal behaviors in terms of human properties, as shown in Figure 5.4.

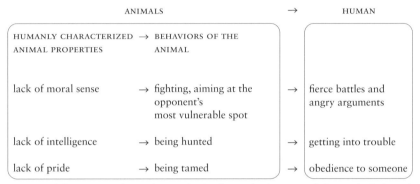

Figure 5.4: The conceptual mapping as a basis of metaphoric senses of phrases depicting animal behaviors indicative of negative evaluations

Animal behaviors, however, are not always negatively evaluated. Animals are well-known for their perceptive abilities which far surpass the human being. Concepts of their perceptive abilities and their behaviors based on those abilities are sometimes used to understand mental activities of human beings:

(49) **get wind of something**: To hear rumors about something that is supposed to be a secret. ... Figuratively, to *get wind of something* is to sense that something secret is going on or is about to happen, although the sense employed is usually hearing rather than smell.
(50) **prick up your ears**: To pay close attention. ...Humans figuratively *prick up their ears* when they suddenly raise their head or cock it toward the source of the sound. This occurs when they hear something interesting or surprising, esp. when it concerns themselves.
(51) **track down**: To search for someone or something until you find them/it. ...

Police investigators *track down* perpetrators of crime and corruption by following both a physical trail and a paper trail. Once they are *on the track of* the criminals, their goal is to *keep track of* them until they are apprehended. If the objects of pursuit *backtrack*, or *double back* on their tracks, the pursuers may *lose track of* them temporarily. When the criminals are surrounded, however, with no way out, they usually *stop dead in their tracks*. Private investigators, insurance investigators, scientific investigators, and investigative reporters employ the same techniques, although their goal is more likely evidence, knowledge, or the solution to a problem. Ordinary people try to *track down* the cause of a leaky roof; they sometimes *backtrack* to an earlier issue when speaking; they try to *keep track of* their friends; they sometimes *lose track of* their friends; and they *stop dead in their tracks* when they finally spot them again.

(52) **prowl**: To wander about stealthily. Predatory humans *prowl around* on someone else's property looking for trouble (i.e., *prowlers*); they *prowl around* in squad cars (i.e., *prowl cars*) looking for lawbreakers; and they *prowl around* (or go *on the prowl*) looking for sexual partners.

Animals have a keen sense of smell, and recognize the scent of another animal some distance away by "getting wind of it." In addition, animals like dogs and horses "prick up their ears" when they hear a sudden or unfamiliar sound. Making free use of the keen sense, predatory animals "prowl" around "tracking down" their prey. These abilities and behaviors peculiar to the animal are mapped onto human activities of discovering some secret, paying close attention on what they hear, searching for information on someone or something, and moving carefully around an area in search of someone or something.

Some of the other behaviors peculiar to animals are also compared to human activities:

(53) **burrow**: To tunnel; to penetrate; to nestle. …Humans *burrow* into the ground to build a tunnel; they *burrow* into the rubble to rescue survivors of an earthquake; they *burrow* into a pile of papers on their desk to find the one that is lost; they *burrow* into a crime syndicate to uncover their secrets; and they *burrow* under the covers to get some sleep.

(54) **browse**: To examine an assortment of things randomly and casually. … People *browse* when they examine the contents of something, such as a department store, a library, a bookstore, or an individual book. *Browsing* is indoor window-shopping: You're not there to buy anything, just to sample it — much like the animal that stretches its neck to reach a single leaf on a low-hanging limb.

(55) **ruminate**: To contemplate, meditate, or mull something over in your

mind. ...People who *ruminate* do not regurgitate their food, but they do turn a thought over and over in their mind — and they do assume the preoccupied look of a contented cow standing still, *chewing its cud*.

(56) **(grow) by leaps and bounds**: To grow rapidly and beneficially. ...When a business — or the productivity of a business — grows *by leaps and bounds*, it is making rapid progress, breaking records every quarter. Industries also grow this way as do institutions and governments.

(57) **claw your way out; claw your way to the top**: To achieve freedom or success the hard way. ...Figuratively, people who find themselves in a predicament try to *claw their way out* by any means possible; and people who *claw their way to the top* manage to achieve success by working their fingers to the bone.

(58) **lick your wounds**: To attempt to recover from a psychological blow. ... Mammals attempt to cure their physical wounds by licking them, i.e., keeping them clean and coating them with saliva. Humans sometimes do the same thing to treat superficial cuts on their hands, but their method of curing psychological wounds, such as loss of face, loss of a job, or rejection by a lover, is to apply lots of denial and self pity.

The animal's behavior of "burrowing" in the ground for the purpose of building a nest is identified with human activities of building a tunnel, rescue work, and various kinds of investigations.[12] The behaviors of "browsing" and "ruminating," peculiar to herbivorous animals, are mapped onto human mental activities of a quick survey of goods or texts and recurrent meditations. Behaviors of spectacular "leapers" and "bounders" like the deer, the rabbit, and the kangaroo are compared to how a human business makes rapid progress. Animals like the cat and the mouse that are caught in a pit "claw their way out" of the hole, whose behavior is used as a metaphoric vehicle for a person's achievement of success through a long struggle. Mammals, including the human, "lick their wounds" in order to cure them. Human attempt to cure psychological damage is also understood in terms of the behavior of "licking."

As we have seen, metaphorical phrases shown in (49) through (58) imply positive evaluation of their keen sense, predators' reasoning about where their prey is, their physical capabilities, herbivorous animals' powers of concentration, and rational behaviors for the purpose of avoiding danger and recovering from a wound. We evaluate them highly in terms of human properties, and then map their abilities and behaviors back onto the human domain once again, as shown in Figure 5.5.

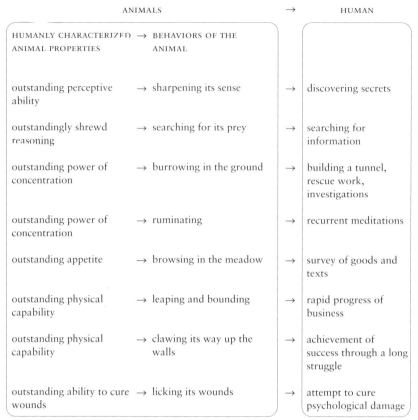

Figure 5.5: Conceptual mapping as a basis of metaphoric senses of phrases depicting animal behaviors indicative of positive evaluations

5.5 Conclusion

Human personalities and characters are various, encompassing haughtiness and humbleness, as well as courage and cowardice. The cultural model of the Great Chain of Being where the human is regarded as superior to the animal, though it has exerted a great influence on the conceptual mapping for understanding and talking about qualities of human beings in terms of animals in general, does not fully explain the positive aspects of the animal metaphor. When we narrow the scope of investigation from generic terms for the animal through family names to specific animal names, a close observation of physiological qualities and behaviors of the specific animals reveals that our understanding of the animal sometimes releases itself from the spell of the Great

CHAPTER V BESTIALITY AND HUMANITY THROUGH ANIMAL METAPHORS   137

Chain of Being. Bestiality, which is supposed to be inferior, is placed on an unexpectedly higher position than humanity in the hierarchy of creatures. Whereas insects are lower in position than quadrupeds or birds in the conceptual chain, the human is able to learn a lesson from small insects like ants, as suggested by *Proverbs*, saying "Go to the ant, thou sluggard; consider her ways, and be wise: / Which having no guide, overseer, or ruler, / Provideth her meat in the summer, and gathereth her food in the harvest" (6. 6–8). It is human wisdom to treat the whole of creation as an exemplar that enables us to praise people for their physical, intellectual, aesthetic and moral superiority by animal metaphors. [13]

Notes

1   "J." in the definitions in the *OED* cited in (2) and (6) is an abbreviation of "quoted from Johnson's Dictionary," namely, *A Dictionary of the English Language* by Samuel Johnson, 1755.
2   "Nature proceeds little by little from things lifeless to animal life in such a way that it is impossible to determine the exact line of demarcation, nor on which side thereof an intermediate form should lie. Thus, next after lifeless things comes the plant, and of plants one will differ from another as to its amount of apparent vitality; and, in a word, whole genus of plants, whilst it is devoid of life as compared with an animal, is endowed with life as compared with other corporeal entities. Indeed, as we just remarked, there is observed in plants a continuous scale of ascent towards the animal. So, in the sea, there are certain objects concerning which one would be a loss to determine whether they be animal or vegetable. For instance, certain of these objects are fairly rooted, and in several cases perish if detached; thus the pinna is rooted to a particular spot, and the razor-shell cannot survive withdrawal from its burrow. Indeed, broadly speaking, the entire genus of testaceans have a resemblance to vegetables, if they be contrasted with such animals as are capable of progression." Aristotle, *History of Animals*, Book 8, Chapter 1, 588b. "[S]eals and bats are ambivalent, the former between land and water animals, and the latter between animals that live on the ground and animals that fly; and so they belong to both kinds or to neither. For seals, if looked on as water-animals, are yet found to have fins. For their hind feet are exactly like the fins of fishes; and their teeth also are sharp and saw-like as in fishes. Bats again, if regarded as winged animals, have feet; and, if regarded as quadrupeds, are without them. So also they have neither the tail of a quadruped nor the tail of a bird; no quadruped's tail, because they are winged animals; no bird's tail, because they are terrestrial. This absence of tail is the result of necessity. For they are skin-winged; but no animal, unless it has barbed feathers, has the tail of a bird; for a bird's tail is composed of such feathers. As for a quadruped's tail, it would be an actual impediment, if present among the feathers." *Parts of Animals*, Book 4, Chapter 13, 697b.
3   According to Genesis (1. 20–27), God created the fish of the sea and the fowl of the air on the fifth day, and the beast of the earth and finally man on the sixth day. Since God created man in his own image, beings seem to have been created in ascending order, namely, from the lowest to the highest.
4   Lakoff and Turner (1989: 172) define the Great Chain Metaphor as "an ensemble consisting

of the common-sense theory of the Nature of Things + the Great Chain + the GENERIC IS SPECIFIC metaphor + the Maxim of Quantity."

5 On positive connotations in the figurative meanings of *dog* and a group of words semantically related to *dog*, see Watanabe (2006).
6 According to the *OED*, "lion heart" is commonly used to translate *Cœur de Lion*, the traditional appellation of Richard I of England.
7 Nesi (1995) argues on the role of animal metaphor, stating that it is used "to maximize personal impact, both endearments and, perhaps more frequently, in insults" (p. 274). Similarly, Halupka-Rešetar and Radić (2003) classify animal names used in adressing people in Serbian into "terms of abuse" and "terms of endearment." The positive evaluation of animal qualities as the basis of the figurative use of animal terms shown in Figure 5.3 goes beyond mere "endearment" and can be characterized as admiration and yearning toward those animals.
8 It is Shoyo Tsubouchi who first completed Japanese translations of the whole Shakespearian dramas and three poems. His translation of *The Taming of the Shrew* with a Japanese title *Jaja-uma Narashi* was published by Waseda University Press in 1920. Later, many translators such as Toshiko Oyama, Yushi Odashima, Tsuneari Fukuda and others followed Tsubouchi in the struggle for domestication of this drama, adopting the same title as Tsubouchi.
9 It should be noted that Petruchio in this line uses only male animal terms, avoiding female ones like *mare* and *cow*, which could be metaphorically used to talk contemptuously about a woman.
10 According to Nilsen (1996), some metaphoric senses of animal names assigned to people are gender-specific: *wolf*, for example, is linked to the male, whereas *bitch* is linked to the female. When those names are converted into verbs, however, *wolf* can be used to describe a female, as in "She wolfed down the food," and *bitch* can be used for a male, as in "He's going to bitch and moan until he gets what he wants," because in those cases the comparison are not made to the entire animal but instead to its specific characteristic or action. Deignan (2005) also argues that "when a word referring to an animal is used metaphorically to describe human characteristics or behaviour, an adjective or verb is often formed" (Chapter 7). The word class shift occurring in animal terms and the metaphoric use of verbs referring to animal behaviors observed in this section seem to be based on the same reason.
11 *Henpeck* is one of uncommon expressions applied to the situation in which a female is dominant over a male.
12 *To dig* and *to mine* as well as *to burrow* can be used to describe the mental activity of investigation. The metaphoric sense seems to be based on a conceptual metaphor where THE EARTH is mapped on to THE MENTAL ACTIVITY (for further details, see Omori 2004b). The figurative sense of *burrow* seems to be related to both of the source domains of THE ANIMAL and THE EARTH.
13 In his study on figurative senses of bird terms, Watanabe (2005b) points out that *eagle* and *hawk* have a sense of "vigor," *nightingale* "melodious singers or speakers," *chicken* and *duck* "a cute young girl," *swan* "faultlessness and excellence," and *dove* "a gentle woman." A comparison between the positive meanings of bird terms and those of quadruped terms shown in Figure 5.3 reveals that cuteness, a typical characteristic of small birds, is not clearly recognized in beasts, whereas brawn and sturdiness, a typical characteristic of physically strong beasts, are not generally recognized in birds. However, quadrupeds are interestingly equivalent to birds when both of them are positively evaluated as vigorous, beautiful, gentle and innocent.

Appendix

Appendix 5.1

Animal terms metaphorically applied to the human in the OED, *the Merriam-Webster Dictionary*, and *Kenkyusha's English-Japanese Dictionary for the General Reader*

Family	Term	OED	Merriam-Webster Dictionary	Kenkyusha's
cat	cat	As a term of contempt for a human being; esp. one who scratches like a cat; a spiteful or backbiting woman. spec. an itinerant worker (U.S. slang).	2: a malicious woman / 7: a: a player or devotee of jazz / b: guy	2a《口》(陰口をきく) 意地悪女；悪意のあるゴシップ；すぐひっかく子供；夜盗, b《俗》人, やつ, 仲間 (guy),《特に》ジャズ奏者 [狂]；女の尻を追う男. vi. 1《俗》吐く, もどす (vomit). 2《俗》ぶらぶらする, 女を求めてうろつきまわる, ナンパする〈around〉. catty a. 抜き足差し足の (stealthy);《特に女性の言動に関して》ずるい, 陰険な, 辛辣な, 意地悪な, 意地の悪いうわさをする
	kitten	Applied to a young girl, with implication of playfulness or skittishness. In extended use: a girl-friend; a young woman; often as a form of address.	—	n. おてんば娘. vi., vt.〈猫が子を〉産む；じゃれつく, こびを見せる.
	wild-cat	Applied to a savage, ill-tempered, or spiteful person, esp. a woman.	a savage quick-tempered person	《口》[fig.] 短気者, むこうみず, 猛烈な闘士. attrib. a. 1〈計画など〉無謀な, むこうみずな；試掘井の;《口》奔放な〈娘〉. ·a ~ idea 大それた考え.【リーダーズプラス】《黒人俗》盛り場の遊び人. vi., vt.《石油・ガスを求めて》(未知の鉱区を) 試掘する；あぶない事業に手を出す.
	lion	3. fig. (chiefly after biblical usage; cf. Rev. v. 5). a. Taken (in a good sense) as the type of one who is strong, courageous, or brave. / b. In a bad sense: A fiercely cruel, tyrannical or 'devouring' creature or person.	2 a: a person felt to resemble a lion (as in courage or ferocity) / b: a person of outstanding interest or importance <a literary lion>	勇猛な人；名物男, 流行児, 人気作家《など》. ·the ~ of the day 当時の花形 [人気者]. · make a ~ of sb 人をもてはやす. lionhearted a. (心が広く) 勇猛な, 豪胆な

	lioness	1.b. fig. Applied to persons. / 1413 Pilgr. Sowle (Caxton 1483) i. xv. 12 Yet wote I wel that leon is he nought ne thou ne myght no leonesse be. / 1595 Shakes. John ii. i. 291 Were I at home At your den sirrah, with your Lionnesse, I would set an Oxe-head to your Lyons hide. / 1847 Tennyson Princess vi. 147 O fair and strong and terrible! Lioness That with your long locks play the Lion's mane / 2. A female celebrity; a woman who is lionized. Also (Oxford University slang), a lady visitor to a member of the university.	—	—
	tiger	A person of fierce, cruel, rapacious, or blood-thirsty disposition; also sometimes, a person of very great activity, strength, or courage.	a fierce, daring, or aggressive person or quality <aroused the tiger in him> <a tiger for work>	2a 荒くれ者, 残忍な男；勇猛な人, 猛者(もさ)；ばりばり仕事をする人, すごいやり手；放蕩無頼の男；《口》《テニスなどで》強敵 (cf. → RABBIT 1). tigerish a. 獰猛 [凶暴, 残忍] な.
	leop-ard	—	—	【リーダーズプラス】1 [L~]《ボリビア警察の》麻薬対策班員.
	pan-ther	Applied to a fierce or savage man.	—	【リーダーズプラス】《口》凶暴なやつ.
	chee-tah	—	—	—
	puma	—	—	—
	jaguar	—	—	—
dog	dog	3. Applied to a person; / a. in reproach, abuse, or contempt: A worthless, despicable, surly, or cowardly fellow. / b. playfully (usually in humorous reproof, congratulation, or commiseration): A gay or jovial man, a gallant; a fellow, 'chap'. Usually with adj. such as cunning, jolly, lucky, sad, sly, etc. / c. = bull-dog n. 2. [→ See below.] / d. = watch-dog b. (Schoolboys' slang.) [→ fig. and in fig. context, esp. denoting a commission or other group appointed as a safeguard against abuses by the authorities (in government, foreign policy, etc.), business interests, etc.] / e. An informer; a traitor; esp. one who betrays fellow criminals. U.S. and Austral. slang.	2 a: a worthless or contemptible person / b: fellow, chap <a lazy dog> <you lucky dog> / 9: an unattractive person; especially: an unattractive girl or woman	2a くだらない [卑劣な] やつ；《米俗・豪俗》密告者 [人], 裏切り者, 犬；《俗》つまらん [魅力のない, もてない] 女, ブス；《俗》娼婦；《ののしって》ちくしょう！ b《俗》《大学の》新入生, 新米労働者；自動車点検工. c [通例 cunning, gay, jolly, lucky, sad, sly などの形容詞を伴って][軽蔑・戯言・愛称] やつ(fellow). ・a sad [jolly] ～ 困った [愉快な] やつ. ・a dirty ～ やくざ男. vt. 1 尾行する (shadow); 犬で追いかける；〈不幸などが〉…に付きまとう. 2【機】鉄釘で掛ける, 鉤(かぎ)でつかむ. vi.《古》〈災難・不幸などが〉どこまでも付きまとう. doggy a.《口》いきで派手な, きざな (stylish and showy).

CHAPTER V BESTIALITY AND HUMANITY THROUGH ANIMAL METAPHORS   141

puppy	Applied to a person as a term of contempt; especially, in modern use, a vain, empty-headed, impertinent young man; a fop, a coxcomb.	baby 4 [→ person, thing]	生意気な青二才．〜hood, 〜dom n. 子犬であること［時代］；生意気時代［盛り］．〜ish a. 子犬のような；生意気な．〜ism n. 生意気.
whelp	2. b. transf. A young child; a boy or girl. Now only jocular. / 3. b. An ill-conditioned or low fellow; later, in milder use, and esp. of a boy or young man: A saucy or impertinent young fellow; an 'unlicked cub', a 'puppy'. Also attrib.	a young boy or girl	[derog.] がき, 小僧, 嫌われ者, [joc.] ちびすけ；[W-] Tennessee 州人《俗称》.
hound	4. Transferred, in various senses, to persons. / a. Applied opprobriously or contemptuously to a man: cf. dog n.1 3 a; a detested, mean, or despicable man; a low, greedy, or drunken fellow. / b. Cambridge slang: see quot. 1879. [→ 1879 E. Walford in N. & Q. 5th Ser. XII. 88 In the Anecdotes of Bowyer.. we are told that a Hound of King's College.. is an undergraduate not on the foundation, nearly the same as a 'sizar'.] / c. U.S. One of an organized gang of ruffians in San Francisco, in 1849; also called 'Regulators'. / d. transf. A player who follows the 'scent' laid down by the 'hare' in the sport hare and hounds or paper-chase. Cf. hare 3 b. / e. Used with a preceding substantive to designate a person who has a particular enthusiasm for, or interest in, the object or activity specified; esp. in news-hound (see news n. pl. 6 c). colloq. (orig. U.S.).	2: a mean or despicable person / 4: a person who pursues like a hound; especially: one who avidly seeks or collects something <autograph hounds>	《紙まき競走 (hare and hounds) の》追跡者,「犬」; [derog.] 卑劣漢,「犬」,《口》《趣味などを》追う人, 熱中者, [compd.] すごい...好き［ファン］；《俗》《大学の》新入生. vi. 激しく追跡する；悩ます, 迫害する, いじめる, せき立てる［けしかける (set)〈at〉; 激励する〈on〉
greyhound	—	—	《俗》てきぱきした肉屋［セールスマン］

wolf	5. a. A person or being having the character of a wolf; one of a cruel, ferocious, or rapacious disposition. In early use applied esp. to the Devil or his agents (wolf of hell); later most freq., in allusion to certain biblical passages (e.g. Matt. vii. 15, Acts xx. 29), to enemies or persecutors attacking the 'flocks' of the faithful. / † b. Applied to a person, etc. that should be hunted down like a wolf. (Cf. wolf's-head.) Obs. / c. slang. (a) A sexually aggressive male; a would-be seducer of women; (b) orig. U.S., a male homosexual seducer or one who adopts an active role with a partner. Occas. applied to a woman: see quot. 1968 s.v. wolfess 2.	2 a (1): a fierce, rapacious, or destructive person (2): a man forward, direct, and zealous in amatory attentions to women	1a オオカミ・(as)greedy as a～(狼のように)貪欲な。 2a 残忍な人,貪欲な人；《口》女をあさる男,色魔,「狼」,色男；《俗》相手をあさるホモの男. wolfish a. 貪欲な,残忍な
bitch	2. a. Applied opprobriously to a woman; strictly, a lewd or sensual woman. Not now in decent use; but formerly common in literature. In mod. use, esp. a malicious or treacherous woman; of things: something outstandingly difficult or unpleasant. (See also son of a bitch.) / b. Applied to a man (less opprobrious, and somewhat whimsical, having the modern sense of 'dog'). Not now in decent use.	2 a: a lewd or immoral woman / b: a malicious, spiteful, or overbearing woman — sometimes used as a generalized term of abuse	女,いやな［意地の悪い,いやらしい］女,「めす犬」；(うわさばっかりするような)ホモ野郎. vi 不平［文句］を言う〈about sth, at sb〉；みだら［意地悪］である. vt だいなしにする,ぶちこわす〈up〉；…にみだらなこと［意地悪］をする；だます；…について不平を言う.
bull-dog	1. c. transf. Applied to persons: One that possesses the obstinate courage of the bulldog. /2. † A sheriff's officer (obs.); one of the Proctors' attendants at the Universities of Oxford and Cambridge. colloq.	a proctor's attendant at an English university	n. 勇敢で粘り強い人物,一徹者；《口》《Oxford, Cambrige 大学の》学生監補佐. a. ブルドッグのような,勇猛で粘り強い. ・the ～ breed 英国人《俗称》. vt. 勇猛に行動［攻撃］する；《焼き印をおすためなどに》〈牛を〉角をつかみ首をひねって倒す；《俗》大げさに言う
poodle	fig. A lackey or cat's-paw.	—	こびる者,追従者.
spaniel	2. fig. / a. One who pries into, or searches out, something. / b. A submissive, cringing, or fawning person.	a fawning servile person	おべっか者,卑屈でへいへいする人.
pug	—	—	狆に似た顔の,ずんぐりした短毛の中国原産の愛玩犬.《古俗》大家の召使頭；《一・BUN 1 状の》束髪.

CHAPTER V BESTIALITY AND HUMANITY THROUGH ANIMAL METAPHORS   143

beagle	fig. One who makes it his business to scent out or hunt down; a spy or informer; a constable, sheriff's officer, bailiff.	—	ビーグル《ウサギ狩り用の小猟犬》; スパイ, 探偵; 執達吏 legal beagle《韻 俗》n. やり手の［辣腕の］弁護士; 証拠をあさり歩く人.
jackal	fig. A person who acts like a jackal, esp. one who does subordinate preparatory work or drudgery for another, or ministers to his requirements.	2 a: a person who performs routine or menial tasks for another / b: a person who serves or collaborates with another especially in the commission of base acts	2 [fig.］下働き, お先棒かつぎ, だしに使われる人《ジャッカルはライオンのために獲物をあさると信じられたところから》; 悪者, 詐欺師；[〈a.〉] 先棒かつぎ的な. vi. (-ll-) 下働きをつとめる〈for〉.
coyote	transf. / 1872 S. Powers Afoot & Alone 277 Many slouching fellows.. are really squatters or 'coyotes'. 1890 Chicago Advance 20 Nov., Many 'coyotes,' as the Mexicans call the half breed population. 1909 'O. Henry' Roads of Destiny xvi. 266 She's married to Benton Sharp, a coyote and a murderer. 1948 New Mexico Q. Rev. Summer 198 Often coyote is used as a synonym for native, and is applied to Indians and mestizos (mixed bloods), as readily as to plants.	one who smuggles immigrants into the United States	1 コヨーテ (= prairie wolf)《北米西部大草原のイヌ科の肉食獣; 米西部のインディアンの伝説中ではトリックスターの役を果たすことが多い》. 2 悪党, 狡猾なやつ, 卑劣な男.

fox		2. fig. a. A man likened for craftiness to a fox. / b. ? Used as adj.: Fox-like, cunning. / c. An attractive woman. U.S. slang.	2: a clever crafty person / 5: a good-looking young woman or man	1・The ～ is known by its brush. 人それぞれに特徴があるもの. ・When the ～ preacheth then beware your geese. うまい話には乗るな. ・set the ～ to keep the geese 人をうっかり信用して［見誤って］ばかを見る. ・An old ～ is not easily snared. 老いたる狐は用心深い. ・Every ～ must pay his skin to the furrier. 才ある者は才におぼれる. ・The ～ preys farthest from home. 簡単にしっぽをつかまれるようなことはしない. ・a ～ that has lost its tail 人の不幸を願うやつ. 2 狡猾な［ずるい］人;【聖】似非預言者;《俗》魅力的な若い女［若者］. ・an old ～ 老獪な人. ・play the ～ ずるを決め込む. vt., vi. 1 《口》a 欺く, ずるをする; ふりをする, そらとぼける. b 困らせる, 惑わす;《廃》泥酔させる. 2a 〈本のページ・写真など〉きつね色に変色させる［する］. ・be badly ～ de ひどく変色して［色が焼けて］いる. b 味が変わる,〈ビールなど〉(発酵の際)酸っぱくする［なる］. 3〈靴〉の甲を修繕する,〈靴〉に革の装飾を付ける. 4《豪口》ひそかに追跡する,〈ボールを〉追いかけて取ってくる. foxy a. 狡猾な, ずるい(顔つきをした).《俗》魅力的な, セクシーな〈女の子〉.
	vixen	2. An ill-tempered quarrelsome woman; a shrew, a termagant. / † b. In the phrase to play the vixen. Obs. / † c. Applied to a child or a man. Obs. rare.	1: a shrewish ill-tempered woman / 3: a sexually attractive woman	口やかましい女, がみがみ女.
hyena	hyena	transf. Applied to a cruel, treacherous, and rapacious person; one that resembles the hyena in some of its repulsive habits.	—	1【動】ハイエナ《アジア・アフリカ産;死肉を食べ, ほえ声は悪魔の笑い声にたとえられる》. 2 残酷な人, 裏切り者, 欲の深い人.

CHAPTER V BESTIALITY AND HUMANITY THROUGH ANIMAL METAPHORS   145

weasel	weasel	1. a. transf. and fig. 1599 Shakes. Hen. V, i. ii. 170 For once the Eagle (England) being in prey, To her vnguarded Nest, the Weazell (Scot) Comes sneaking, and so sucks her Princely Egges. / 1632 Chapman & Shirley Ball i. (1639) A 4, Co. Dee not know him, tis the Court dancing Weesill. Ma. A Dancer, and so gay. / 1633 B. Jonson Tale Tub i. vi, Wherefore did I, Sir, bid him Be call'd, you Weazell, Vermin of a Huisher? / 1638 Ford Fancies ii. ii, Whoreson, lecherous weazle! / 1790 Wolcot (P. Pindar) Advice to Future Laureat ii. 39 Brudenell, thou stinkest! weasel, polecat, fly! / 1886 P. Robinson Teetotum Trees 39 A thin little weasel of a Bengalee Baboo. / 5. U.S. A nickname for a native of S. Carolina.	a sneaky, untrustworthy, or insincere person	1b こそこそするやつ, ずるい男;《俗》密告者.
	ferret	1. b. transf. and fig. / 1626 L. Owen Spec. Jesuit. (1629) 66 These Ferrets (or if you will Iesuites). / 1641 Milton Reform. i. (1851) 31 Many of those that pretend to be great Rabbies in these studies.. have bin but the Ferrets and Moushunts of an Index. / 1856 G. H. Boker Poems (1857) II. 25 A cunning ferret after doubtful phrases. / 1891 Daily News 19 June 7/3 He engaged him as a kind of ferret or detective. / 1946 Brickhill & Norton Escape to Danger xv. 140 Night and day.. German security guards patrolled and snooped... These guards were known by us as 'ferrets'. / 1960 Times 2 Dec. 17/2 A more recent approach starts from a device known as a 'ferret' which operates in the mains themselves. Its ordinary use is in cleaning out mains and it consists of an arrangement of water-propelled cleaning brushes. / 2. slang. a. A dunning tradesman (see quot. 1700). ? Obs. / b. (See quot. 1889.) [→ 1889 Barrère & Leland Slang Dict., Ferret, a young thief who gets into a coal barge and throws coal over the side to his confederates.] / † c. A pawnbroker (Bailey 1736). Obs.	an active and persistent seacher	熱心な捜索者, 探偵. vt., vi. ケナガイタチを使って〈ウサギ・ネズミを〉狩る[狩り出す]〈out, away〉;〈秘密・犯人などを〉捜し出す, 探索する〈out〉;捜しまわる〈about〉;せんさくする;苦しめる, 悩ます (harass).
	mink	—	—	2《俗》魅力的でいきのいい娘［女］;《黒人俗》ガールフレンド

	sable	—	—	【紋・詩】黒色；[pl.]《詩》喪服. a. クロテン毛(皮)の；[後置]【紋】黒色の；《詩》暗黒の, 陰気な. ·his ～ Majesty 悪魔大王(the Devil).
	marten	—	—	—
	otter	—	—	—
	skunk	colloq. A thoroughly mean or contemptible person. Also in playful use.	an obnoxious or disliked person	《口》いやなやつ；《俗》ブスでいやな女の子；《俗》黒人；《西部》《交替勤務者の》目覚まし係の少年, 雑役ボーイ.
	badger	1. fig. 1642 Fuller Holy & Prof. St. ii. viii. 80 Erasmus was a badger in his jeeres, where he did bite he would make his teeth meet. / 2. (in U.S.) Nickname of natives or inhabitants of Wisconsin.	capitalized: a native or resident of Wisconsin — used as a nickname	2 [B～] アナグマ(Wisconsin 州人の俗称). vt. しつこく苦しめる［いじめる, 悩ます］；しつこくせがむ.
	stoat	fig., esp. a treacherous fellow; a sexually aggressive man, a lecher.	—	—
	ermine	fig. With reference to the use of ermine in the official robes of judges and the state robes of peers.	a rank or office whose ceremonial or official robe is ornamented with ermine	1 オコジョ, エゾイタチ, ヤマイタチ, アーミン 2a アーミンの白い毛皮《詩語では純潔の象徴》；アーミン毛皮のガウン［外套］《王侯・貴族・裁判官用》. b《権威などの象徴として》アーミンを着る役職［地位］. ·wear [assume] the ～ 裁判官の職に就く
bear	bear	1. e. slang (orig. and chiefly U.S.). A policeman; ellipt. for Smokey Bear 2. Freq. attrib. or in phr.: see also feed the bears s.v. feed v. 4 b. / 2. fig. A rough, unmannerly, or uncouth person. to play the bear: to behave rudely and roughly; const. with (colloq.): to play the deuce with, inflict great damage upon (? obs.). Also in obs. colloquial sense: see quot. 1832.	2: a surly, uncouth, burly, or shambling person <a tall, friendly bear of a man> / 3 (probably from the proverb about *selling the bearskin before catching the bear*): one that sells securities or commodities in expectation of a price decline –compare bull	2a がさつ者, 不作法者；《俗》醜い女, ブス. ·a regular ～ がさつ者. b《ある事に》強い［熱心な］人, 《俗》目をみはるもの, すごいやつ. ·a ～ at mathematics 数学のできる人. ·a ～ for punishment [work] 虐待に耐える［仕事に熱心な］人, 悪条件［労働］にも屈しない人. c【証券】(弱気の)売方, 弱気筋 (opp. bull). d [the B～] ロシア (Russia), ソ連《俗称》. e《CB 無線俗》警官 (cf. → SMOKEY). bearish a. 熊のような；乱暴な (rough)；【証券】弱気の, 下がりぎみの (opp. bullish)；《一般に》がっかりさせる(ような), 悲観的な.
	racoon	raccoon	—	—	—
	panda	panda	—	—	—

CHAPTER V BESTIALITY AND HUMANITY THROUGH ANIMAL METAPHORS 147

walrus	walrus	—	—	《俗》背の低い太ったやつ;《俗》泳げないやつ, ダンスのできないやつ.
cow	cattle	4. e. Applied by slaveholders to their slaves. / 7. In various extended uses; mostly contemptuous: b. of men and women, with reference to various preceding senses. arch.	human beings especially en masse	pl. 畜牛 (cows and bulls);《古》家畜 (livestock);《人間を軽蔑的に》畜生ども, 虫けら;《古》害虫.
	cow	4. transf. / † a. A timid, fainthearted person, a coward. Obs. / b. Applied to a coarse or degraded woman. Also, loosely, any woman, used esp. as a coarse form of address. / c. An objectionable person or thing, a distasteful situation, etc. Austral. and N.Z. slang.	—	《口》(太った)だらしない女, のろまな女, いやな女;《豪俗・ニュ俗》いやなやつ, 不愉快なもの.
	sacred cow	2. fig. (orig. U.S.). a. Journalism. (a) someone who must not be criticized;	one that is often unreasonably immune from criticism or opposition	《インドにおける》聖牛;[fig.] 神聖で侵す[批判する]ことのできない人[もの], いつも好意的に[慎重に]扱われる人[機関].
	bull	7.c. A policeman. U.S. slang. / 8. Stock-Exchange [see bear n.1 8]. One who endeavours by speculative purchases, or otherwise, to raise the price of stocks. Bulls and Bears, the two different classes of speculators. Bull was originally a speculative purchase for a rise.	2: one who buys securities or commodities in expectation of a price rise or who acts to effect such as a rise / 3: one that resembles a bull (as in brawny physique)	《大きさ・強さなどに関して》雄牛のような男;【証券】買方, 強気筋 (opp. bear);《俗》おまわり, ポリ公, サツ, デカ, 看守; vi., vt. 1a 押し進む, ...に対し乱暴にする;《俗》〈雄牛が〉さかりがつく;《卑》〈女〉と性交する.・~ ahead 前方へ進む.・~ one's way 反対を押し切って進む. b【証券】買いあおる,《高価になるよう》〈株・市場〉の操作をする. 2《口》...にはったりをかける;大口をたたく, ほらを吹く, 自慢をする;かつぐ. bullish a.《たくましさなどの点で》雄牛のような;頑固な;愚かな;【証券】強気の (opp. bearish);楽観的な
	ox	4. fig. a. A fool; esp. in phr. to make an ox of (any one). dumb ox: see dumb a. 7 b. / b. the black ox, misfortune, adversity; old age: in proverb, the black ox has trod on (his, etc.) foot.	—	牛のように力持ちの[落ちついた, 鈍重な, ぶかっこうな]人.
	calf	transf. Applied to human beings: A stupid fellow, a dolt; sometimes a meek inoffensive person. Also as a term of endearment. Essex calf: a nickname for a native of that county.	an awkward or silly youth	《口》愚かな若者, まぬけ

buf-falo	(With capital initial.) A member of the Royal Antediluvian Order of Buffaloes, founded in 1822 for sociable and benevolent purposes.	—	《俗》vt. 困らせる, めんくらわせる, ごまかす (baffle);(虚勢を張って)おどす；だます, 利用する.【リーダーズプラス】《俗》黒いの, 黒人;《俗》娘っ子, 女,《特に》太った女, 大女, デブ女, カバ;《俗》亭主,《広く》男, 野郎, やつ.
sheep	2. Similative (often passing into figurative) uses. / a. In allusions to: (a) The sheep's timidity, defencelessness, inoffensiveness, tendency to stray and get lost: chiefly in echoes of biblical passages, and sometimes with allusion to sense 4. (b) The fabled assumption by a wolf (or other beast of prey) of the skin of a slaughtered sheep. (c) The division into 'sheep' and 'goats' (saved and lost) at the Last Judgement. Also attrib., as sheep-and-goat. (d) The infection of the whole flock by one sheep. (e) The shearing of sheep; with suggestion of 'fleecing' or robbing. / b. lost sheep: one who has strayed from the right way. (Cf. 2 a (a) and see lost 2.) / c. black sheep: a bad character. Cf. 3. / 4. fig. In biblical and religious language, applied (as collective plural) to persons, in expressed or implied correlation with shepherd. With varying specific reference: said, e.g., of Israel, the Church, or mankind generally, viewed as under the guidance and protection of God, and as owing obedience to Him; of those who are led by Christ as the Good Shepherd (John x. 1–16); and of those who are under the charge of a spiritual pastor, or who are viewed as needing to be spiritually fed or directed. Hence occas. in sing. / 5. a. A person who is as stupid, timid, or poor-spirited as a sheep. † b. Sheep and shrew are contrasted as types of wives of opposite characters (see quots.).	a timid docile person; especially: one easily influenced or led	おとなしい人, 臆病者, 愚か者;信者たち, 教区民 ・like [as] a sheep to the slaughter ひどく柔順に, おとなしく. ・separate [tell] the sheep from [and] the goats【聖】善人と悪人［すぐれた者と劣った者］とを区別する《Matt. 25:32》.
lamb	2. fig. Applied to persons. / a. A young member of a flock, esp. of the church. / b. One who is as meek, gentle, innocent, or weak as a lamb. / c. used as a term of endearment. / d. A simpleton; one who is cheated; esp. one who speculates and loses his money.	2 a: a gentle or weak person / b: dear, pet / c: a person easily cheated or deceived especially in trading securities	無邪気な人, 柔和な人；教会の年少信者;《口》だまされやすい人, 投機の初心者;《愛称》いい子, 坊や. 3 [the Lamb] (神の) 小羊, キリスト (= the Lamb of God). ・like [as] a lamb (to the slaughter) (危険を知らずに)柔順に.

CHAPTER V BESTIALITY AND HUMANITY THROUGH ANIMAL METAPHORS 149

	ram	1. † b. As the reward given to the victor in a wrestling match. Obs. / c. transf. A sexually aggressive man; a lecher. colloq.	—	《俗》好色な男, 助平
	ewe	2. transf. / 1610 B. Jonson Alch. v. v, [To his sister] Kas. Come on, you yew, you haue match'd most sweetly, ha you not? / a1700 B. E. Dict. Cant. Crew, Ewe, or the White Ewe, a Top-woman among the Canting Crew, very Beautiful. / Ibid., Strowling-morts.. Travel the Countries, making Laces upon Ewes. / 1725 New Cant. Dict., Yews. / 18.. Jamieson Rotten yow, metaph., Applied to a person.. subjected to much expectoration.	—	―(雌羊, 雌緬羊)
	goat	3. fig. a. A licentious man. / b. to play the (giddy) goat: to frolic foolishly; to play the fool; to behave in an irresponsible manner. Also, to act the goat. colloq. / c. to get (a person's) goat: to make (him) angry; to annoy or irritate. slang (orig. U.S.). / d. A fool; a dupe. colloq.	2: a licentious man: lecher / 3: scapegoat 2 [→ a: one that bears the blame for others / b: one that is the object of irrational hostility]	好色漢, 助平;《口》なぶり者, あざけり［からかい］の的, とんま; 他人の罪を負わされる人, 身代わりの犠牲者 (scapegoat);《陸軍俗》部隊士官.
	ante-lope	—	—	―(レイヨウ(羚羊), アンテロープ)
	gazelle	—	—	―(ガゼル属の羚羊の総称)
	serow	—	—	―(カモシカ属の各種のヤギレイヨウ, シーロー)
deer	deer	3. small deer: transf. 1857 H. Reed Lect. Eng. Poets x. II. 17 The small deer that were herded together by Johnson as the most eminent of English poets.	—	small deer《古》小動物, 雑輩, つまらないもの《集合的》.
	stag	6. dial. and colloq. A big, romping girl; a bold woman. / 7. slang. [Prob. from sense 1; but the reason for the use is obscure.] a. An informer; esp. in phrase to turn stag. Also see quot. 1725. [→ 1725 New Canting Dict., Stag,.. as, I spy a Stag, used by.. Shepherd, lately executed, when he first saw the Turnkey of Newgate, who pursu'd and took him.] / f. U.S. A man who attends a social function without a female partner. Also quasi-adv. in phr. to go stag. / 8. Comm. slang. a. A person who applies for an allocation of shares in a joint-stock concern solely with a view to selling immediately at a profit.	5 a: a social gathering of men only / b: one who attends a dance or party without a companion	1a 雄鹿《特に5歳以上のシカ》. 2《口》《パーティーなどに》女性を同伴せずに出席する男性;《俗》独身男, 一人者;《口》→ STAG PARTY. ・No Stags Allowed ご婦人同伴でない方お断わり. 3【証券】《取引所の》のみ屋; 短期利食いが目的で新株買いをする者. 4《黒人俗》→ DETECTIVE;《俗》密告者.

	buck	2. transf. Applied to a man (in various associations). / b. A gay, dashing fellow; a dandy, fop, 'fast' man. Used also as a form of familiar address. / c. the word indicated rather the assumption of 'spirit' or gaiety of conduct than elegance of dress; the latter notion comes forward early in the 19th century, and still remains, though the word is now arch. / d. A man: applied to native Indians of S. America, and to any male Indian, Negro, or Aboriginal. So buck Aborigine, Indian, Maori, Negro, nigger. Also (illogically) buck-woman. Chiefly U.S.	2 a: a male human being: man / b: a dashing fellow: dandy	1a 雄鹿(stag)　2《口》男, 元気な若者,［voc.］おい, 若いの;［derog.］インディアン［黒人］の男［若造］;《古》しゃれ者, ダンディー.
	doe	—	—	雌鹿.《俗》《パーティーなどで》男性パートナーのいない女性.
	hart	—	—	—（雄鹿《特に5歳以上のアカシカ》）
	hind	—	—	—（雌鹿《特に3歳以上のアカシカ》）
	fawn	fig. 1609 Heywood Brit. Troy xv. xxxii, That her commensed spleene may be withdrawne From them, whose violence spar'd not her Fawne.	—	—（《特に1歳以下の》子鹿）
boar	wild boar	—	—	—
	swine	Applied opprobriously to a sensual, degraded, or coarse person; also (in mod. use) as a mere term of contempt or abuse.	a contemptible person	《俗》卑劣なやつ, 強欲な男, 好色漢.・You ~ ! この野郎!
	pig	5. a. Applied, usually contemptuously or opprobriously, to a person, or to another animal. (Cf. F. cochon.) / b. Colloq. phr. to make a pig of oneself, to gluttonize. / 6. slang. b. A police officer. Now usu. disparaging. / c. A pressman in a printing-office. / d. An informer. ? Obs.	3: a dirty, gluttonous, or repulsive person / 5 slang: an immoral woman / 6 slang usually disparaging: police officer	《口》豚のような人［動物］, うすぎたない人, 食いしんぼう, 貪欲者, 頑固者;《俗》ポリ公;《俗》自堕落な女;
	hog	IV. 7. fig. Applied opprobriously to a person. / a. A coarse, self-indulgent, gluttonous, or filthy person. / b. A nickname for the members of St. John's College, Cambridge. / c. A person who behaves in a rude mannerless fashion without respect for the safety or convenience of others; esp. in road hog n.	3 a: a selfish, gluttonous, or filthy person / b: one that uses something to excess <old cars that are gas hogs>	1a・eat [behave] like a ~ がつがつ食う［無作法にふるまう］.・What can you expect from a ~ but a grunt?《諺》豚にはブーしか期待できない. 2a《口》豚みたいなやつ, 下品な男, 貪欲なやつ, 大食家, 不潔な人物.《俗》薬（やく）を多く使うやつ. b《俗》ポリ(公), マッポ. c《俗》囚人(yard pig). d《鉄道俗》機関車, 機関士

CHAPTER V BESTIALITY AND HUMANITY THROUGH ANIMAL METAPHORS 151

	boar	fig. (or heraldically) applied to persons. / 1297 R. Glouc. 133 Cornewailes bor.. þat was Kyng Arthure. / 1594 Shakes. Rich. III, iv. v. 2 In the stye of the most deadly Bore, My Sonne George Stanley is frankt vp in hold. / 1651 Proc. in Parl. No. 122 The Wild Boare of Antichristianity.	—	—(《去勢しない》雄豚)
	sow	2. Applied to persons (male or female) as a term of abuse, opprobrium, or reproach, esp. to a fat, clumsy, or slovenly woman.	—	《学生俗》だらしない女(の子), 雌豚;《俗》 ブス. ・(as) drunk as a 〜 酔っぱらって.
camel	camel	fig. A great awkward hulking fellow.	—	【リーダーズプラス】play camels《古俗》酒をたらふく［がぶがぶ］飲む, 酔っぱらう.
hippo-potamus	hippo-potamus	—	—	—(見出し語 hippopotamic には「カバのような；大きくてぶかっこうな」の記述あり)
giraffe	giraffe	—	—	—

horse	horse	Applied contemptuously or playfully to a man, with reference to various qualities of the quadruped.	an athlete whose performance is consistently strong and reliable <a team with the horses to win the pennant>	1a・eat like a 〜 馬食［大食］する．・work like a 〜 大元気で［がむしゃらに，忠実に］働く．・You can take [lead] a 〜 to water, but you can't make him drink.《諺》いやがることはさせられない．・All lay loads on a willing 〜．《諺》進んで働く者には仕事をさせるものだ．・Don't change 〜 s in the midstream.《諺》川中で馬を乗り換えるな《A. Lincoln のことばから．・If two men ride on a 〜, one must ride behind. 二人が一頭の馬に乗るなら一人は後ろ《指導者は一人がよい》．・It is useless to flog a dead 〜．《諺》死に馬にむち打ってもむだだ《過ぎたことはあきらめよ》．b 騎兵，騎兵隊 (cavalry)《集合的》; c [derog./joc.] 人，やつ (fellow)．・a willing 〜 (一手に引き受けて) 手伝ってくれる人；《俗》頑固者；《スポ俗》強い攻撃的プレーヤー．vt 2 《俗》…と性交する；《俗》虎の巻で勉強する；《海・口》〈人を〉酷使する，〈新入生を〉いじめる；《口》からかう；《俗》だます；《俗》派手に演技する vi ばか騒ぎをする，ふざける 〈around, about;《口》のらくら［ちんたら］する 〈around〉
	thorough-bred	2.b. transf. Applied to human beings or their attributes: sometimes implying characteristics like those of a thoroughbred horse, as gracefulness, energy, distinction, etc. (Cf. B. 2.) / B.2. transf. and fig.: A well-born, well-bred, or thoroughly trained person. Also a first-rate motorcar, bicycle, or other vehicle.	a thoroughly educated or skilled person	n. 毛並みのよい人，教養ある人 a.〈人が〉毛並みのよい，上品な，優雅な；意気盛んな，元気な；訓練の行き届いた，老練な．
	stallion	2. Applied to a person. / † a. A begetter. Obs. / b. A man of lascivious life; in 17th and 18th-c., a woman's hired paramour. Now only in former sense. / † 3. a. A courtesan. Obs. / b. Among U.S. Blacks, a tall, good-looking girl or woman. colloq.	—	《俗》男，いかしたやつ，遊び人，わかってる男 (stud)；《黒人俗》色気のある女［大女］
	pony	4. slang. b. A small chorus girl or dancer.	—	《俗》コーラスガール

colt	2. fig. (mostly humorous or slang.) Applied to persons having the characteristics of a colt: / a. A young or inexperienced person, a 'green hand'; now in Sport (orig. Cricket), a young or inexperienced player; a member of a junior team; also in pl., the team itself; in dial. an awkward young person who needs to be broken in; / b. A lively or spirited person; / † c. A lascivious fellow, a wanton. / † 3. A cunning fellow, a cheat. Obs. rare. (Cf. colt v. 2.)/ 4. Legal slang. The barrister that attended on a serjeant-at-law at his induction.	a young untried person	ちゃめな若者, とんまな男の子; 青二才;【競技】初心者(tyro),《特にクリケットチームの》新米, ジュニアチームの選手.
filly	transf. Applied to a young lively girl.	a young woman: girl	雌の子馬 (cf. → COLT);《口》おてんば娘, 元気な小娘;《口》魅力のある若い女.
jade	2. A term of reprobation applied to a woman. Also used playfully, like hussy or minx. / c. Rarely applied to a man: usually in some figure drawn from sense 1.	2 a: a disreputable woman / b: a flirtatious girl	[derog./joc.] 女, あばずれ, 浮気娘. vt.《馬を》《へとへとになるほど》こき使う;《一般に》疲れさせる;《廃》ばかばかしくする, さらしものにする.
ass	2. Hence transf. as a term of reproach: An ignorant fellow, a perverse fool, a conceited dolt. Now disused in polite literature and speech.	sometimes vulgar: a stupid, obstinate, or perverse person <made an ass of himself> — often compounded with a preceding adjective <don't be a smart-ass>	頑迷な人,《頑固でのろまな》ばか. ·Every ~ likes to hear itself bray.《諺》ばかはおしゃべり好きなものだ. ·an ~ in a lion's skin ライオンの皮をかぶったロバ, 虎の威を借る狐. ·make an ~ of sb 人を愚弄する. ·make an ~ of oneself 笑いものになる. ·play the ~ ばかなまねをする. vi《俗》ぶらつく.
donkey	2. transf. a. A stupid or silly person.	a stupid or obstinate person	ばか者, とんま, 頑固なやつ
mule	2. transf. a. A person having the characteristics of a mule; chiefly, a stupid or obstinate person. / † b. ? A strumpet, concubine. Obs. / c. One who is 'neither one thing nor the other'.	a very stubborn person	1a ラバ《雄ロバと雌馬との子》. ·(as) obstinate [stubborn] as a ~ とても頑固な. 2《口》意地っぱり, 頑固者, ばか.
hinny	—	—	—(ケッテイ《雄馬と雌ロバとの交配子》)
steed	—	—	—(《乗馬用の》馬)

zebra		—	[from the shirts patterned in black-and-white stripes worn by football referees]: referee 2 [→ a sports official usually having final authority in administering a game]	《俗》【フット】《縞模様のシャツを着た》審判員, オフィシャル
elephant	elephant	fig. of a man of huge stature.	one that is uncommonly large or hard to manage	巨大な物［人］
rabbit	rabbit	Applied contemptuously to a person; spec. (slang) a poor performer at any game; a novice; also attrib.	a runner in a long-distance race who sets a fast pace for the field in the first part of the race	1a・(as) scared [weak, timid] as a ~ ひどくこわがって［弱虫で, 臆病で］. 2b《長距離競走で》スタート直後速いペースで仲間をひっぱる走者. 3 臆病者, 弱虫;《口》おしゃべり. 4《口》《クリケット・ゴルフ・テニスなどが》へたな人, へぼ, 新米(cf. → TIGER). vi.《口》(だらだら)しゃべる, くどくどと言う〈on, away; about〉. rabbity a. ウサギのような; 小心な.
	hare	3. fig. Applied to a person, in various allusive senses. / c1325 Poem Times Edw. II, 252 in Pol. Poems (Camden) 334 Nu ben theih liouns in halle, and hares in the feld. / 1650 R. Stapylton Strada's Low C. Warres vi. 7 At the very first charge.. this hare in a Helmet fled out of the Field. / 1729 Swift Libel on Dr. Delany, etc. 53 Thus Gay, the hare with many friends, Twice seven long years the Court attends. / 1864 Tennyson Aylmer's F. 490 The.. distant blaze of those dull banquets made The nightly wirer of their innocent hare Falter before he took it.	—	1a.・(as) timid as a ~ 非常にはにかみ屋で気の小さい.・He who runs after two ~ s will catch neither.《諺》二兎を追う者は一兎をも得ず.・First catch your ~ (then cook him).《諺》まず現物を手に入れよ(料理はそれから), まず事実を確かめよ.・You cannot run with the ~ and hunt with the hounds.《諺》ウサギといっしょに逃げて犬といっしょに狩りをすることはできない(⇒ → 成句). 2a《俗》無賃乗車の旅客;《紙まき遊びの》ウサギ役の子..・(as) mad as a (March) hare (三月の交尾期のウサギのように)狂気じみた, 気まぐれな, 乱暴な・make a hare of... ...をばかにする. vi 疾走する〈off, after, away〉
	coney	† 5. a. A term of endearment for a woman. Obs. / b. Also indecently. / † 6. A dupe, a gull; the victim of the 'cony-catcher'. Obs.	—	《古》(すぐだまされる)お人よし, ばか.

CHAPTER V BESTIALITY AND HUMANITY THROUGH ANIMAL METAPHORS

squirrel	squirrel	—	—	2a《口》がらくたを後生大事にしまい込んでいる人. b《俗》心理学者, 精神科医《nuts を診るから》. c《俗》ホットロッドのむちゃな［すぐかっとなる］ドライバー;《俗》気違い, けったいなやつ;《俗》グループに入りたがっているやつ, メンバーみたいな顔をするやつ.
rat	mouse	2. Phrases. a. In various similes: *drunk as a mouse*, earlier † *drunk as a dreynt (= drowned) mouse*; *mum, mute, quiet, still, etc., as a mouse* († *in a cheese*). Also, † *(to speak) like a mouse in a cheese*, i.e. with a muffled voice, inaudibly; *like a drowned mouse*, i.e. in a miserable plight. / b. In alliterative association with man. (a) See man n.1 7; (b) neither man nor mouse, not a creature; mouse and man, every living thing. / † 3. a. As a playful term of endearment, chiefly addressed to a woman. Obs.	a timid person	1a・(as) drunk as a (drowned) ～ ひどく酔っぱらって. ・(as) quiet as a ～ 実に静かで. ・like a drowned ～ びしょぬれになって; しょんぼりして. ・Burn not your house to fright the ～ away.《諺》ネズミ退治に家を焼くな《極端な手段をとるな》. ・Don't make yourself a ～, or the cat will eat you.《諺》みずからネズミになれば猫に食われる《毅然としないと人にしてやられる》. ・The ～ that has but one hole is quickly taken.《諺》穴一つだけのネズミはすぐにつかまる《一つのことだけにたよるのは危険だ》. 2a 臆病者, 内気者. b かわいい子, いい子《女の子などに対する愛称》;《俗》女(の子); ガールフレンド, 婚約者. vi. あさり歩く〈*about*〉; 忍び足で歩く〈*along*〉

rat		3. b. Preceded by a specifying n., applied to one who is associated with or frequents the place specified (originally esp. a dock or riverside: in this context occas. without defining word); see also *rink-rat* (rink n.2 5), *river rat* (river n.1 5 e), *wharf-rat* (b) (wharf n.1 3). Chiefly U.S. / 4. spec. / † a. A pirate. Obs. / † b. (See quots.) Obs. / c. In Politics: One who deserts his party. (From the alleged fact that rats leave a house about to fall or a ship about to sink: see sense 1, quots. 1610, 1625.) / d. A workman who refuses to strike along with others, or takes a striker's place; also (esp. among printers), one who works for lower wages than the ordinary (or trade-union) rate. Chiefly U.S. / e. U.S. A new student or freshman, esp. a newly-recruited cadet. / f. A police informer; an informer in a prison. slang.	2: a contemptible person: as / a: one who betrays or deserts friends or associates / b: scab 3b [→ (1) a worker who refuses to join a labor union (2) a union member who refuses to strike or returns to work before a strike has ended (3) a worker who accepts employment or replaces a union worker during a strike (4) one who works for less than union wages or on nonunion terms] / c: informer 2 [→ one that informs against another; specifically: one who makes a practice especially for a financial reward of informing against others for violations of penal laws] / 4: a person who spends much time in a specified place <a mall rat>	1・(as) drunk [poor, weak] as a ～ 酔いつぶれて［無一文で, 全く力を失って］. ・like [(as) wet as] a drowned ～ ぬれねずみのようになって. ・R～s desert a sinking ship.《諺》ネズミは沈みかけた船を見捨てる. 2a《俗》脱党者, 裏切り者《ネズミは火事の家・沈没する船から退散するとの俗信から》. b《俗》組合協定より安く働く労働者［職工］, スト破り労働者(scab). c《俗》密告者, スパイ;《俗》卑劣漢, 恥知らず, いやなやつ;《俗》身持ちの悪い女;《俗》こそ泥;《豪》浮浪児 vi 2《俗》組合協定より安い賃金で働く, スト破りをする;《俗》脱党する, 裏切る, 密告する;《俗》卑劣なふるまいをする. vt *《豪俗・ニュ俗》《盗む目的で》…をさぐる, …から盗む. rat around《俗》うろちょろ［のらくら, ぶらぶら］する. rat on…《俗》〈人を〉裏切る, 見捨てる, 密告する;〈企て〉から逃げ出す,〈約束〉を破る. rat out《俗》見捨てる, 手を引く, 逃げをうつ〈on〉
dormouse	dormouse	2. transf. A sleepy or dozing person.	—	眠たがり屋.
shrew	shrew	A person, esp. (now only) a woman given to railing or scolding or other perverse or malignant behaviour; freq. a scolding or turbulent wife. For the proverbial collocation of sheep and shrew see sheep n. 5 b. / 3. attrib. Dormouse-like, sleepy.	an ill-tempered scolding woman	口やかましい女, がみがみ女, 荒々しい女.
beaver	beaver	(eager beaver a glutton for work; an over-zealous or officious person; also attrib. and transf. (colloq., orig. U.S.).)	(eager beaver a person who is extremely zealous about performing duties and volunteering for more)	b ビーバーの毛皮;【織】ビーバークロス《強度に縮充した綾織二重織りの毛織物》;《俗》あごひげ(男);《卑》女性の性器, 陰部;《CB 無線俗》女. d《口》働き者, 勤勉家(cf.→EAGER BEAVER) vi.《口》せっせと［がむしゃらに］働く〈away (at)〉.

CHAPTER V BESTIALITY AND HUMANITY THROUGH ANIMAL METAPHORS 157

porcu-pine	porcu-pine	Applied allusively to a person. / 1594 ? Greene Selimus Wks. (Grosart) XIV. 286 What are the vrchins crept out of their dens, Vnder the conduct of this porcu-pine? / 1606 Shakes. Tr. & Cr. ii. i. 27 Ther. Thou art proclaim'd a foole... Aia. Do not Porpentine, do not; my fingers itch.	—	—
kanga-roo	kanga-roo	3. b. One who advances by fitful jumps. / c. humorous. A native of Australia. /	—	オーストラリア人；[pl] 西オーストラリア鉱山株
pos-sum	pos-sum	fig. In various slang uses (see quots.). / 1833 N.Y. Mirror 7 Sept. 80 A 'possum, the western phrase for a paltry fellow – a coward. / 1900 Dialect Notes II. 51 Possum, a negro, or negress. / 1943 Baker Dict. Austral. Slang (ed. 3) 61 Possum, a 'ring-in'. / 1945 – Austral. Lang. vi. 130 Fools of one kind and another.. flathead, possum, gammy, [etc.]. / Ibid. vii. 138 Thieves are described variously as.. dwelling dancers, stoops and possums. / Ibid. 142 Jay and possum, a trickster's victim. / e. *like a possum up a gum-tree*: contented; (see also quot. 1898); *to stir (or rouse) the possum*: to stir up controversy, to liven things up. See also gum-tree 2. Austral. colloq.	—	play possum 眠った［死んだ］ふりをする；知らないふりをする, 仮病をつかう.
wom-bat	wom-bat	—	—	《俗》変人, 変わり者, いかれたやつ.

Appendix 5.2

Major animal similes in Wilkinson (2002) *Thesaurus of Traditional English Metaphors*

Dogs: fierce/ greedy / howerly [dirty] / hungry / lame / mad / mucky / sick / stalled [surfeited] / tired / true as a dog; proud as a gardener's dog with a nosegay tied to his tail; pleased / proud as a dog with two tails; look like a dog that has lost its tail; mim [prim and proper, prudently restrained] as a dog without a tail; blush like a black dog ((which could not) Be incapable of shame.); stare like a terrier dog watching a ratton

Wolves: hungry as a wolf / she-wolf with pups; dark as a wolf's mouth; like an Irish wolf she barks at her own shadow (Makes wild accusations.)

Foxes: crazy [cunning, shrewd] / fause [shrewd, sharp, clever in a cunning/deceitful way] / ram [rank, fetid] / rank / red as a fox; greedy as a fox in a hen-roost; thieving as a fox's snout; dark as a fox's mouth; grin like a fox eating yellow-jackets [wasps or hornets]

Vixens: cunning as a clicket / klyket [vixen on heat]; fow [angry] as a vixen with a sore head; worried as a pregnant fox in a forest fire

Boars: rattle like a boar in a holme [holly] bush

Cats: fierce / lame / lish [lithe, loose-moving] melancholy / nervous / nimble / sick / waffly = waffy [weak, ailing, shaky, easily blown about] / whist [silent] waukrife [wakeful] as a cat; common as backfence cats; lean as an alley-cat; dark as a stack of black cats; mawngy [surly] as an old cat; girn [grin] like a cat; cat-witted (Spiteful, wayward; silly and conceited.); pleased as a cat with two tails; like a cat on ice (Very cautiously and warily.); like a cat, he'll lig anywhere [lie, sleep anywhere]; like a cat, he will fall / land on his feet (Come out of the trouble unaffected.); has as many (nine) lives as a cat (Of someone who seems to lead a charmed life.)

Wildcats: glower like a wullicat [wild-cat]; mean as a wild-cat; looks like a wild-cat out of a bush (Dishevelled, savage.)

Badgers: blue / greasy / grey / wry as a badger; smell like a badger's touch-hole (Smell foul — often of someone over-perfumed.); stink like a brock [a badger]

Otters: greedy / hard [hardy] / keen / nice [fussy, particular — because of taking only one bite out of a fish] as an otter; bites as keen as an otter; grin like a she-otter

Stoats: screech like a whitneck / whitrack / whitret/ whitterick [stoat / weasel]; wacken /waken /wakken [lively, quick-witted, wide awake] as a whitterick; clever as a whitret; harmless as a whitret without teeth; souple [= supple] as a whitterick; fuck like a stoat (Vigorously and promiscuously, of both sexes.);

run like a whitneck

Weasels: cross / sharp [quick-moving] / wick [lively] as a weasel / wizzel; soft-hearted as a rezzil / wizzel (Ironic.); fause [shrewd, sharp, cunningly clever] as a weasel with its een bored out; grin like a weasel in a trap; sken [squint, peer sideways] like a trapped weasel; glower like a weasel frae a humplock [hillock] of stones

Deer: hearty / mad / wild / as a buck; like a buck of the first head (Brisk, pert, forward)

Hares: fleet / hearty / mad / wild as a (March) hare;

Rabbits: rabbit-hearted / rabbit-scared (As timorous or panic-stricken as a rabbit.); like a rabbit, fat and lean in twenty-four hours; goes like a rabbit (Of someone's sexual activities, frequent and enthusiastic.)

Squirrels: squirrel-hearted / minded (Scatterbrained, shallow.); lively / nimble / ruddy as a squirrel; lish [active, nimble, supple] as a squirrel; crozzled up [huddled together] like a squirrel

Rats: dead as a mawky ratton [= maggoty rat]; cold / drunk / fause [shrewd, sharp, clever in a cunning way] / fierce / poor / rank / sick / weak as a rat; fierce as a buck rat; fit as a buck rat; flash as a rat with a gold tooth; rough as rats (Of a ruthless, aggressive, uncouth, selfish person.); hungry as a rotton [= ratton, rat]; look like a drowned rat

Mice: drunk / dun / mim [prim, precise] / mum [silent, secret] / mute /quiet /shy / still / timid / trig [full, stuffed to the limit] / whisht / whist [quiet] as a mouse; sleep like / drowsy as a dormouse (Very soundly.); warm as a dormouse; full as a blowed [fly-blown] mouse; looks like a chowed / chewed mouse; looks like a drowned mouse

CHAPTER VI
Case Study: Lucifer's Metamorphosis in Milton's *Paradise Lost*

6.1 Introduction

Milton's *Paradise Lost*, an epic in 12 books, treats of biblical stories of the war in Heaven, the Fall of Lucifer, the Creation of the world, and the Fall of Man. In describing these stories, the poet frequently uses a poetic device called "epic simile," a lengthy and detailed comparison between two highly complex objects, events or relations. Whaler (1931), who analyzes logical patterns of Miltonic similes, highly evaluates the device, saying that without it the tone and landscape of an epic "would be too often austere and bleak" (p. 1034). He lists five functions of the epic simile, three of which are distinctive with Milton.[1] The first one is "illustration," a function of defining an abstract idea or a relation by presenting an analogous concrete thing or experience, often homely and familiar, and letting the readers see or image it clearly. The second function, "aggrandizement," is to ennoble the subject by making use of classic myth and of encyclopedic reference to scientific research, geography, history, the Bible, and to *belles lettres*, which are the unusual or less familiar part of the readers' experience or knowledge. And the third is "prolepsis," a function of anticipating event in the fable by means of simile.[2]

This chapter focuses on the first two functions, Miltonic similes used to "illustrate" and "aggrandize" Satan's ambitious and hazardous attempt to take revenge on God.[3] In the epic, the events which happen to the fallen angel are not told in the order of their occurrence.[4] The chronological rearrangement of the rebel's story brings some conceptual metaphors as a religious background of the epic similes to the fore part of the narrative. In the following sections consideration will be given to the relations between those metaphors and Satan's strong and complex emotions occasionally described in the text.

6.2 The change of Satan's figure and his acts

The epic vividly describes how Satan, formerly a high-ranking angel called Lucifer, upright and pure in Heaven, raises a rebellion against God, is defeated and banished to Hell, cherishes a hope of regaining Heaven and meditates revenge on the Almighty. In those detailed descriptions a number of epic similes play an enormously important role. The vehicles adopted in those similes minutely and clearly depict the gradual change of Satan's figure according to his acts, and his internal change, too, properly fulfilling illustrative and ennobling functions mentioned by Whaler (1931). It is noteworthy that the poet's references to Satan's "pretense," "incarnation," and "transformation" as well as similes contribute to the description of the change from a celestial figure of a fair angel to a hideous and disgusting one, a literally "hellish" figure. Whereas a simile, for the purpose of illustration of Satan's change, creates a picture of something referred to by the vehicle, an imaginative production in the reader's mind, Satan not only imaginarily but also "actually" metamorphoses himself by feigning an angel and various animals, incarnating himself as a serpent, and finally being transformed by God into a monstrous serpent as a punishment. These metamorphoses also reflect the gradual change of his inner self and correspond to his acts. This gradual change is shown in Table 6.1. Here Satan's story is divided into seven phases, in each of which he changes his figure according to his act. Figures formed by pretense, incarnation and transformation are enclosed in square brackets.

Phase	Satan's act	Satan's figure
1	Satan's rebellion against God	Lucifer, a God, tower, mountain
2	Satan's agony in Hell and plot to revenge on God	gigantic beings, Leviathan, the morning sun in the misty air, the sun in eclipse, the evening sun, a monarch, a tower, a comet, a thundercloud
3	Satan's escape from Hell and flight to the new world	a gryphon, Jason and Ulysses on the voyage
4	Satan's arrival on the earth	a vulture, a scout, a sunspot, [a Cherub]
5	Satan's invasion upon Paradise and unsuccessful approach to Eve	a wolf, a thief, a cormorant, [a lion], [a tiger], a toad, a heap of nitrous powder, a steed, Teneriff, Atlas
6	Satan's temptation accomplished	[a serpent], a traveler, a wandering fire, a Greek or Roman orator
7	Satan's return to Hell and divine punishment inflicted upon him	[a bright angel], a bright star or false glitter, [a monstrous serpent]

Table 6.1: The gradual change of Satan's figure according to his acts

6.3 Conceptual metaphors related to the changes of Satan's figure

This section offers a detailed observation of the changes of Satan's figure in each phase and conceptual metaphors related to them.

6.3.1 Phase 1: Satan's rebellion against God

The first phase of the revolter's story is chiefly described in Books V and VI. When he resided in Heaven, he was a high-ranking angel called "Lucifer" (VII. 131), the morning star,[5] whose brilliancy eclipsed all other angels, as described in quotation (1) (the italics in the quotations below are mine).

(1) ... *brighter* once amidst the host
Of Angels than that star the stars among ... (VII. 132–133)

When God, in front of an innumerable host of angels, declares his Son to be their "head" (V. 606) and commands their absolute obedience to him, Satan, at that time a celestial being who is "great in power, / In favor, and pre-eminence," (V. 660–661), thinks himself "impaired" (V. 665) out of envy at the Son of God. He determines to revolt against his creator, secretly mustering all his legions. In spite of his arrogant attempt, his brilliancy remains when he takes his angels with him, as described in quotation (2), and in the chariot he still possesses a divine presence, as in quotation (3). At the war in Heaven among the angelic powers, Satan and the archangel Michael confront each other, who are equivalent in stature, motion, arms, and above all, divinity, as in quotation (4).

(2) His countenance, as *the morning-star* that guides
The starry flock, allured them, and with lies
Drew after him the third part of Heaven's host. (V. 708–710)
(3) High in the midst, exalted as *a God*
The Apostate in his sun-bright chariot sat, ... (VI. 99–100)
(4) ... likest *gods* they seemed,
Stood they or moved, in stature, motion, arms,
Fit to decide the empire of great Heaven. (VI. 301–303)

These descriptions are all based on a Christian view: God is identified with light; Heaven, the home of God, is flooded with the light; and the virtuous character which accords with divinity is the light. This view is expressed by the poet at the beginning of Book III: "Hail, holy Light, offspring of Heaven first-born! / Or of the Eternal coeternal beam / May I express thee unblamed? since *God is light*, / And never but *in unapproached light / Dwelt* from eternity — dwelt then in thee, / Bright effluence of bright essence increate!" (III. 1–6), and is also shown in a number of biblical passages like "God is light, and in him is no darkness at all" (1 John 1.5), and "The light of the righteous rejoiceth: but the lamp of the wicked shall be put out" (Proverbs 13.9). It is a cultural model which imparts an important aspect of Christianity.[6] Following the conceptual metaphor literature, this mode of thought can be indicated as follows:

VIRTUE IS LIGHT. THE VIRTUOUS IS A CELESTIAL ENTITY.

A seraph named Abdiel, who has intense and unswerving loyalty to God, sees Satan's divine presence up close in the battlefield, deploring "O Heaven! that such resemblance of the Highest / Should yet remain, where faith and realty / Remain not!" (VI. 114–116). However, Satan himself never doubts his own justifiability, stubbornly believing that the fault is on the side of God who has glorified his Son and neglected Satan, and he swaggeringly says to Michael, "Err not that so shall end / The strife which thou call'st evil, but we style / The strife of glory; which we mean to win (VI. 288–290)." It is this strong pride that makes him shine, as depicted by the vehicle shown in quotations (2) to (4).

Satan's figure is also portrayed by vehicles referring to "towering" objects. See quotations (5) and (6).

(5) Satan, with vast and haughty strides advanced,
     Came *towering*, armed in adamant and gold.   (VI. 109–110)
(6) Ten paces huge
     He back recoiled; the tenth on bended knee
     His massy spear upstayed: as if, on earth,
     Winds under ground, or waters forcing way,
     Sidelong had pushed a *mountain* from his seat,
     Half-sunk with all his pines.   (VI. 193–198)

These vehicles are based on orientational metaphors VIRTUE IS UP (Lakoff and Johnson 1980)[7]. Satan's figure expressed by them also seems to be formed by his confident belief that it is him who is right.

6.3.2 Phase 2: Satan's agony in Hell and plot to revenge on God

The second phase of Satan's story is chiefly described in Books I and II. The rebellion by Satan and his powers aroused the anger of God, and they are overwhelmingly defeated and forced to leap down with horror and confusion into Hell, as stated by the poet: "Him the Almighty Power / Hurled headlong flaming from the ethereal sky" (I. 44–45). The place of punishment prepared for them is completely different from the celestial realms flooded with the light. See quotations (7) and (8).

(7) At once, as far as Angel's ken, he views
    The dismal situation waste and wild.
    A dungeon horrible, on all sides round,
    As one great furnace flamed; yet from those flames
    No light; but rather *darkness visible*
    Served only to discover sights of woe,
    Regions of sorrow, *doleful shades*, ... (I. 59–65)

(8) ... here their prison ordained
    In *utter darkness*, and their portion set,
    As *far removed from God and light of Heaven*
    As from the centre thrice to the utmost pole.
    Oh how unlike the place from whence they fell! (I. 71–75)

These descriptions of Hell, the place provided for the rebels, realize the following conceptual metaphors, which form a parallel to the conceptual metaphors above.

VICE IS DARKNESS. THE VICIOUS IS A TERRESTRIAL ENTITY.[8]

In spite of his miserable fall, however, Satan keeps his pride and power. The high-ranking angels subordinate to Satan are compared to "demi-gods" (I. 796), but Satan's mighty power far surpasses the others. Hence he is likened to giants in Greek mythology[9] and the hugest marine creature Leviathan as in quotation (9).[10]

(9) ... in bulk as huge
    As whom the fables name of monstrous size,
    Titanian or Earth-born, that warred on Jove,
    Briareos or Typhon, whom the den
    By ancient Tarsus held, or that sea-beast
    Leviathan, which God of all his works
    Created hugest that swim the ocean-stream. (I. 196–202)

The vehicles for Satan in the following quotations, *a monarch*, *a tower*, and *the sun*, also suggest his authoritative manner:

(10) ... at last,
    Satan, whom now *transcendent glory* raised
    Above his fellows, with *monarchal pride*
    Conscious of highest worth, unmoved thus spake: (II. 426–429)
(11) He, above the rest
    In shape and gesture proudly eminent,
    Stood like a *tower*.   (I. 589–591)
(12) His form had yet not lost
    All her original brightness, nor appeared
    Less than Archangel ruined, and the excess
    Of glory obscured: as when the *sun* new-risen
    Looks through the horizontal misty air
    Shorn of his beams, or, from behind the moon,
    In *dim eclipse*, disastrous twilight sheds
    On half the nations, and with fear of change
    Perplexes monarchs. Darkened so, yet shone
    Above them all the Archangel: (I. 591–600)
(13) ... the radiant *sun*, with farewell sweet,
    Extend his *evening beam*, ...   (II. 492–493)

The sun adopted as the vehicles for the apostate in the quotations (12) and (13) is not a satisfactory source of the VIRTUE-AS-LIGHT metaphor: in (12) its beams are decreased through the horizontal misty air in the morning, or because of an eclipse by the moon; and in (13) the last light of day is about to die out. Thus the light is dim or dying because the tenor is not a resident of Heaven any more. However, despite his cardinal sin, it is the heavenly body that Satan is compared to ("Darkened so, yet shone / Above them all the Archangel" (I. 599–600)). Worthy of these vehicles, he is still the mighty and compassionate leader of a host of angels, feeling deep "remorse and passion" (I. 605) for them, bursting into tears, undertaking a highly dangerous mission in order to save them from Hell, and thus receiving profound veneration, loyalty and gratitude from his followers (cf. I. 600–620, II. 486–495).

   To ascertain the truth of the prophecy concerning another world and another kind of creatures, not much inferior to angels, to be created, Satan alone sets out on a voyage, and tries to pass through Hell-gate. There he is disturbed by monstrous beings who guard the gate, so he goes into a rage standing up like a huge comet, and attempts to give one of them a deadly blow. Satan and the monster glare at each other like two black thunderclouds, as described in quotation (14):

(14) Satan stood
  Unterrified, and like a *comet* burned,
  That fires the length of Ophiuchus huge
  In the arctic sky, and from his horrid hair
  Shakes pestilence and war. Each at the head
  Levelled his deadly aim; their fatal hands
  No second stroke intend; and such a frown
  Each cast at the other as when two *black clouds*,
  With heaven's artillery fraught, come rattling on
  Over the Caspian,— then stand front to front
  Hovering a space, till winds the signal blow
  To join their dark encounter in mid-air.   (II. 707–718)

Though a comet and a black thundercloud are both the celestial, they are eerie and ominous beings, without any positive connotation like that of the sun and the stars which emit bright light. Here the two conceptual metaphors, THE VIRTUOUS IS A CELESTIAL ENTITY and VICE IS DARKNESS, opposite to each other, are simultaneously realized to describe the complicated characteristics of Satan.

6.3.3 Phase 3: Satan's escape from Hell and flight to the new world

In the third phase of the story, described in Book 2, Satan escapes from Hell and makes his solitary flight through Chaos. He goes over a number of dangerous spots by swimming, sinking, wading, creeping, and flying. This manner of pursuing his way is likened to a gryphon, an imaginative animal in Greek mythology having the head and wings of an eagle and the body and hind quarters of a lion (cf. *OED* "griffin" 1), as described in quotation (15). His arduous and perilous journey is linked to fabulous characters such as Jason and Ulysses, as in quotation (16).[11]

(15) As when a *gryphon* through the wilderness
  With winged course, o'er hill or moory dale,
  Pursues the Arimaspian, who by stealth
  Had from his wakeful custody purloined
  The guarded gold; so eagerly the Fiend
  O'er bog or steep, through strait, rough, dense, or rare,
  With head, hands, wings, or feet, pursues his way,
  And swims, or sinks, or wades, or creeps, or flies.   (II. 943–950)

(16) harder beset
>And more endangered than when *Argo* passed
>Through Bosporus betwixt the justling rocks,
>Or when *Ulysses* on the larboard shunned
>Charybdis, and by the other Whirlpool steered. (II. 1016–1020)

These similes perform Whaler's (1931) "aggrandizing" function. Satan, the courageous adventurer who braves obstacles and difficulties, is "ennobled" by these legendary vehicles. Unlike those in the first and the second phases, they are no longer celestial entities, but these mythical characters nevertheless have an atmosphere of solemnity. The eagle and the lion, the constituents of a gryphon, have conventionally received a positive evaluation. The former is given the title of "the king of birds" because of its strength, keen vision, and graceful and powerful flight (cf. *OED* "eagle" 1.a); and the latter is also powerful and has a noble appearance, and thus called "the king of beasts"[12] (cf. *OED* "lion" 1.a).[13] In comparison with the preceding and following phases, Satan in this phase is figuratively regarded as a being intermediate between celestial and terrestrial entities.[14]

6.3.4 Phase 4: Satan's arrival on the earth

In the fourth phase described in Book III, Satan alights upon the world's outermost orb, passes through the sun and finally reaches the earth. It is a stage of transition in that the rebel arrives at his destination and his revenge against God begins to loom as a real possibility. This transition causes a considerable change in vehicles for Satan: in this phase appears an animal, the terrestrial, for the first time; and at the same time it is the last phase the celestial being is applied to him as a vehicle. This change is influenced by the conceptual metaphors given above: VIRTUE IS LIGHT and THE VIRTUOUS IS A CELESTIAL ENTITY, and the opposing metaphors VICE IS DARKNESS and THE VICIOUS IS A TERRESTRIAL ENTITY. Figure 6.1 roughly shows the change in vehicles for Satan.

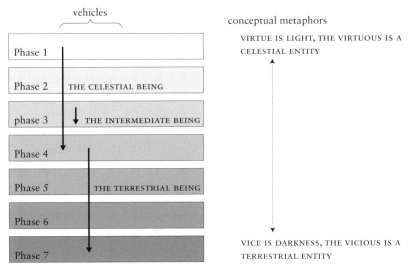

Figure 6.1: Change in vehicles for Satan and related conceptual metaphors

The first terrestrial vehicle for Satan is a vulture, as described in quotation (17). Here he has just landed on the surface of the celestial sphere and walks around, as if the hungry raptor hunts lambs or yeanling kids:

(17) As when a *vulture*, on Imaus bred,
   Whose snowy ridge the roving Tartar bounds,
   Dislodging from a region scarce of prey,
   To gorge the flesh of lambs or yeanling kids
   On hills where flocks are fed, flies toward the springs
   Of Ganges or Hydaspes, Indian streams,
   But in his way lights on the barren plains
   Of Sericana, where Chineses drive
   With sails and wind their cany waggons light;
   So, on this windy sea of land, the Fiend
   Walked up and down alone, bent on his prey: (III. 431–441)

Since it flies high in the sky, the vulture is akin to the celestial being (see Section 6.3.5). However, it is culturally evaluated as of a vile and rapacious disposition (cf. *OED* "vulture" 2.b), contrastive to the eagle as the king of birds (cf. Section 6.3.3). This low-ranked raptor serves as a quite suitable vehicle to depict Satan's vicious attempt to revenge against God, foreboding that Eve will fall into his prey. Interestingly, as Satan's story develops and he comes closer to his final goal, animal vehicles chosen for him gradually become lower in rank, as observed below.

The last vehicle related to the celestial is a sunspot, which is applied to Satan's figure on the orb of the sun, as quoted in (18).[15] It is not a heavenly body emitting the celestial light but a black spot which appears on its surface, a peripheral element of the domain of THE CELESTIAL ENTITIES. Hence, it is no longer to be mapped onto the domain of THE VIRTUOUS.

(18) There lands the Fiend, *a spot* like which perhaps
     Astronomer *in the Sun's lucent orb*
     Through his glazed optic tube yet never saw.   (III. 588–590)

In this story of revenge, Satan several times disguises himself to conceal his identity. His first act of disguise occurs in the fourth phase, when he encounters Uriel the archangel, and, in order to safely ask him the way to Man's habitation, he changes himself into the shape of an angel:

(19) But first he casts to change his proper shape,
     Which else might work him danger or delay:
     And now a *stripling Cherub* he appears,
     Not of the prime, yet such as in his face
     Youth smiled celestial, and to every limb
     Suitable grace diffused; so well he feigned.   (III. 634–639)

As described in this quotation, his pretense is absolutely perfect, and therefore Uriel is entirely deceived by his bright appearance diffusing grace, quite suitable for a cherub. But this is the last time Satan disguises himself as a sacred being. From the next phase on, he changes his appearance into animals, coarse terrestrial beings.

6.3.5 Phase 5: Satan's invasion upon Paradise and unsuccessful approach to Eve

The fifth phase described in Book IV is characterized by Satan's notable step toward the Fall of Man. Here solely terrestrial beings of vicious character appear as vehicles for the Fiend. Quotation (20) describes how he trespasses upon Paradise by overleaping the bounds. His fierce and greedy manner is likened to a wolf which leaps over the fence into the sheepfold, and a thief who attempts to steal money from a rich burgher's house. This carnivorous animal is conventionally characterized as cruel, ferocious and rapacious (cf. the *OED* "wolf" 5.a), and thus regarded as equivalent of a brazen thief, as suggested in the biblical phrase: "He that entereth not by the door into the sheepfold, but climbeth up some other way, the same is a thief and a robber." (John 10. 1.)

(20) As when a prowling *wolf*,
   Whom hunger drives to seek new haunt for prey,
   Watching where shepherds pen their flocks at eve,
   In hurdled cotes amid the field secure,
   Leaps o'er the fence with ease into the fold;
   Or as a *thief*, bent to unhoard the cash
   Of some rich burgher, whose substantial doors,
   Cross-barred and bolted fast, fear no assault,
   In at the window climbs, or o'er the tiles;
   So clomb this first grand Thief into God's fold: (IV. 183–193)

The next animal vehicle is a cormorant. It depicts the shape of Satan sitting on the Tree of Life, the highest point in Paradise, as shown in the quotation below:

(21) Thence up he flew, and on the Tree of Life,
   The middle tree and highest there that grew,
   Sat like a *cormorant*; ...   (IV.193–195)

The large and voracious sea-bird [16] is conventionally applied to an insatiably greedy or rapacious person (cf. the *OED* "cormorant" 2), and in English poetry it is interpreted as "obscene," "greedy," and "ill-omened" (cf. Robinson 1883, p. 9 and pp.124–127). The cormorant appears together with the bittern in a passage of Isaiah and that of Zephaniah, which prophesy that the land of Idumea and Assyria will be desolated due to God's fury and that these birds will settle there.[17] Similarly, the scene of the vicious visitor to Paradise in the shape like the sinister bird depicted in quotation (21) suggests a bleak future before Adam and Eve in which their disobedience provokes anger of God and hence causes the loss of Paradise.

On the Tree of Life Satan finds Adam and Eve, and so he descends to the earth and mingles with the animals around them, in order to observe them closely without being noticed ("Then from his lofty stand on that high tree / Down he alights among the sportful herd / Of those four-footed kinds, himself now one, / Now other, as their shape served best his end / Nearer to view his prey, and, unespied, / To mark what of their state he more might learn / By word or action marked." (IV. 395–401)). He enters the body of a lion, then of a tiger (see quotation (22)), and at night of a toad (see quotation (23)). His disguise of the "lower" animals demonstrates the change of his angelic quality into the lower, vicious one, as suggested by Himes (ed. 1898) who aptly states that "The scene probably signifies that Satan has here determined to make his approach to man through the animal instincts and appetites" (p. 333).

(22) About them round
    A *lion* now he stalks with fiery glare;
    Then as a *tiger*, ...   (IV. 401–403)
(23) Him there they found
    Squat like a *toad*, close at the ear of Eve,
    Assaying by his devilish art to reach
    The organs of her fancy, and with them forge
    Illusions as he list, phantasms and dreams;   (IV. 799–803)

Quotation (23) describes how the Fiend is crouching at the side of sleeping Eve in the shape like a toad, tempting her in a dream. The name of the non-blooded creature is perfectly suitable for his evil attempt: *toad* is metaphorically applied to anything hateful or loathsome (cf. *the OED* "toad" 1.b). According to Himes (ed. 1898, p. 343), the toad is an emblem of the tempter because of its bloated appearance and (supposed) venom. Milton himself mentions a toad in another poem, treating it as an object of aversion: "Thy age, like ours, O soul of Sir John Cheke, / Hated not learning worse than *toad or asp*; / When thou taught'st Cambridge, and King Edward Greek" (Sonnet XI, ll. 12–14). This passage shows that the amphibian with a short stout body and the small poisonous snake are closely connected in the poet's imagination. Hence, in the scenes of Satan's temptation described here and in the next phase, the Tempter's shape turns into a toad and a serpent respectively.

    This cold-blooded Tempter, in the midst of his effort to seduce Eve by his "devilish art" (line 801), is discovered by Ithuriel and Zephon, the guardian Angels subsequent to Gabriel. A light touch of Ithuriel's spear startles Satan, as described below:

(24) Him thus intent Ithuriel with his spear
    Touched lightly; for no falsehood can endure
    Touch of celestial temper, but returns
    Of force to its own likeness. Up he starts,
    Discovered and surprised. As, when a spark
    Lights on *a heap of nitrous powder*, laid
    Fit for the tun, some magazine to store
    Against a rumored war, the smutty grain,
    With sudden blaze diffused, inflames the air;
    So started up, in his own shape, the Fiend.   (IV. 810–819)

Nitrous powder, adopted in (24) as a vehicle for Satan, is the material of a

CHAPTER VI   CASE STUDY: LUCIFER'S METAMORPHOSIS IN MILTON'S PARADISE LOST   173

genocidal weapon invented by Satan and manufactured by his legions during the Angelic war in the first phase of the rebel's story ("sulphurous and nitrous foam / They found, they mingled, and, with subtle art / Concocted and adusted, they reduced / To blackest grain, and into store conveyed" (VI. 512–515)). Now in the fifth phase of the story, a heap of the devilish explosives, that is fired and goes up in flames, corresponds to the ferocious character of the Devil himself.

Since his arrival on the surface of the cosmos, Satan has changed himself into one shape after another, gradually adding viciousness: from the raptorial birds, through the quadrupeds and the non-blooded creature, to the inanimate object with infernal nature. As the story develops, the habitats of the animals adopted as vehicles get lower: the vulture flies in the air, the quadrupeds are land-based, the cormorant flies but also dives into water in order to hunt fish, and the toad, an amphibian, can live both on land and in water. On habitats of the animals, Milton states in the epic as follows: [18]

(25) O Adam, one Almighty is, from whom
All things proceed, and up to him return,
If not depraved from good, created all
Such to perfection; one first matter all,
Endued with various forms, various degrees
Of substance, and, in things that live, of life;
But more refined, more spiritous and pure,
As nearer to him placed or nearer tending
Each in their several active spheres assigned,   (V. 469–477)

This view of the correlation between the height of the habitat and the nature of the habitant reflects the conceptual metaphors shown above: THE VIRTUOUS IS A CELESTIAL ENTITY and THE VICIOUS IS A TERRESTRIAL ENTITY. The habitats of the animal vehicles appearing in the story one after another make a gradual descent, a gradual increase in the distance to God, and accordingly the natures of those animals show a gradual deterioration, contributing to the structural description of Satan's nature downgraded as he gets closer to his goal.

It is to be noted that the vehicle for Satan is slightly upgraded at the time when Satan is arrested by the guardian angels and brought to the archangel Gabriel. His figure is compared to a proud steed, not a non-blooded creature but a four-footed animal, as described in quotation (26), and when he tries to intimidate his interrogator, to mountains named Teneriff and Atlas, notable for their height, as in (27):

(26) The Fiend replied not, overcome with rage;

But like a *proud steed* reined, went haughty on,
Champing his iron curb. (IV. 857–859)

(27) Satan, alarmed,
Collecting all his might, dilated stood,
Like *Teneriff or Atlas*, unremoved: (IV. 985–987)

Since he escaped from Hell, he has continued the solitary journey, bending his efforts to attain the evil goal all by himself, and simply getting worse and worse in nature. Now, coming face to face with Gabriel, one of his ex-companions and an opponent in the Angelic war, he stirs up the pride of a high-ranking angel once again. It is probably this change of his mental state that has caused the subtle change of the rank of the vehicle in the opposite direction.

6.3.6 Phase 6: Satan's temptation accomplished

Satan escapes from Gabriel and the guardian angels at the end of the previous phase, and the sixth phase, described in Book IX, starts with his return into Paradise. As a result of careful consideration of every creature in terms of a tool for his purpose, he comes to realize that the serpent is the most opportune for his insidious wiles, and determines to enter its body:

(28) Thus the orb he roamed
With narrow search, and with inspection deep
Considered every creature, which of all
Most opportune might serve his wiles, and found
The *Serpent* subtlest beast of all the field.
Him, after long debate, irresolute
Of thoughts revolved, his final sentence chose
Fit vessel, fittest imp of fraud, in whom
To enter, and his dark suggestions hide
From sharpest sight; (IX. 82–91)

Without limbs and creeping upon the earth, the serpent holds a remarkably low rank among the animal vehicles for Satan. After the incarnation in the mean creature, Satan succeeds in making direct contact with Eve. With skillful flattery, the Tempter arouses her acute interest in the "alluring fruit" (IX 588), and in raptures leads her to the Tree of Knowledge forbidden. Quotation (29) describes this scene, where his figure is likened to a wandering fire. It is also known as "will-o'-the-wisp," "Jack-o'-lantern" or "ignis fatuus" (cf. the *OED* "wandering" 2.f, "will-o'-the-wisp," "Jack-o'-lantern, Jack-a-lantern" and "ignis fatuus"). According to the *OED*, it is a "phosphorescent light seen

CHAPTER VI CASE STUDY: LUCIFER'S METAMORPHOSIS IN MILTON'S PARADISE LOST 175

hovering or flitting over marshy ground, and supposed to be due to the spontaneous combustion of an inflammable gas (phosphuretted hydrogen) derived from decaying organic matter; popularly called *Will-o'-the-wisp*, *Jack-a-lantern*, etc. It seems to have been formerly a common phenomenon but is now exceedingly rare. When approached, the *ignis fatuus* appeared to recede, and finally to vanish, sometimes reappearing in another direction. This led to the notion that it was the work of a mischievous sprite, intentionally leading benighted travellers astray. Hence the term is commonly used allusively or fig. [i.e., figuratively] for any delusive guiding principle, hope, aim, etc." (the *OED* "ignis fatuus").

(29) Hope elevates, and joy
   Brightens his crest. As when a *wandering fire*,
   Compact of unctuous vapor, which the night
   Condenses, and the cold environs round,
   Kindled through agitation to a flame
   (Which oft, they say, some evil spirit attends),
   Hovering and blazing with delusive light,
   Misleads the amazed night-wanderer from his way
   To bogs and mires, and oft through pond or pool,
   There swallowed up and lost, from succor far;
   So glistered the dire Snake, and into fraud
   Led Eve, our credulous mother, to the Tree
   Of Prohibition, root of all our woe;   (IX. 633–645)

The *OED* picks up this passage above as the first example for "wandering fire" (the *OED* "wandering" 2.f.), and the definition column for this phrase gives no other sense but "Will-o'-the-wisp." The global search for this item in the whole dictionary (the *OED2 on CD-ROM*) reveals that it appears only twice, under the headword "wandering" (just mentioned above), and in the quotation "Floating bodies of fire .. the ignis fatuus, or wandering fire." (1774 Goldsm. *Nat. Hist.* (1862) I. xxi. 134) under the headword "ignis fatuus," demonstrating that this dictionary takes the sense of "wandering fire" as a phosphorescent light seen hovering or flitting over marshy ground, and nothing else. However, in the text of *Paradise Lost* this phrase appears at one further point, i.e., in the morning hymn by Adam and Eve in Book V, where it refers to a planet, as follows:

> (30) And ye five other *wandering Fires*, that move
> In mystic dance, not without song, resound
> His praise who out of Darkness called up Light. (V. 177–179)

Verity (ed. 1910) mentions the referent of "five other wandering Fires," stating that "He has already mentioned the Sun, Moon (then reckoned planets) and Venus (166–70): hence only four planets remain — Mercury, Mars, Jupiter and Saturn. Possibly M. [i.e., Milton] by a mere error said five instead of four (which Bentley read); but I think that he intended to include Venus again." Assuming the validity of this statement, the readers, by comparing their orisons in (30) with the scene of Satan's temptation quoted in (29), can interpret the devotions addressed to the planets, especially Venus, as indicative of an ironic fate of the bright star and the two earnest and innocent prayers themselves. That is to say, their solemn request to praise the glorious Maker would not be answered; instead, Venus or Lucifer, called a "wandering fire" in the hymn, is tragically doomed to curse God and would soon turn into a damnable "wandering fire," lead Eve into temptation, and make her fall together with her husband. "Wandering fire" with these conflicting senses symbolizes Satan's contradictory (or "oxymoronic," as it were) nature, that is, both a shining archangel and a shameless apostate.

The word "planet" etymologically represents "a *wanderer*" (cf. the *OED* "planet" *n.* 1). In this epic Milton himself describes the paths of planets on the celestial sphere as "Their *wandering* course, now high, now low, then hid, / Progressive, retrograde, or standing still" (VIII. 126–127). The fact that Satan was called by the name of a planet implies that he is a "wandering" being from the beginning, who is destined to wander from the right path that an angel should take. He is originally a wanderer in Heaven, and is later degraded to a wanderer on the earth. Similarly, at the very end of the epic, the fallen pair Adam and Eve leave Paradise and take their solitary way "with *wandering* steps" (XII. 648).

6.3.7 Phase 7: Satan's return to Hell and divine punishment inflicted upon him

The last phase of Satan's story is described in Book X. After he succeeds in making Eve commit the sin and witnesses her making her husband commit the same sin in turn, he leaves Paradise for Hell to inform his followers on his success. On his way, he meets his children Sin and Death, who have just built a broad bridge over Chaos to make the way from Hell to the place of Man to and fro. They see their parent in disguise, which they easily penetrate:

(31) And now their way to Earth they had descried,
   To Paradise first tending, when, behold
   Satan, in likeness of an *Angel bright*,
   Betwixt the Centaur and the Scorpion steering
   His zenith, while the Sun in Aries rose!
   Disguised he came; but those his children dear
   Their parent soon discerned, though in disguise.   (X. 325–331)

Satan has so far changed his appearance various ways in order to deceive his enemies and his preys. His figure in disguise has been gradually degraded: from a pretense of a cherub, through four-footed animals, to the incarnation in a serpent. However, now in the scene of reunion with his children, his appearance is drastically upgraded to a bright angel. It is noteworthy that, although his disguise has been wholly successful, now he is correctly identified by his children. The failure is probably caused by his true figure, which is too ugly because of his sinful deed in Paradise and is completely different from that of an angel (though once he was *actually* a bright angel). Conversely, his success in disguise of mean animals so far demonstrates that his pretense is *not* in fact a pretense but what shows his true character. In fact, in the fifth phase, his ugliness is already indicated by the guardian angel Zephon, who states that "Think not, revolted Spirit, thy shape the same, / Or undiminished brightness, to be known / As when thou stood'st in Heaven upright and pure. / That glory then, when thou no more wast good, / Departed from thee; and thou resemblest now / Thy sin and place of doom obscure and foul" (IV. 835–840), making Satan grieve over the loss of his brightness ("Abashed the Devil stood, / And felt how awful goodness is, and saw / Virtue in her shape how lovely — saw, and pined / His loss; but chiefly to find here observed / His lustre visibly impaired" (IV. 846–850)).

Arriving at Hell, Satan sits on the high throne without being noticed by any angels who have all been waiting for the return of their great Adventurer, and amazes them by suddenly emitting the bright light, as in quotation (32):

(32) Down a while
   He sat, and round about him saw, unseen.
   At last, as from a cloud, his fulgent head
   And shape *star-bright* appeared, or *brighter*, clad
   With what permissive glory since his fall
   Was left him, or *false glitter*. All amazed
   At that so sudden blaze, the Stygian throng
   Bent their aspect, and whom they wished beheld,
   Their mighty Chief returned: loud was the acclaim.   (X. 447–455)

His brilliance, described as "star-bright ... or brighter," is also actually "false" glitter. Quotations (31) and (32) show that his attempt to pretend a celestial or shining being is fruitless and his figure no longer merits the metaphoric conceptions VIRTUE AS LIGHT or THE VIRTUOUS AS A CELESTIAL ENTITY, now that he has accomplished his vicious purpose, i.e., corruption of Man.

In full assembly Satan triumphantly relates his success against Man, but, instead of applause, he receives a dismal hiss by all his audience. Soon he notices that he as well as his followers are all transformed to serpents:

(33) He wondered, but not long
    Had leisure, wondering at himself now more.
    His visage drawn he felt to sharp and spare,
    His arms clung to his ribs, his legs entwining
    Each other, till, supplanted, down he fell,
    A *monstrous serpent* on his belly prone,
    Reluctant, but in vain; a greater power
    Now ruled him, punished in the shape he sinned,
    According to his doom. He would have spoke,
    But hiss for hiss returned with forked tongue
    To forked tongue; for now were all transformed
    Alike, to serpents all, as accessories
    To his bold riot.   (X. 509–521)

The transformation described in quotation (33) is intrinsically different from his pretense of something or the resemblance to a vehicle in a simile. It is a punishment "in the shape he sinned" (line 516) given by the "greater power" (line 515). This penalty inflicted by the Almighty God in the last phase of Satan's story has brought a perfect accord between the rebel's appearance and his wicked nature.

6.4 Metaphor and Satan's emotion

In last section the rebel's story was divided into seven phases, and a detailed observation was made about his mental and physical changes according to his acts. It has revealed that the fourth phase is the turning point of his revenge on God, where his arrival at the cosmos and at the earth considerably enhances the possibility for achievement of his goal, and the vehicles for his figure turn from celestial to terrestrial entities accordingly. From this phase on, the readers see several scenes where Satan clearly manifests his strong feelings. Here I will closely look at these scenes, considering how his feelings are related to the development of the story and to the conceptual metaphors which form the background of the story.

6.4.1 Satan's awareness of falling down and his anguish (1)

In the fifth phase of the story, Satan reaches the earth "inflamed with rage" (IV. 9), and is just about to put his plan into practice, when suddenly feelings of "horror and doubt" (IV. 18) distract his thoughts. They awaken his conscience, which relentlessly reminds him of the deterioration of his moral nature through his past, present, and future:

(34) Now conscience wakes despair
 That slumbered; wakes the bitter memory
 Of what he was, what is, and what must be
 Worse; of worse deeds worse sufferings must ensue! (IV. 23–26)

Revolving upon his profound guilt, he talks to himself with sighs. Quotations (35) and (36) are parts of his long, plaintive monologue. As shown in (35), his words are filled with remorse for his cruel action against God, who is entirely free from fault and instead deserves Satan's gratitude, praise, and service. Lamenting his misery, he confusedly pronounces a curse on his Creator who lavished love upon him, and on himself who acted against the Creator. This mental state is characterized by himself as Hell in his mind, the inner space that gives him far greater pain than the actual Hell, as described in (36).

(35) Ah, wherefore? He deserved no such return
 From me, whom he created what I was
 In that bright eminence, and with his good
 Upbraided none; nor was his service hard.
 What could be less than to afford him praise,
 The easiest recompense, and pay him thanks,
 How due? (IV. 42–48)
(36) Me miserable! which way shall I fly
 Infinite wrath and infinite despair?
 Which way I fly is Hell; myself am Hell;
 And, in the lowest deep, a lower deep
 Still threatening to devour me opens wide,
 To which the Hell I suffer seems a Heaven. (IV. 73–78)

Thus Satan expresses an intense conflict between his hatred and his regret. These opposing emotions correspond to his double character as a high-ranking angel and the Adversary of God and Man, giving the readers an impression that he is quite similar to the human being, an alloy of good and evil. Here an especially noteworthy mental state of Satan is his awareness that he is still falling headlong, in spite of his followers' worship of him on the throne of Hell:

(37) Ay me! they little know
    How dearly I abide that boast so vain,
    Under what torments inwardly I groan.
    While they adore me on the throne of Hell,
    With diadem and sceptre high advanced,
    The lower still I fall, only supreme
    In misery: such joy ambition finds! (IV. 86–92)

What he calls falling, needless to say, is not a movement as a physical phenomenon. His downward motion was already complete when he fell from Heaven to Hell over a period of nine days (cf. VI. 871). The "fall" he recognizes above is a metaphoric understanding of the continual change of his moral nature. It is to be characterized as a conceptual movement structured by the metaphors THE VIRTUOUS IS A CELESTIAL ENTITY and THE VICIOUS IS A TERRESTRIAL ENTITY.

Seized with "infinite wrath and infinite despair" (line 74), and urged by his consciousness of his inner Hell (cf. "myself am Hell" in (36)) and by his awareness that he is still now falling lower and lower in his inner space, Satan says farewell to emotions of hope, fear, and remorse ("So farewell hope, and, with hope farewell fear, / Farewell remorse! All good to me is lost; / Evil, be thou my Good:" (IV. 108–110)).[19] His parting from those favorable emotions brings about a further deterioration of himself as depicted by the animal vehicles.

6.4.2 Satan's awareness of falling down and his anguish (2)

As observed in Section 6.3.6, Satan determines to enter the body of a serpent in the sixth phase when the achievement of his goal is close at hand. The incarnation in a serpent is essentially different from other changes of his figure: it is neither a similized state in which he *looks* like a serpent, nor a disguise by which he *pretends* to be a serpent. It is to *be united* with a serpent. Satan so far has been likened to, or has pretended, various animals such as quadrupeds, raptors, and a toad. Now he is about to turn into a still meaner creature, not into anything *like* the creature but into the creature *itself*. Immediately after this agonizing decision, Satan speaks out his "bursting passion" that explodes from his "inward grief" (IX. 97–98), expressing his view of this incarnation as a further fall:

(38) O *foul descent*! that I, who erst contended
   With Gods to sit the highest, am now constrained
   Into a beast, and, mixed with bestial slime,
   This essence to incarnate and imbrute,
   That to the highth of deity aspired!   (IX. 163–167)

He knows well that the incarnation in a serpent is the most effective way to achieve his purpose, as observed in Section 6.3.6, but even so the proud memory of the angelic war in which he challenged the Supreme makes him reluctant to mix himself with "bestial slime." Rethinking that he first has to descend to the basest being in order to soar up and accomplish the ambition and carry out revenge (as described in (39)), he finally turns into the base creature.

(39) But what will not ambition and revenge
   Descend to? Who aspires must *down* as *low*
   As *high* he *soared*, obnoxious, first or last,
   To basest things.   (IX. 168–171)

6.4.3 Satan wandering between good and evil

As observed above, Satan, enduring anguish caused by his awareness of falling, incessantly strives to carry out revenge on God, and gradually degrades his own figure as he gets closer to his goal and gains his viciousness accordingly. His step-by-step deterioration, recognized by Satan himself as "falling," is readily comprehensible to the readers owing to the various vehicles, each of which is successively replaced to a degraded one, regarded as "lower" in the hierarchy of creatures.

A detailed observation of the similes describing his figure, however, reveals that sometimes the vehicle is upgraded, namely, from the mean animal to the human being. The upgrade reflects the solitary rebel's wavering emotions.

Quotation (40) represents a scene in which Satan, who has reached the cosmos in the fourth phase, finds a gold flight of stairs up to the gate of Heaven. Standing on the lower stair, he looks down at the magnificent view of the entire world created by God.

(40) As when a *scout*,
   Through dark and desert ways with peril gone
   All night, at last by break of cheerful dawn
   Obtains the brow of some high-climbing hill,
   Which to his eye discovers unaware
   The goodly prospect of some foreign land

>   First seen, or some renowned metropolis
>   With glistering spires and pinnacles adorned,
>   Which now the rising sun gilds with his beams;
>   Such wonder seized, though after Heaven seen,
>   The Spirit malign, but much more envy seized,
>   At sight of all this World beheld so fair.   (III. 543–554)

Satan at that time has already been likened to a vulture (cf. quotation (17)), whereas the vehicle in this scene in (40) is a scout, who on a dangerous mission makes a night journey and, at dawn on the summit of a high hill, is captivated by a beautiful view of a foreign land or of a metropolis glittering in the morning sunlight. Just like him, Satan is fascinated by the outlook over the cosmic space, a beautiful product of his adversary, the Creator.

The following quotation describes how Satan, who has already turned into a serpent in the sixth phase, sees Eve at a flowery plat in the early morning.

(41) Much he the place admired, the person more.
>   As *one* who, long in populous city pent,
>   Where houses thick and sewers annoy the air,
>   Forth issuing on a summer's morn, to breathe
>   Among the pleasant villages and farms
>   Adjoined, from each thing met conceives delight —
>   The smell of grain, or tedded grass, or kine,
>   Or dairy, each rural sight, each rural sound —
>   If chance with nymph-like step fair virgin pass,
>   What pleasing seemed for her now pleases more,
>   She most, and in her look sums all delight:
>   Such pleasure took the Serpent to behold
>   This flowery plat, the sweet recess of Eve
>   Thus early, thus alone.   (IX. 444–457)

Here Satan's delight at the beautiful garden and the fair woman is compared to that of a traveler, who is tired of a densely populated city and visits pleasant villages and farms, where he sees a fair maiden whose look is the essence of delight felt in the entire rural sight. Watching Eve up close and deeply moved by her divine beauty and graceful innocence, Satan temporarily forgets his fierce intent and evil emotions altogether; namely, guile, hate, envy, and revenge:

(42) Her heavenly form
>   Angelic, but more soft and feminine,
>   Her graceful innocence, her every air

>   Of gesture or least action, overawed
>   His malice, and with rapine sweet bereaved
>   His fierceness of the fierce intent it brought.
>   That space the Evil One abstracted stood
>   From his own evil, and for the time remained
>   Stupidly good, of enmity disarmed,
>   Of guile, of hate, of envy, of revenge.   (IX. 457–466)

Each of the similes in the quotations above adopts a person as a vehicle, i.e., a person who innocently feels delighted at something beautiful. These vehicles effectively show that Satan is never completely evil but occasionally — and fleetingly — regains his original virtue. His character somewhat resembles that of the human being, who has both virtue and vice. For Milton, the human being is "the master-work" of the Creator, "the end" of all the creatures, provided with "sanctity of reason," "self-knowing," gratefully acknowledging "whence his good descends," and adoring and worshiping "God Supreme, who made him chief of all his works" (cf. VII. 505–516). After the trespass into our cosmos, Satan is sometimes likened to a human who is endowed with this good nature, whereas he is chiefly compared to base creatures. These fluctuating vehicles representing the gradual change of his figure and his nature (i.e., a vulture (lower) — a scout (upper) — base beasts and lower creatures (still lower) — a traveler (upper) — a wandering fire (lower than ever)) correspond to his tragic destiny, in which he is unable to avoid falling, wavering between good and evil just like the planet which follows a "wandering" course (cf. Section 6.3.6). This correspondence is indicated in Figure 6.2, where the change of hierarchical rank of Satan's figure shown in graphic form is coherently mapped onto the moral tones of his character.

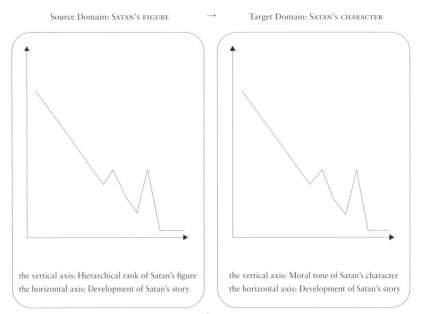

Figure 6.2: Metaphoric description of Satan's fall

6.5 The power of Milton's rhetoric

The final section focuses on a scene immediately before Satan obtains his goal. Disguised as a serpent he has approached Eve, and in the shape like a wandering fire he has led her to the Forbidden Tree. But she, giving a glance at the tree, tells him that God commanded her and her husband not to taste nor touch that tree. The Tempter, getting even bolder, attempts to persuade her to eat the forbidden fruit. His manner of speaking to her is compared to a zealous orator in an ancient city of Athens or Rome, who displays skillful methods of attracting attention of his audience even before his speech begins:

> (43) She scarce had said, though brief, when now more bold
> The Tempter, but, with show of zeal and love
> To Man, and indignation at his wrong,
> New part puts on, and, as to passion moved,
> Fluctuates disturbed, yet comely, and in act
> Raised, as of some great matter to begin.
> As when of old some *orator* renowned
> In Athens or free Rome, where eloquence

> Flourished, since mute, to some great cause addressed,
> Stood in himself collected, while each part,
> Motion, each act, won audience ere the tongue
> Sometimes in highth began, as no delay
> Of preface brooking through his zeal of right:
> So standing, moving, or to highth upgrown,
> The Tempter, all impassioned, thus began: (IX. 664–678)

The deed of the Enemy of Mankind described in this quotation is the final trigger for Eve's transgression. Why is a human vehicle, not an animal one, adopted to describe this vicious act? It does not appear to be suited to the conceptual basis of the Satan's story, the coherent mappings which relate a hierarchy of creatures to moral nature.

A clue is provided by the term *act* in the quotation above (line 668). Satan in this scene is about to perform an "act," to play a role of one who feels indignation at the wrong done to the Man. This performance reminds us of a scene in the fourth phase, where he borrows a visage of a cherub and attempts to deceive Uriel the archangel with his eloquence, playing a role of an admirer of the "wondrous" works by God, and saying that "Unspeakable desire to see and know / All these his wondrous works, but chiefly Man, / His chief delight and favor, him for whom / All these his works so wondrous he ordained, / Hath brought me from the quires of Cherubim / Alone thus wandering" (III. 662–667). In explanation of the reason why Uriel, the "sharpest-sighted Spirit of all in Heaven" (III. 691), is artfully deceived by "the false dissembler" (III. 681), Milton emphasizes the mysterious power of hypocrisy, stating that "neither man nor angel can discern / Hypocrisy — the only evil that walks / *Invisible*, except to God alone, / By his permissive will, through Heaven and Earth" (III. 682–685). Similarly, the scene described in quotation (43) displays Satan's hypocrisy, his pretense of expressing righteous indignation, by which his true feelings or true intentions are "invisible" to Eve.

That offers a hint as to the choice of the vehicle in the scene of Satan's final temptation. So far, we have been given various vehicles each of which is replaced by another, and with the aid of those gradually demoted vehicles we have perceived the deterioration of Satan's nature as if we are seeing a falling object with our own eyes. Thus the conceptual metaphors let the readers perceive abstract, invisible conceptions like good and evil as if they were facing something visible. Those successive vehicles give us, as it were, the eyes of God that see through the internal change of the character. In the scene described in quotation (43), however, the vehicle serves as a smoke screen. An orator is different from other persons adopted as vehicles so far, each of whom has been innocently pleased with fair scenery or a fair woman. A good orator is a man of irresistible eloquence, whose audience is overwhelmed by his compelling appeal and is *unable to see* whether he gives expression to his true feelings or he employs sophistry. With the apt comparison given to an orator, not to a wolf or a raptor or a snake clearly indicative of vice, we come to be momentarily *blind* to the character's truth. At that moment we lose the eyes of God that penetrate the true nature of the object, and we are forced to see the Tempter from the same point of view as of Eve who is unable to ascertain the truth of his words, being puzzled over but fascinated by them. In other words, we are forced to experience vicariously the moment of her Fall.

That is the reason why an orator is adopted here as a vehicle. It functions as a device for making the readers experience an invisible vice of hypocrisy together with Eve. Following the figure of Satan and the wandering course of his journey of revenge, and witnessing Man's transgression, the readers enjoy Miltonic power of rhetoric that provides us with, and sometimes deprives us of, an insight into the nature of the subject.

Notes

1 The remaining two functions given by Whaler (1931) are to "relieve" the readers in the midst of a scene of strife, pain, or crisis, which is characteristically Homeric; and to "please" them, as frequently seen in William Browne, by inserting vignettes of rural life more for the sake of their intrinsic charm than for their application of the story. Whaler states that Milton exhibits the former sparingly, while he never does the latter. We should note, however, that Milton also gives "pleasing" expressions in which a pastoral scene is depicted. See quotation (41) in Section 6.4.3.

2 Milton refers to his own similes in the epic by having the angel Michael tell Adam that "what surmounts the reach / Of human sense I shall delineate so, / By likening spiritual to corporal forms" (V. 571–573). Major descriptions in *Paradise Lost* are of what happened in Heaven before and immediately after the Creation, and the tragic destiny of Adam and Eve, the "ancestors" of the human race, so most of the vehicles adopted in the similes refer to things which may be familiar to the readers but do not exist yet at the time of the narrative, hence "prolepsis."

3 The texts of *Paradise Lost* quoted in this chapter are from John A. Himes ed. (1898).

4 The epic starts with a description of Satan in the Hell. The preceding event of the Angelic War before he was cast out of Heaven is delayed and described in Books V and VI.

5 According to a 17th-century collocations dictionary compiled by Poole (1657), a contemporary of Milton, the term "lucifer" collocates with "watchfull," "ushering," "blushing," "radiant," "beaming," "bright," and "Aurora's harbinger," which together indicate a connotative image of the term. This image of brightness is approximately consistent with a description of the morning star in *Paradise Lost*, published ten years later: "Fairest of Stars, last in the train of Night, / If better thou belong not to the Dawn, / Sure pledge of day, that crown'st the smiling morn / With thy bright circlet, praise him in thy sphere / While day arises, that sweet hour of prime" (V.166–170).

6 According to Tillyard (1943, Ch. 5), in the Elizabethan period the upper regions in the sky were esteemed to be filled with a pure and clear gas called "ether," brilliantly shining day and night.
7 These vehicles are also related to GOD IS UP mentioned by Kövecses (2002).
8 These metaphors are related to DEPRAVITY IS DOWN (Lakoff and Johnson 1980) and DOING EVIL IS FALLING (Kövecses 2005).
9 According to A. W. Verity ed. (1910), *Earth-born* is defined as "the Giants; like the Titans ... they were reputed the offspring of Uranus and Ge (Earth)," and *Briareos* and *Typhon* as "the former ..., being the son of Uranus, is meant to represent the Titans — the latter, the Giants" (p. 375).
10 Leviathan in Isaiah is identified with a serpent, that pursues a similar destiny to Satan: "In that day the Lord with his sore and great and strong sword shall punish leviathan the piercing serpent, even leviathan that crooked serpent; and he shall slay the dragon that is in the sea" (Isaiah 27.1).
11 "Argo" in the quotation (16) refers to a vessel in which Jason, a Greek mythological hero, and the 50 Argonauts sailed to fetch the Golden Fleece (cf. A.W. Verity ed., 1910, p. 427). Book II also contains several other expressions which compare Satan to a vessel and his journey to a sea voyage.
12 Edwards (1999) in Chapter 5 gives a detailed review of arguments about the mythical beast griffin, i.e., its reality, the propriety of using the fabulous creature in a simile, and its symbolic potentiality and significance, by Milton scholars, philosophers and scientists including Kester Svendsen, Francis Bacon, and Thomas Browne. Among them, Browne's treatment of the griffin in *Pseudodoxia Epidemica* (1646) especially is closely connected with our discussion on the connotative meaning of the legendary vehicle. He speculates on its usefulness as a symbol, stating that it is "an Embleme of valour and magnanimity, as being compounded of the Eagle and Lion, the noblest animals in their kinds."
13 See Chapter V, where I discuss the *OED* definition and the cultural implication of "lion."
14 A gryphon is a monstrous animal in Greek mythology, whereas in Christianity it is emblematic of Christ, as in *Purgatorio, Divina Comedia* by Dante Alighieri: "Lo spazio dentro a lor quattro contenne / un carro, in su due rote, trionfale, / ch'al collo d'un *grifon* tirato venne. / Esso tendea in su l'una a l'altr'ale / tra la mezzana e le tre liste, / si ch'a nulla fendendo facea male. / Tanto salivan, che non eran viste; / le membra d'oro avea, quanto era uccello, / e bianche l'altre di vermiglio miste." (The space within the four of them contained a car triumphal, upon two wheels, which came drawn at the neck of *grifon*. And he stretched upwards one wing and the other, between the middle and the three and three bands, so that he did hurt to none by cleaving. So high they rose that they were not seen; his members had he of gold, so far as he was a bird, and the others white mingled with vermilion.) (Canto XXIX, 106–114: pp. 368–370, *The Purgatorio of Dante Alighieri*. ed. by Israel Gollancz. 1926. London: J. M. Dent & Sons).
15 Milton's mention of a sunspot, an astronomer, and an "optic tube" indicates that he is well informed of the contemporary knowledge of science. According to Verity (ed. 1910), "probably he is thinking of Galileo, who in 1609 constructed a telescope ("optic tube") by which the spots on the solar disc were perceptible."
16 Immediately before his trespass on Paradise, Satan is pleased with the sweet odor from Paradise ("So entertained those odorous sweets the Fiend / Who came their bane, though with them better pleased / Than Asmodeus with the fishy fume / That drove him, though enamored, from the spouse / Of Tobit's son, and with a vengeance sent / From Media post to Egypt, there fast bound."(IV. 166–171)). Here the poet mentions Asmodeus, one of the fallen angels in the Apocryphal *Book of Tobit*, who is fascinated by the fishy fume. The name of the

lustful demon evokes an association of a cormorant in anticipation: for Satan the odor from Paradise is like the odor of fish that comes to a cormorant, stimulating the appetite instead of nauseating (cf. Himes, ed., 1898, p. 329).

17 The birds of evil omen are described in Isaiah and Zephaniah as follows: "And the streams thereof shall be turned into pitch, and the dust thereof into brimstone, and the land thereof shall become burning pitch. / It shall not be quenched night nor day; the smoke thereof shall go up for ever: from generation to generation it shall lie waste; none shall pass through it for ever and ever. / But *the cormorant and the bittern* shall possess it; the owl also and the raven shall dwell in it: and he shall stretch out upon it the line of confusion, and the stones of emptiness." (Isaiah 34, 9–11.), and "And flocks shall lie down in the midst of her, all the beasts of the nations: both *the cormorant and the bittern* shall lodge in the upper lintels of it; their voice shall sing in the windows; desolation shall be in the thresholds: for he shall uncover the cedar work" (Zephaniah 2.14).

18 The quotation (25) is a part of words by Raphael the archangel, who explains to Adam the relationships among all the creatures, and between the nature and the Creator. Adam correctly understands his explanation and aptly calls the relationships "the scale of Nature," stating that "O favorable Spirit, propitious guest, / Well hast thou taught the way that might direct / Our knowledge, and the scale of Nature set / From centre to circumference, whereon, / In contemplation of created things, / By steps we may ascend to God" (V. 507–512). This notion of the scale is to be characterized as Miltonic version of the conception of "the Great Chain of Being" mentioned in Chapter V.

19 It can be gathered from Satan's deep despair and his farewell to hope, fear, and remorse that these emotions are closely related to each other. On the relationships among the emotion concepts of hope, fear and despair, see Chapter III.

Conclusion:
Entering in at the Strait Gate

The present study investigated the structure of conceptual metaphors for the emotions. I used two types of linguistic data: a large corpus (BNC) and smaller corpora such as literary works and dictionaries, both of which are suitable for a cognitive metaphor study in that they have synchronically and/or diachronically infiltrated into people's mind. Focusing on both ordinary and literary language data, I attempted to take account of the systematic nature of metaphor in language and thought.

Zoltán Kövecses, a leading researcher on metaphors for emotion for the last two decades, has regarded the conceptual domain of CONTAINER as the major metaphorical source domain, offering a cognitive model indicating correspondences between thermodynamics of a fluid in a container and generation of emotion (1990, 2000, etc.). The research of mine, however, has examined a substantial number of corpus examples in the form of "[source-domain nominal] + *of* + [target-domain nominal]," and has revealed that the source domain most frequently mapped onto the target domain of EMOTION IS NATURAL PHENOMENA, and that the major source sub-domain is A HUGE MASS OF MOVING WATER IN THE NATURAL WORLD like SEA and RIVER.

The first half of the present study, therefore, concentrated on the conceptual domain of NATURAL PHENOMENA. In Chapter I, I studied on WATER metaphors describing the mental activity of emotion in English poetry. Detailed analyses of poetic works have revealed that poets use conceptual domain of WATER as a source for A MENTAL ACTIVITY and that the entities belonging to the domain like STAGNANT WATER, RUNNING WATER, SURGING WAVES, EBB AND FLOW OF THE TIDE, A WHIRL, and OVERFLOWING WATER are consistently mapped onto mental activities.

Chapter II reported a corpus study on conventional metaphors for emotion containing both source and target-domain lexemes in the conventional form of two nominals connected by the preposition "*of*." Through observation of a number of citations retrieved from BNC, I revealed that the prevalent source domain in conventional metaphors for emotion is A HUGE MASS OF MOVING WATER IN THE NATURAL WORLD, and the specific emotions close to the emotion prototype are ANXIETY, RELIEF, DESIRE, and PLEASURE. The results offered an alternative to the long-accepted idea on the prototype of emotion formed by the introspective method adopted in traditional cognitive linguistic studies.

Chapter III concentrated on specific emotions like PLEASURE, SADNESS, HOPE, FEAR, and DESPAIR. I adopted the same corpus methodology as I did in the preceding chapter for retrieval and analysis of conventional metaphors used to talk about those emotions, classifying them into four domains subordinate to the source domain NATURAL PHENOMENA; i.e., AIR, WATER, FIRE, and EARTH. This study indicated that semantic relationships between antonymous pairs of emotion concepts can be characterized in terms of whether or not a particular aspect of a source domain, or the domain itself, is used in metaphorical mappings. The antonymous relationships between PLEASURE and SADNESS are demonstrable, for example, by the presence and absence of citations derived from the source domain FIRE. It also revealed that an unexpected relationship of antonymy between two emotion concepts like HOPE and FEAR emerges through identification of the presence and absence of source domain words in corpus citations, and that an unexpected relationship of synonymy between two emotion concepts like FEAR and DESPAIR is also acknowledged through the examination of source domain words in corpus citations.

The second half of the present study focused on the conceptual domain of ANIMAL as a source used to describe emotions. The study showed how various qualities of various animals are linked to aspects of human emotions in metaphorical mappings. Chapter IV observed animal metaphors in English idioms and poetic texts retrieved by dictionaries, and considered a systematic nature of correspondences between source and target domains. A detailed study of dictionaries revealed that there are many animal idioms for PLEASURE AND HAPPINESS, ANGER, and FEAR, while idioms for SADNESS AND UNHAPPINESS and ANXIETY are scarce; and that typical animal idioms for emotions include vehicles related to animals familiar to daily lives of human beings, i.e., pets, domestic fowls, and small creatures, whereas large animals are not frequently adopted as vehicles of animal idioms. And through a study of animal metaphors in poetry I found that traits of song birds present a remarkable contrast with those of carnivorous birds, and that the antonymous relation between those two types of birds is coherently, and tenaciously, mapped onto the domain of EMOTION, exhibiting correspondences between SONG BIRDS and JOY AND HOPE, and between CARNIVOROUS BIRDS and FEAR.

Chapter V was a study on quadruped metaphors, with special reference to the Great Chain of Being, a widespread cultural model providing a background to European literature and the history of ideas. In that model the human is regarded as superior to the animal. A close observation of metaphoric senses of specific animal terms and conventional expressions evoking animal behaviors, however, revealed that our understanding of the animal sometimes releases itself from the spell of the Great Chain of Being, when bestiality, which is supposed to be inferior, is placed on an unexpectedly higher position than humanity in the hierarchy of creatures.

Chapter VI was a case study on *Paradise Lost*. Focusing on a number of epic similes in the Miltonic work, which vividly describe how Satan attempts to take revenge on God and gradually changes his own figure and emotion as he gets closer to his goal, I postulated conceptual metaphors indicating a Christian view of the world, and investigated a relationship between those conceptual metaphors and the descriptions of the fallen angel's physical and internal change. The vehicles describing them fluctuate in terms of the hierarchical rank of creatures in the Christian world picture, coherently corresponding to the moral tones of his character and indicating that he is unable to avoid "falling," wavering between good and evil just like the planet which follows a "wandering" course, as his former name Lucifer tragically suggests.

Much more still remains to be done. Concerning NATURAL PHENOMENA metaphors I focused on a linguistic pattern of "[source-domain nominal] + *of* + [target-domain nominal]," and have not yet observed other conventional patterns such as verbal metaphors like "emotion *surged up* within her." The study of ANIMAL metaphors reported here is not an exhaustive research either. More comprehensive collection of animal terms used to talk about human emotions might trigger another discovery and understanding of our conceptualization of animals and metaphoric comprehension of emotions. But a study of this scale could provide a new perspective on cognitive mechanisms of conceptual metaphors for emotions, with an important implication that we linguists should not attempt to enter a "wide gate." Although the researcher's own introspection is highly accessible and seemingly the most convenient research tool, it does not necessarily provide appropriate data for the cognitive metaphor theory. Corpus analyses, on the other hand, reveal some semantic relationships between concepts that are hard to notice by unsupported intuition. We should also notice that although a software program can process a large number of citations in a corpus swiftly and accurately, careful study of the meaning and the use of metaphorical expressions can only be done by a human researcher, not by a computer. We should enter in at "the strait gate" and follow the "narrow" way. Only close and diligent investigation into authentic data appearing in large and small corpora brings important insights, and makes a valuable contribution to cognitive linguistic theories on metaphor.

Bibliography

Aristotle (1963) [*Poetics*]. *Aristotle's Poetics, Demetrius on Style, Longinus on the Sublime*, translated by John Warrington. London and New York: Everyman's Library.
Barnes, Jonathan (1984) *The Complete Works of Aristotle (The revised Oxford translation)*. Vols. 1–2. New Jersey: Princeton University Press.
Bednarek, Monica (2008) *Emotion Talk across Corpora*. Basingstoke: Palgrave Macmillan.
Black, Max (1962) *Models and Metaphors: Studies in Language and Philosophy*. Ithaca and London: Cornell University Press.
Black, Max (1979) "More about Metaphor." Andrew Ortony (ed.), 19–43.
Cameron, Lynne (2003) *Metaphor in Educational Discourse*. London: Continuum.
Charteris-Black, Jonathan (2002) "Second Language Figurative Proficiency: A Comparative Study of Malay and English." *Applied Linguistics* 23: 104–133.
Charteris-Black, Jonathan (2004) *Corpus Approaches to Critical Metaphor Analysis*. Basingstoke: Palgrave Macmillan.
Cruse, D. A. (1986) *Lexical Semantics*. Cambridge: Cambridge University Press.
Cummins, Juliet Lucy (2011) "The Ecology of *Paradise Lost*," Angelica Duran (ed.), *A Concise Companion to Milton*, 161–177. West Sussex: Wiley-Blackwell.
Davidson, Donald (1978) "What Metaphors Mean." Sheldon Sacks (ed.), *On Metaphor*, 29–46. Chicago and London: The University of Chicago Press.
Deane, Paul (1988) "Polysemy and Cognition." *Lingua* 75: 325–361.
Deignan, Alice (1995) *Collins Cobuild English Guide 7: Metaphor*. London: Harper Collins.
Deignan, Alice (1997) "Metaphors of Desire." Harvey, Keith and Shalom, Celia, *Language and Desire: Encoding Sex, Romance and Intimacy*. London: Routledge.
Deignan, Alice (1999) "Metaphorical Polysemy and Paradigmatic Relations: A Corpus Study." *Word* 50: 319–338.
Deignan, Alice (2005) *Metaphor and Corpus Linguistics*. Amsterdam: John Benjamins.
Deignan, Alice (2007) "'Image' Metaphors and Connotations in Everyday Language." Francisco José Ruiz de Mendoza Ibáñez (ed.), *Annual Review of Cognitive Linguistics* 5. Amsterdam: John Benjamins.
Deignan, Alice (2008) "Corpus Linguistics and Metaphor." Gibbs, Raymond Jr. (ed.), 280–294.
Deignan, Alice and Potter, Liz (2004) "A Corpus Study of Metaphors and Metonyms in English and Italian." *Journal of Pragmatics* 36: 1231–1252.
Edwards, Karen L. (1999) *Milton and the Natural World: Science and Poetry in Paradise Lost*, Cambridge: Cambridge University Press.
Evans, Nicholas and Wilkins, David (2000) "In the Mind's Ear: The Semantic Extensions of Perception Verbs in Australian Languages." *Language* 76–3: 546–592.
Evans, Vyvyan and Green, Melanie (2006) *Cognitive Linguistics: An Introduction*. Edinburgh: Edinburgh University Press.
Fauconnier, Gilles (1985) *Mental Spaces*. Cambridge: Cambridge University Press.
Fortescue, Michael (2001) "Thought about Thought." *Cognitive Linguistics* 12: 15–45.
Fujii, Haruhiko (1974) *Time, Landscape and the Ideal Life: Studies in the Pastoral Poetry of Spenser and Milton*. Kyoto: Apollon-sha.
Gibbs, Raymond W. Jr. (1992) "What Do Idioms Really Mean?" *Journal of Memory and Language* 31: 485–506.
Gibbs, Raymond W. Jr. (1993) "Process and Products in Making Sense of Tropes." Andrew

Ortony (ed.), 2nd edition., 252–276.
Gibbs, Raymond W. Jr. (1994) *Poetics of Mind: Figurative Thought, Language, and Understanding*. Cambridge: Cambridge University Press.
Gibbs, Raymond W. Jr. (ed.) (2008) *The Cambridge Handbook of Metaphor and Thought*. Cambridge: Cambridge University Press.
Gibbs, Raymond W. Jr., Bogdanovich, Josephine M., Sykes, Feffrey R. and Barr, Dale J. (1997) "Metaphor in Idiom Comprehension." *Journal of Memory and Language* 37: 141–154.
Gibbs, Raymond W. Jr. and O'Brien, Jennifer E. (1990) "Idioms and Mental Imagery: The Metaphorical Motivation for Idiomatic Meaning." *Cognition* 36: 35–68.
Goatly, Andrew (1997) *The Language of Metaphors*. London: Routledge.
Goossens, Louis, Pauwels, Paul, Rudzka-Ostyn, Brygida, Simon-Vanderbergen, Anne-Marie and Vanparys, Johan (1995) *By Word of Mouth: Metaphor, Metonymy and Linguistic Action in a Cognitive Perspective*. Amsterdam: John Benjamins.
Grady, Joseph E. (1997) "Theories are Buildings Revisited." *Cognitive Linguistics* 8: 267–290.
Grice, H. Paul (1975) "Logic and Conversation," Peter Cole and Jerry L. Morgan (eds.), *Syntax and Semantics Vol. 3: Speech Acts*, 41–58. New York: Academic Press.
Halupka-Rešetar, Sabina and Radić, Biljana (2003) "Animal Names Used in Addressing People in Serbian," *Journal of Pragmatics* 35: 1891–1902.
Hirose, Yukio (1986) *Referential Opacity and the Speaker's Propositional Attitudes*. Tokyo: Liber Press.
Ikegami, Yoshihiko (1996) "Some Traditional Japanese Visual Tropes and their Perceptual and Experiential Bases." *Poetica* 46: 89–99.
Ingram, William and Swaim, Kathleen (eds.) (1972) *A Concordance to Milton's English Poetry*, Oxford: Oxford at the Clarendon Press.
Jackendoff, Ray (1983) *Semantics and Cognition*. Cambridge and MA: MIT Press.
Jakobson, Roman (1956) "Two Aspects of Language and Two Types of Aphasic Disturbances." R. Jakobson and M. Halle, *Foundations of Language*, 55–82. The Hague: Mouton.
Jakobson, Roman (1987) "Linguistics and Poetics." *Roman Jakobson: Language in Literature*, Krystyna Pomorska and Stephen Rudy (eds.), 62–94. Cambridge and Massachusetts: The Belknap Press of Harvard University Press.
Jäkel, Olaf (1995) "The Metaphorical Concept of Mind: 'Mental Activity Is Manipulation.'" John R. Taylor and Robert E. MacLaury (eds.), *Language and the Cognitive Construal of the World*, 197–229. Berlin: Mouton de Gruyter.
Johnson, Mark (1987) *The Body in the Mind: The Bodily Basis of Meaning, Imagination, and Reason*. Chicago: The University of Chicago Press.
Kawakami, Seisaku (1984) "Bun no Imi ni Kansuru Kiso-teki Kenkyu: Ninshiki to Hyogen no Kanren-sei wo Megutte (A Basic Study on Meaning: With a Special Reference to the Relationship between Cognition and Expression)." *Memoirs of the Faculty of Letters* 24. Osaka University.
Kawakami, Seisaku (1996) "Metaphor and Metonymy in Japanese Nicknames." *Poetica* 46: 77–99.
Koguchi, Ichiro (2005) "Reinventing Epic Simile: Wordsworth and the Miltonic Tradition." *Shi-teki Gengo to Rhetoric: Gengo Bunka Kyoudou Kenkyu Project 2004 (Poetic Language and Rhetoric: Joint Research Project on Language and Culture 2004)*, 41–54. Graduate School of Language and Culture, Osaka University.
Kövecses, Zoltán (1986) *Metaphors of Anger, Pride, and Love: a Lexical Approach to the*

Structure of Concepts. Amsterdam: John Benjamins.
Kövecses, Zoltán (1990) *Emotion Concepts*. New York: Springer-Verlag.
Kövecses, Zoltán (1991) "Happiness: A Definitional Effort." *Metaphor and Symbolic Activity* 6: 29–46.
Kövecses, Zoltán (2000) *Metaphor and Emotion: Language, Culture, and Body in Human Feeling*. Cambridge: Cambridge University Press.
Kövecses, Zoltán (2002) *Metaphor: A Practical Introduction*. Oxford: Oxford University Press.
Kövecses, Zoltán (2005) *Metaphor in Culture: Universality and Variation*. Cambridge: Cambridge University Press.
Kövecses, Zoltán (2008a) "On Metaphors for Emotion: A Reply to Ayako Omori (2008)." *Metaphor and Symbol* 23: 200–203.
Kövecses, Zoltán (2008b) "Metaphor and Emotion." Gibbs, Raymond W. Jr. (ed.), 380–396.
Lakoff, George (1987) *Women, Fire, and Dangerous Things: What Categories Reveal about the Mind*. Chicago and London: The University of Chicago Press.
Lakoff, George (1993) "The Contemporary Theory of Metaphor." Andrew Ortony (ed.) 2nd edition, 202–251.
Lakoff, George (2008) "The Neural Theory of Metaphor." Gibbs, Raymond W. Jr. (ed.), 17–38.
Lakoff, George and Johnson, Mark (1980) *Metaphors We Live By*. Chicago: The University of Chicago Press.
Lakoff, George and Johnson, Mark (1999) *Philosophy in the Flesh: The Embodied Mind and Its Challenge to Western Thought*. New York: Basic Books.
Lakoff, George and Kövecses, Zoltán (1987) "The Cognitive Model of Anger Inherent in American English," in D. Holland and N. Quinn (eds.), *Cultural Models in Language and Thought*, 195–221. Cambridge: Cambridge University Press.
Lakoff, George and Turner, Mark (1989) *More than Cool Reason: A Field Guide to Poetic Metaphor*. Chicago: The University of Chicago Press.
Langacker, Ronald W. (1995) "Raising and Transparency." *Language* 71: 1–62.
Leech, Geoffrey N. (1969) *A Linguistic Guide to English Poetry*. London and Harlow: Longmans.
Leech, Geoffrey N. (1983) *Principles of Pragmatics*. London: Longman.
Levinson, Stephen C. (1983) *Pragmatics*. Cambridge: Cambridge University Press.
Lindquist, Hans (2009) *Corpus Linguistics and the Description of English*. Edinburgh: Edinburgh University Press.
Lovejoy, Arthur O. (1936) *The Great Chain of Being: A Study of the History of an Idea*. Massachusetts: Harvard University Press. [Harper Torchbook edition, 1960, New York: Harper & Brothers.]
Lyons, John (1981) *Language and Linguistics*. Cambridge: Cambridge University Press.
McGlone, Matthew S. (1996) "Conceptual Metaphors and Figurative Language Interpretation: Food for Thought?" *Journal of Memory and Language* 35: 544–565.
Miller, George A. (1979) "Images and Models, Similes and Metaphors." Andrew Ortony (ed.), 202–250.
Moon, Rosamund (1998) *Fixed Expressions and Idioms in English: A Corpus-based Approach*. Oxford: Clarendon Press.
Nayak, Nandini P. and Gibbs, Raymond Jr. (1990) "Conceptual Knowledge in Idiom Comprehension." *Journal of Experimental Psychology: General* 119: 315–330.
Nesi, Hilary (1995) "A Modern Bestiary: A Contrastive Study of the Figurative Meanings of Animal Terms." *ELT Journal* 49/3: 272–278.

Nilsen, Alleen Pace (1996) "Of Ladybugs and Billy Goats: What Animal Species Names Tell About Human Perceptions of Gender." *Metaphor and Symbolic Activity* 11: 257–271.

Nomura, Masuhiro (1996) "The Ubiquity of the Fluid Metaphor in Japanese: a Case Study." *Poetica* 46: 41–75.

Ogden, C. K. and Richards, I. A. (1923) *The Meaning of Meaning*. London: Routledge & Kegan Paul.

Oishi, Akira (2006) "Mizu no Metaphor Saikou: Corpus wo Mochii-ta Metaphor Bunseki no Kokoromi (Water Metaphor Reconsidered: An Attempt at Corpus Analysis of Conceptual Metaphors)." *Proceedings of the Sixth Annual Meeting of the Japanese Cognitive Linguistics Association* 6: 277–286.

Omori, Ayako (1996) "Meaning and Metaphor." *Poetica* 46: 119–136.

Omori, Ayako (2004a) "A Mental Activity Is a Flow of Water: Poetic Metaphor and Cognition," Shin-ichiro Watanabe and Risto Hirtunen (eds.) *Approaches to Style and Discourse in English*, 183–207. Osaka: Osaka University Press.

Omori, Ayako (2004b) "Chi no Metaphor to Kokoro no Ninchi (Earth Metaphor and Cognition of Mind)." *Studies in Language and Culture* 30: 105–127. Graduate School of Language and Culture, Osaka University.

Omori, Ayako (2005a) "Eigo Konchu-mei no Metaphor Kenkyu (A Study on Metaphoric Use of English Terms for Insects)." *Shi-teki Gengo to Rhetoric: Gengo Bunka Kyoudou Kenkyu Project 2004 (Poetic Language and Rhetoric: Joint Research Project on Language and Culture 2004)*, 23–38. Graduate School of Language and Culture, Osaka University.

Omori, Ayako (2005b) "Joji-shi-teki Hiyu no Ninchi-teki Houryaku (Cognitive Strategy of Epic Similes: On "Reinventing Epic Simile: Wordsworth and the Miltonic Tradition")." *Shi-teki Gengo to Rhetoric: Gengo Bunka Kyoudou Kenkyu Project 2004 (Poetic Language and Rhetoric: Joint Research Project on Language and Culture 2004)*, 55–59. Graduate School of Language and Culture, Osaka University.

Omori, Ayako (2006) "Doubutsu Hiyu ni Arawareru Jusei to Ningensei (Bestiality and Humanity through Animal Metaphors)." *Shi-teki Gengo to Metaphor: Gengo Bunka Kyoudou Kenkyu Project 2005 (Poetic Language and Metaphor: Joint Research Project on Language and Culture 2005)*, 47–60. Graduate School of Language and Culture, Osaka University.

Omori, Ayako (2007a) "Shizen Genshou to Kanjou no Metaphor Shazo: 'A-Flood-of Joy' Gata no Hyougen wo Megutte (Metaphorical Mappings between Natural Phenomena and Emotion: Research into Metaphor of 'A-Flood-of-Joy' Type)." Sachiko Takagi (ed.), *Perspectives on Language and Culture*, 639–655. Tokyo: Eihosha.

Omori, Ayako (2007b) " Kanjou ni Kansuru Metaphor to Shazo no Tokusei: 'A-Flood-of-Joy' Gata no Hyougen wo Megutte (2) (Metaphor for Emotion and Properties of Mapping: Research into Metaphor of 'Flood-of-Joy', Part 2)." *Bunka to Rhetoric: Gengo Bunka Kyoudou Kenkyu Project 2006 (Culture and Rhetoric: Joint Research Project on Language and Culture 2006)*, 5–19. Graduate School of Language and Culture, Osaka University.

Omori, Ayako (2007c) "Metaphor no Dynamics to Shiten: *Paradise Lost* no Joji-shi-teki Hiyu wo Megutte (Viewpoint and Dynamics of Metaphor: With Special Reference to Epic Similes in *Paradise Lost*)." Seisaku Kawakami and Kazumi Taniguchi (eds.), *Kotoba to Shiten (Language and Viewpoint)*, 5–19. Tokyo: Eihosha.

Omori, Ayako (2008) "Emotion as a Huge Mass of Moving Water." *Metaphor and Symbol* 23: 130–146.

Omori, Ayako (2009) "Idiom to Shi-teki Hyougen ni Mirareru Doubutsu wo Baitai to Shita Kanjo Metaphor (Animal Metaphors for Emotion in Idioms and Poetic Expressions)."

Gengo no Rekishi-teki Henka to Ninchi no Wakugumi: Gengo Bunka Kyoudou Kenkyu Project 2008 *(Historic Change of Language and Cognitive Frames: Joint Research Project on Language and Culture 2008)*, 23–36. Graduate School of Language and Culture, Osaka University.

Omori, Ayako (2011) "Da-tenshi no Hen-you to Kanjou: *Paradise Lost* ni Okeru Metaphor no Kouzou-sei wo Megutte (Metamorphosis and Emotion of the Fallen Angel: Structure of Metaphors in *Paradise Lost*)." *Bunka to Rhetoric Ninshiki: Gengo Bunka Kyoudou Kenkyu Project* 2010 *(Culture and Cognition of Rhetoric: Joint Research Project on Language and Culture 2010)*, 21–34. Graduate School of Language and Culture, Osaka University.

Omori, Ayako (2012) "Conventional Metaphors for Antonymous Emotion Concepts." Paul Wilson (ed.), *Dynamicity in Emotion Concepts (Łódź Studies in Language 27)*. Frankfurt am Main: Peter Lang.

Ortony, Andrew (ed.) (1979) *Metaphor and Thought*. Cambridge: Cambridge University Press.

Ortony, Andrew (1979) "The Role of Similarity in Similes and Metaphors." Andrew Ortony (ed.), 186–201.

Ortony, Andrew (ed.) (1993) *Metaphor and Thought*, 2nd edition. Cambridge: Cambridge University Press.

Partington, Alan (1998) *Patterns and Meanings: Using Corpora for English Language Research and Teaching*. Amsterdam: John Benjamins.

Patthey-Chavez, G. Genevieve, Clare, Lindsay and Youmans, Madeleine (1996) "Watery Passion: The Struggle between Hegemony and Sexual Liberation in Erotic Fiction for Women." *Discourse and Society* 7: 77–106.

Reddy, Michael J. (1979) "The Conduit Metaphor: A Case of Frame Conflict in Our Language about Language." Andrew Ortony (ed.), 284–310.

Richards, I. A. (1936) *The Philosophy of Rhetoric*. New York: Oxford University Press.

Ricoeur, Paul (1977) *The Rule of Metaphor: Multi-disciplinary Studies of the Creation of Meaning in Language*. Translated by Robert Czerny. Toronto and Buffalo: University of Toronto Press.

Ritchie, David (2003) "'ARGUMENT IS WAR' –Or Is It a Game of Chess? Multiple Meanings in the Analysis of Implicit Metaphors." *Metaphor and Symbol* 18: 125–146.

Rohrer, Tim (1995) "The Metaphorical Logic of (Political) Rape: The New Wor(l)d Order." *Metaphor and Symbolic Activity* 10: 115–137.

Saito, Toshio, Nakamura, Junsaku and Akano, Ichiro (eds.) (2005) *Eigo Corpus Gengogaku (Kaitei Shinban) (English Corpus Linguistics (A Revised Version))*.Tokyo: Kenkyusha.

Searle, John R. (1969) *Speech Acts: An Essay in the Philosophy of Language*. Cambridge: Cambridge University Press.

Searle, John R. (1979) "Metaphor." Andrew Ortony (ed.), 92–123.

Semino, Elena (2005) "The Metaphorical Construction of Complex Domains: The Case of Speech Activity in English." *Metaphor and Symbol* 20: 35–70.

Semino, Elena (2008) *Metaphor in Discourse*. Cambridge: Cambridge University Press.

Seto, Ken-ichi (1986) *Rhetoric no Uchu (The Universe of Rhetoric)*. Tokyo: Kaimeisha.

Silaški, Nadežda and Đurović, Tatjana (2011) "The Natural Force Metaphor in the Conceptualisation of the Global Financial Crisis in English and Serbian." *Zbornik Matice Srpske za Filologiju i Lingvistiku* 54: 227–245.

Sinclair, John (1991) *Corpus, Concordance, Collocation*. Oxford: Oxford University Press.

Sperber, Dan and Wilson, Deirdre (1986) *Relevance: Communication and Cognition*. Cambridge and Massachusetts: Harvard University Press.

Stefanowitsch, Anatol and Gries, Stefan Thomas (eds.) (2006) *Corpus-Based Approaches to Metaphor and Metonymy.* Berlin: Mouton de Gruyter.

Stewart, David W. Morris, Jon and Grover, Aditi (2007) "Emotions in Advertising." Gerard J. Tellis and Tim Ambler (eds.) *The Sage Handbook of Advertising,* 120–134. Los Angeles: Sage Publications.

Sticht, Thomas G. (1979) "Educational Uses of Metaphor." Andrew Ortony (ed.), 474–485.

Stockwell, Peter (2002) *Cognitive Poetics: An Introduction.* London: Routledge.

Sweetser, Eve (1990) *From Etymology to Pragmatics.* Cambridge: Cambridge University Press.

Taylor, John R. (1989) *Linguistic Categorization: Prototypes in Linguistic Theory.* Oxford: Oxford University Press.

Tillyard, E. M. W. (1943) *The Elizabethan World Picture.* London: Chatto & Windus.

Tomlinson, Barbara (1986) "Cooking, Mining, Gardening, Hunting: Metaphorical Stories Writers Tell about Their Composing Processes." *Metaphor and Symbolic Activity* 1: 57–79.

Turner, Mark (1991) *Reading Minds: The Study of English in the Age of Cognitive Science.* Princeton: Princeton University Press.

Ullmann, Stephen (1951) *The Principles of Semantics.* Oxford: Basil Blackwell.

Ungerer, Friedrich and Schmid, Hans-Jörg (1996) *An Introduction to Cognitive Linguistics.* London: Longman.

Urban, Wilbur Marshall (1939) *Language and Reality: The Philosophy of Language and the Principles of Symbolism.* London: George Allen & Unwin.

van Teeffelen, Toine (1994) "Racism and Metaphor: The Palestinian-Israeli Conflict in Popular Literature." *Discourse and Society* 5: 381–405.

Watanabe, Hideki (1993) "Some Neglected Aspects of Meaning of the Old English Noun-Verb Combination *Egesa Stod,*" *Studies in Medieval English Language and Literature* 8: 25–37. Tokyo: The Japan Society for Medieval English Studies.

Watanabe, Hideki (2005a) *Metaphorical and Formulaic Expressions in Old English Reconsidered: With Special Reference to Poetic Compounds and Their Modern English Counterparts.* Tokyo: Eihosha.

Watanabe, Hideki (2005b) "Eigo Chou-mei no Metaphor Kenkyu (On Metaphoric Use of English Bird Terms)." *Shi-teki Gengo to Rhetoric: Gengo Bunka Kyoudou Kenkyu Project 2004 (Poetic Language and Rhetoric: Joint Research Project on Language and Culture 2004),* 1–19. Graduate School of Language and Culture, Osaka University.

Watanabe, Hideki (2006) "Inu-ka no Doubutsu-mei no Ningen Hiyu no Imi Han'i to Kouzou (Figurative Meaning and Structure of Canine Terms Used to Talk about Human Beings)." *Shi-teki Gengo to Metaphor: Gengo Bunka Kyoudou Kenkyu Project 2005 (Poetic Language and Metaphor: Joint Research Project on Language and Culture 2005),* 35–44. Graduate School of Language and Culture, Osaka University.

Watanabe, Hideki (2008) "Inu-ka Meishi, Hasei-go no Ningen Hiyu no Level to Kouzou (Figurative Meaning and Structure of Nouns and Derivatives for the Canine Used to Talk about Human Beings)." *Studies in Language and Culture* 34: 93–98. Graduate School of Language and Culture, Osaka University.

Watanabe, Hideki (2009) "Meishi Cat wo Fukumu Kotowaza, Seiku, Idiom to Ningen Hiyu-gi no Kouzou (Figurative Meaning and Structure of Proverbs, Set Phrases, and Idioms Including the Noun *Cat* Used to Talk about Human Beings). *Gengo no Rekishi-teki Henka to Ninchi no Wakugumi: Gengo Bunka Kyoudou Kenkyu Project 2008 (Historic Change of Language and Cognitive Frames: Joint Research Project on Language and Culture 2008),* 5–21. Graduate School of Language and Culture, Osaka University.

Whaler, James (1931) "The Miltonic Simile." *Publications of the Modern Language Association of America* 46: 1034–1074.
Whaler, James (1932) "Animal Simile in Paradise Lost." *Publications of the Modern Language Association of America* 47: 534–553.
Yamanashi, Masaaki (1988) *Hiyu to Rikai (Metaphor and Understanding)*. Tokyo: Tokyo University Press.
Yamanashi, Masaaki (1996) "Spatial Cognition and Egocentric Distance in Metaphor." *Poetica* 46: 1–14.
Yu, Ning (1995) "Metaphorical Expressions of Anger and Happiness in English and Chinese." *Metaphor and Symbolic Activity* 10: 59–92.
Zaltman, Gerald and MacCaba, Dara (2007) "Metaphor in Advertising." Gerard J. Tellis and Tim Ambler (eds.) *The Sage Handbook of Advertising*, 135–154.

Dictionaries, References and Literary Works

Boyd, James R. (ed.) (1868) *Paradise Lost by John Milton*. New York: A. S. Barnes.
Bridgwater, William and Kurtz, Seimour (eds.) (1963) *The Colombia Encyclopedia*, Third Edition. New York: Colombia University Press.
Colton, C. C. (1832) *Lacon; or Many Things in Few Words; Addressed to Those Who Think*. Vol. II. Revised Edition. New York: Charles Wells.
Dixon, James Main (published year unknown) *English idioms*. London: Nelson.
Evans, Ifor (ed.) (1966) *Selections from William Wordsworth: Poetry and Prose*. London: Methuen Educational.
Fulk, R. D., Bjork, Robert E., and Niles, John D. (eds.) (2008) *Klaeber's Beowulf and the Fight at Finnsburg*. Toronto: University of Toronto Press.
Gollancz, Israel (ed.) (1926) *The Purgatorio of Dante Alighieri*. London: J. M. Dent & Sons.
Gulland, Daphne M., and Hinds-Howell, David (eds.) (1986) *The Penguin Dictionary of English Idioms*. London: Penguin Books.
Hill, Jimmie, and Lewis, Michael (eds.) (2002) *The Dictionary of Selected Collocations*. Boston: Thomson.
Himes, John A. (ed.) (1898) *Paradise Lost by John Milton*. New York: Harper& Brothers Publishers.
Johnson, Thomas H. (ed.) (1951) *The Poems of Emily Dickinson, Including Variant Readings Critically Compared With All Known Manuscripts*, 3 vols. Cambridge: The Belknap Press.
Karibe, Tsunenori and Koyama, Ryoichi (eds.) (2007) *The Old English Epic Beowulf: A Bilingual Edition*. Tokyo: Kenkyusha.
Lodge, George Cabot, Moody, William Vaughn and Lodge, John Clierton (eds.) (1905) *The Poems of Thumbull Stickney*. Boston: Mifflin.
Mitchel, James (ed.) (1983) *The Random House Encyclopedia*, New Revised Edition. New York: Random House.
Onions, Charles Talbut (1986) *A Shakespeare Glossary*. Oxford: Oxford University Press.
Orgel, Stephen and Goldberg, Jonathan (eds.) (1991) *John Milton: A Critical Edition of the Major Works*. Oxford: Oxford University Press.
Palmatier, Robert A. (1995) *Speaking of Animals: A Dictionary of Animal Metaphors*. Westport: Greenwood Press.
Poole, Josua (1657) *The English Parnassus: or, a Helpe to English Poesie*. London: Thomas Johnson. [Selected and Edited by R. C. Alston, The Scolar Press, Menston, 1972.]
Pope, Alexander (1950) *An Essay on Man*. London: Methuen.

Preminger, Alex and T. V. F. Brogan, (eds.) (1993) *The New Princeton Encyclopedia of Poetry and Poetics*. Princeton: Princeton University Press.
Rundell, Michael and Fox, Gwyneth (2002) *Macmillan English Dictionary for Advanced Lerners*. Oxford: Macmillan Education.
Robinson, Phil (1883) *The Poet's Birds*. London: Chatto and Windus.
Rodale, J. I. (1947) *The Word Finder*. Emmaus, Pennsylvania: Rodale Books, Inc.
Schmidt, Alexander (1971) *Shakespeare Lexicon and Quotation Dictionary*. 2 Vols. New York: Dover Publications.
Selincourt, Ernest de (ed.) (1940–1952) *The Poetical Works of William Wordsworth*. Vols. I–V. Oxford: Oxford University Press.
Skeat, Walter W. (ed.) (1894) *The Complete Works of Geoffrey Chaucer*, Vol. 1: *Romaunt of the Rose and Minor Poems*. London: Oxford University Press.
Sommer, Elyse and Weiss, Dorrie (1996) *Metaphors Dictionary*. Canton, MI: Visible Ink Press.
Verity, A. W. (ed.) (1910) *John Milton, Paladise Lost*. Cambridge: Cambridge University Press.
Wales, Katie (1989) *A Dictionary of Stylistics*. London: Longman.
Wilkinson, P. R. (2002) *Thesaurus of Traditional English Metaphors*. 2nd edition. London: Routledge.
Wilstach, Frank J. (1990) *A Dictionary of Similes*. Reprint (Originally published: 1924). Detroit: Omnigraphics.

(Electronic versions)
Arden Shakespeare CD-ROM. Thomas Nelson & Sons Limited, 1997.
Concise Oxford English Dictionary, 10th edition. Oxford University Press, 2001.
English Poetry Plus. Chadwyck-Healey, 1996.
Great Literature Plus. Bureau of Electronic Publishing, Inc., 1993.
Kenkyusha's English-Japanese Dictionary for the General Reader, 2nd edition. Kenkyusha, 1999.
Merriam-Webster Dictionary HD, Version 1.2. Merriam-Webster Inc., 2011.
The American Poetry Full-Text Database. Chadwyck-Healey, 1996.
The Bible in English. Chadwyck-Healey, 1996.
The Complete Multimedia Bible based on the King James Version. Compton's NewMedia, Inc., 1994.
The Oxford English Dictionary on CD-ROM, Version 1.10. Oxford University Press, 1994.

Index

A
aggrandizement 161
antonymous relationship 56, 113
antonymy 64

B
Bank of English 34
beasts of battle 112
Bible 128
Biblical phrases 5
bodily experience 106, 107
British National Corpus (BNC) 7, 34, 55

C
Christianity 164
cognitive linguistics 4
cognitive metaphor theory 2, 4
cognitive model 38
coherence 101, 114
Comparison Theory 14
conceptual metaphor 2, 18
conventional expressions 5
conventional metaphors 8, 55
corpus 3
corpus search 35, 56, 57, 65

D
dead metaphor 99
discourse 100

E
embodiment 39
emotion in general 33
emotion prototype 32, 43, 66
emotional reaction 15
encyclopaedic knowledge 15

epic 161
epic simile 161
evaluation 168

G
Great Chain Metaphor 123
Great Chain of Being 122
Greek mythology 165, 167

I
idioms 5, 99
illustration 161
imagination 12, 13
incarnation 162
innovative metaphors 5
Interaction Theory 14
interdisciplinary approaches to rhetoric 1
introspective data 3
intuition 2, 34

J
juxtaposition 56

L
large corpus 6
linguistic metaphor 2

M
mapping 2
mental images 100
metamorphoses 162
Miltonic similes 161
motivation 100

N
narrative 161

natural language data 3
negative emotion 62, 72
negative evaluation 125, 133

O
ordinary language 13
orientational metaphors 5, 164

P
paraphrases 5, 100
perceptual information 15
poetic language 13
poetry 11, 105
poets 12
positive emotion 62, 106, 113, 129
positive evaluation 127, 135
pretense 162
prolepsis 161
proverbs 5

R
reason 12
rhetoric 1, 186

S
scarcity of mappings 67
scenario 101
similarity 14
simile 14, 126, 162
small corpus 6
specific emotions 43, 55
synonymous relationship 71

T
tenor 14
the four elements 35
thought process 7
transformation 162

V
vehicle 14

大森文子（おおもり あやこ）

略歴
1963年大阪生まれ。
1986年大阪大学文学部卒業。
1989年大阪大学大学院文学研究科
博士後期課程退学。
2012年博士（文学、大阪大学）。
大阪大学助手、講師を経て、現在、
大阪大学大学院言語文化研究科
准教授。

Ayako Omori was born in Osaka, Japan. She received a Ph.D. degree from Osaka University, Japan in 2012. Ayako was an assistant professor in the Graduate School of Letters, Osaka University, and is currently an associate professor in the Graduate School of Language and Culture, Osaka University.

主な著書・論文
- "Meaning and Metaphor", *Poetica* 46. (1996)
- "Emotion as a Huge Mass of Moving Water", *Metaphor and Symbol* 23. (2008)
- "Conventional Metaphors for Antonymous Emotion Concepts", Paul Wilson (ed.), *Dynamicity in Emotion Concepts* (Łódź Studies in Language 27), Peter Lang. (2012)

Hituzi Linguistics in English No. 24
Metaphor of Emotions in English
With Special Reference to the Natural World and the Animal Kingdom as Their Source Domains

発行	2015年2月16日 初版1刷
定価	9500円＋税
著者	©大森文子
発行者	松本功
ブックデザイン	白井敬尚形成事務所
印刷所	三美印刷株式会社
製本所	小泉製本株式会社
発行所	株式会社 ひつじ書房
	〒112-0011 東京都文京区
	千石2-1-2 大和ビル2F
	Tel: 03-5319-4916
	Fax: 03-5319-4917
	郵便振替 00120-8-142852
	toiawase@hituzi.co.jp
	http://www.hituzi.co.jp/
	ISBN978-4-89476-740-9

造本には充分注意しておりますが、落丁・乱丁などがございましたら、小社かお買上げ書店にておとりかえいたします。ご意見、ご感想など、小社までお寄せ下されば幸いです。

刊行のご案内

Hituzi Linguistics in English

No. 10　The Development of the Nominal Plural Forms in Early Middle English
堀田隆一 著　定価 13,000 円＋税

No. 20　Repetition, Regularity, Redundancy
Norms and Deviations of Middle English Alliterative Meter
守屋靖代 著　定価 13,000 円＋税

No. 21　A Cognitive Pragmatic Analysis of Nominal Tautologies
山本尚子 著　定価 8,800 円＋税

Hituzi Language Studies

No. 1　Relational Practice in Meeting Discourse in New Zealand and Japan
村田和代 著　定価 6,000 円＋税

ひつじ意味論講座
澤田治美 編　定価 各 3,200 円＋税

第 1 巻　語・文と文法カテゴリーの意味
第 2 巻　構文と意味
第 3 巻　モダリティⅠ：理論と方法
第 4 巻　モダリティⅡ：事例研究
第 5 巻　主観性と主体性
第 6 巻　意味とコンテクスト
第 7 巻　意味の社会性（近刊）